Negotiating Multicultural Europe

Palgrave Politics of Identity and Citizenship Series

Series Editors: **Varun Uberoi**, University of Oxford; **Nasar Meer**, University of Southampton and **Tariq Modood**, University of Bristol

The politics of identity and citizenship has assumed increasing importance as our polities have become significantly more culturally, ethnically and religiously diverse. Different types of scholars, including philosophers, sociologists, political scientists, anthropologists, geographers, linguists and historians make contributions to this field and this series showcases a variety of innovative contributions to it. Focusing on a range of different countries, and utilizing the insights of different disciplines, the series helps to illuminate an increasingly controversial area of research and titles in it will be of interest to a number of audiences including scholars, students and other interested individuals.

Titles include:

Heidi Armbruster and Ulrike Hanna Meinhof (*editors*)
NEGOTIATING MULTICULTURAL EUROPE
Borders, Networks, Neighbourhoods

Derek McGhee
SECURITY, CITIZENSHIP AND HUMAN RIGHTS
Shared Values in Uncertain Times

Tariq Modood and John Salt (*editors*)
GLOBAL MIGRATION, ETHNICITY AND BRITISHNESS

Nasar Meer
CITIZENSHIP, IDENTITY AND THE POLITICS OF MULTICULTURALISM
The Rise of Muslim Consciousness

Ganesh Nathan
SOCIAL FREEDOM IN A MULTICULTURAL STATE
Towards a Theory of Intercultural Justice

Michel Seymour (*editor*)
THE PLURAL STATES OF RECOGNITION

Palgrave Politics of Identity and Citizenship Series
Series Standing Order ISBN 978–0–230–24901–1 (hardback)
(outside North America only)

You can receive future titles in this series as they are published by placing a standing order. Please contact your bookseller or, in case of difficulty, write to us at the address below with your name and address, the title of the series and the ISBN quoted above.

Customer Services Department, Macmillan Distribution Ltd, Houndmills, Basingstoke, Hampshire RG21 6XS, England

---

Contents

List of Photographs, Maps and Tables

Photographs

Maps

Tables

Notes on Contributors

Heidi Armbruster is a social anthropologist and Lecturer in German and Transnational Studies at the University of Southampton. Her research and publications have focused on borders, migration and diaspora issues, mostly in the German-speaking context, for a number of years. She codirected the EU framework project *SeFoNe* with Ulrike Hanna Meinhof.

Inken Carstensen-Egwuom currently holds a scholarship at the University of Bremen in Germany to complete her Ph.D. on immigrant entrepreneurship in northern German cities. Her research interests include qualitative migration research methods, immigrant entrepreneurship and city development, migration of Sub-Saharan Africans to the European Union and identity construction in interpersonal communication.

Georgina Christou is a graduate of Law and holds postgraduate degrees in Human Rights and European Studies with a special focus on issues relating to collective memory, education and nationalism in Cyprus and the Balkan region. She has conducted research in the areas of youth, migration and integration, national collective memory and Cypriot education, and gender socialisation. She has worked as a researcher for the University of Nicosia and the Mediterranean Institute of Gender Studies, Cyprus.

Daniela Damigella holds a Ph.D. in Social Psychology from the University of Catania where she currently teaches. Her research interests include social identity and group relations, immigration and contact hypothesis, and action research.

Olga Demetriou is Senior Researcher at the PRIO Cyprus Centre, a branch of the International Peace Research Institute, Oslo. She is a social anthropologist and has worked on issues of marginalisation in Greece and Cyprus, carrying out ethnographic fieldwork among minority and migrant groups over the last ten years. Her work has been published in *Cultural Anthropology*, the *Journal of the Royal Anthropological Institute*, *Ethnic and Racial Studies*, and elsewhere.

Hauke Dorsch is a social anthropologist and Director of the African Music Archives at the Department of Anthropology and African Studies, Johannes-Gutenberg University Mainz, Germany. His research interests include diaspora, migration and transnationalism, performance, popular culture, African and 'World' music.

Cassandra Ellerbe-Dueck studied at the Universities of Paris (VIII) and LMU in Munich, and completed a Ph.D. in Comparative Cultural Studies/Anthropology at the University of Ghent, Belgium in 2006. Cassandra currently works as a Diversity Manager for the city of Mannheim, Germany.

Ágnes Erőss studied at Eötvös Loránd University in Budapest and graduated with an M.A. in History and M.Sc. in Geography. Her fields of interest are ethnic and historical geography with special regard to the patterns and strategies of interethnic coexistence and its spatial and symbolic manifestation in urban space. She is completing a Ph.D. on the meanings and politics of symbolic space in multiethnic towns in the Carpathian Basin.

Béla Filep holds an M.Sc. in Geography (University of Bern) and an M.A. in International Relations and European Studies (Central European University Budapest). He specialises in border studies and interethnic relations in Central and Eastern Europe. Currently he is Visiting Fellow at the Department of Government at Harvard University.

Werner Holly is Professor of German Philology at the Technical University of Chemnitz in Germany. His main areas of research are discourse analysis, especially conversation analysis, text linguistics, language in politics and the media, and audiovisuality. He has published widely in these areas. His most recent publication is the *Handbook for Language, Culture and Communication* (Mouton de Gruyter) that he coedited.

Károly Kocsis is Professor of Geography at the Andrássy University Budapest, member of the Hungarian Academy of Sciences (HAS) and Director of both the Geographical Research Institute of HAS (Budapest) and the Institute of Geography at the University of Miskolc in Hungary. His research has mostly focused on the geographic study of ethnic, religious and political patterns in Central and South-Eastern Europe. The majority of his 300 publications deal with minority and border issues, and the geographic background of the ethnic conflicts in the Carpatho-Pannonian area and in the Balkans.

Orazio Licciardello is Professor of Social Psychology at the University of Catania. His research and publications have addressed subjects such as social identity and intergroup relations, immigration and contact hypothesis, action research and psychosocial research methods, possible selves and human resources.

John C. Mavris is Director of Communications at the University of Nicosia and a Member of the Cyprus Sociological Association. He has an M.A. in Cultural History from the University of Manchester, UK. He recently acted as Project Administrator and Research Fellow for Cyprus in the *SeFoNe* project. His research interests include border studies, ethnic conflict and identity formation.

Ulrike Hanna Meinhof is Professor of German and Cultural Studies and Director of the Centre for Transnational Studies at the University of Southampton. The emphasis of her work is on linguistic ethnography, especially in relation to identity research, borders and transnational studies. She has coordinated three EU Framework research projects (EU Border Discourse, Changing City Spaces, and – with Heidi Armbruster – *SeFoNe*) and is Director of the AHRC-funded project *Diaspora as Social and Cultural Practice*.

Patrik Tátrai has a Ph.D. in geography and is Research Fellow in the Geographical Research Institute of the Hungarian Academy of Sciences. His research interests include ethnic and religious geography, the Roma minorities of Hungary and the Hungarian minorities of Hungary's neighbouring countries.

Monika Mária Váradi is a sociologist and Senior Researcher at the Centre of Regional Studies of the Hungarian Academy of Sciences. Her publications and research interests focus on border studies, minorities and the economic and social restructuring in Hungary's rural regions.

Doris Wastl-Walter is Professor of Cultural Geography at the University of Bern, Switzerland. She is the editor of the *Border Regions Studies* series at Ashgate and has recently edited the *Ashgate Research Companion to Border Studies*. She has published widely on border issues, migration and gender geographies. She served as Chair of the IGU Commission on Geography and Public Policy.

Acknowledgements

Besides its authors, many people have contributed to this book.

Above all we are deeply grateful to all those countless research participants in the different fieldsites whose kindness and support have given reason and substance to the research presented in the following pages. There are too many to list them by name but they can be sure they are remembered by everyone in our team.

We would particularly like to thank Zafimahaleo Rasolofondraosolo, aka Dama, who was consultant to the *SeFoNe* project. Dama was an inspiration to all of us, helping to curate and himself performing in workshops and concerts at key research sites. His participation allowed us to build bridges between researchers, activists and artists.

We would like to thank Nicky Robbins for continuous administrative support, and Akinbode Akinbiyi, Ben Ulke and Franziska Kurz for inspiration and guidance at crucial stages of the research and the preparation of the photographic exhibition. Patrick Tátrai kindly prepared the maps for this book. The Iwalewa House in Bayreuth offered invaluable assistance and cooperation.

At Palgrave Macmillan, Philippa Grand has been a most encouraging and also quite patient commissioning editor and we are most grateful to her and to her editorial assistant Andrew James for guiding us through all the stages of this book.

Our sincere thanks to the EU Commission and the people who supported our stand in the 6th Framework Programme. Special thanks go to our scientific officer in the last year of our work, Wolfgang Bode.

1
Introducing Borders, Networks, Neighbourhoods: Conceptual Frames and Social Practices

Ulrike Hanna Meinhof

The last two decades have seen a plethora of theoretical and empirical work dealing with different facets of European borders, with the EU's continuing expansion to the east calling for a re-theorising and rethinking of Europe within and across its continuously shifting boundaries (e.g. Diez 2006; Delanty and Rumford 2005; Herrmann et al. 2004; O'Dowd 2002). Concurrently and sometimes interdependently, concerns with theories and practices of globalisation and transnationalism have created a whole new body of debates, and reframed conceptual discussions about migration, diasporas, multiculturalism, cosmopolitanism and cultural diversity as both European and global phenomena (e.g. Beck 2000; Vertovec and Cohen 2002; Schuster and Solomon 2002; Meinhof and Triandafyllidou 2006; Bauböck and Faist 2010). Most disciplines across the Humanities and Social and Political Sciences have contributed different conceptual and methodological vantage points from which to observe and engage with these realities: from the often structuralist and institutionalist vision of socio-political sciences to the more discursive-constructivist approaches of ethnographic linguists, human geographers and social anthropologists. The latter in particular have dealt with the interdependency of geopolitical and mental borders, in focusing on the shifting dynamics of in-grouping and out-grouping that define social relations in everyday life contexts at every step. This book is an instance of these concerns. It has arisen from the collaborative work of all the authors published in this volume who were jointly engaged in a research project entitled *Searching for Neighbours: Dynamics of Physical and Mental Borders in the New Europe*, or in short *SeFoNe* (2007–10). *SeFoNe* is the third research project that I (co-)directed under the European Framework initiative in ten years. It builds on two previous thematically related projects, in which some of the current authors also participated. The first was a project on *European Border Identities* (2000–3), that investigated three-generation families living in divided border communities on what was until 2004 the border between Eastern and Western Europe;[1] and the second was a 2002–5 project on *Changing City Spaces* (*CCS*), where we examined cultural diversity in seven capital cities in Europe.[2] In all three projects we were dealing with transnational practices of different orders: within the European Union, old and new; across the borders of the European Union, now and then; within and across the most marginal provincial regions as well as the most central metropolitan ones. The logic that underpins *SeFoNe's* central idea and thus also that of this volume is the interdependency of geopolitical and mental bordering in different contextual settings. This goes beyond the more self-evident observation that geopolitical frontiers between nation-states often closely interact and determine people's perception and self-identification and thus also the 'othering' of those who are not seen as belonging to one's own group. It also and more profoundly throws light on the more subtle and less obvious processes of symbolic 're-bordering' at places where the dissolution of national borders is reshaping cultural affiliations, or in reverse, where the reordering of outer EU-frontiers has created new divisions in formerly interconnecting cross-border social spaces. The former can be geographically located in the regions along the former German–German border, dissolved since 1990, or on the borders on the former 'Iron Curtain' with and between all those states which joined the EU between 2004 and 2007, in particular Poland, Hungary, Slovakia, Slovenia and Romania. The latter can be observed on the new borders of the EU to the east, and southeast, as in the formerly well-interconnected regions on the Hungarian–Ukrainian border which are now much more separated than before 2004, when Hungary joined the EU. In order to capture these fluid processes of bordering, de-bordering and re-bordering, which the last chapter in this volume by Armbruster will further develop, *SeFoNe* is using the metaphor of neighbourhoods or, as we prefer to call it, 'neighbouring'. Neighbouring, we argue, is a useful conceptual and methodological tool for researching and reflecting on interactions and everyday life exchanges between people in and across borderlands, conceived in spatial and virtual, material and symbolic terms.

Retracing the conceptual and empirical trajectory and the continuities and complementarities of all three projects – from border communities and regions to multicultural cities and transnational networks to multilevel neighbourhoods – is thus to imagine the changing map of Europe not only through the material realities of their geopolitical, geosocial contexts, but is also invoking particular conceptual lenses. Borders, networks and neighbourhoods have both a physical reality in the everyday life of European citizens, and a symbolic and metaphorical dimension at the same time. In this introduction, as a way of framing the subsequent discussions in this book, I will attempt to account for both of these realities and give a brief summary of these consecutive projects, their findings and also their limitations.

1.1 Borders and the border identity project, 2000–3

Traditional state borders by their very nature represent the institutional reification of statehood in such a way that it impinges on the everyday life of citizens in material and symbolic ways. Crossing a ***conventional*** geopolitical border usually means showing passports, changing currencies, turning from an insider to an outsider. It also includes the possibility of being denied access. In that sense borders materialise and institutionalise the psychosocial processes of inclusion and exclusion in a very clear-cut and visible way. Yet inversely and paradoxically, borders also offer legal and illegal opportunities of 'border-crossings', subversiveness, liminal spaces for interacting. Nugent and Asiwaju (1996: 11) call border zones 'theatres of opportunity', Diez writes about the 'paradoxes' of borders (Diez 2006), while Sassen (e.g. 1996, 2001) talks about 'analytical borderlands' to capture these new variously interconnecting or disconnecting spaces. Researching border communities and border regions thus becomes a prima facie case of studying multiple processes of in-grouping and out-grouping, of showing the interdependencies of geopolitical borders with mental/psychosocial bordering.

During the decade of our project work – the first decade of the twenty-first century – the map of Europe radically changed with a fundamental reordering of its borders. During the work on the *European Border Identities* project between 2000 and 2003, and with the only exception being the internal German border which had disappeared a decade earlier in 1990, the communities that we were researching were still divided by firmly institutionalised state borders. To cross over from one to the other border community – between Germany and Poland, Germany and the Czech Republic, between Austria and Hungary, Austria and Slovenia, and Italy and Slovenia – while no longer *impossible* in 2003 – was nevertheless regulated by all the paraphernalia and administrative hurdles of separate states. These were the borders where the three Western European states of Germany Austria and Italy – all part of Schengen territory and the Eurozone, and thus effectively 'debordered' – met with their Eastern European neighbours, all applicants for EU-membership but still waiting in line for accession. These borders often marked divisions between different ethnolinguistic national groups which had come about as a result of involuntary population movements in the aftermath of the Second World War, as was the case in Guben/Gubin and Görlitz/Zgorzelec on the German–Polish border (Meinhof and Galasinski 2005; Galasinska and Galasinski 2003; Galasinska et al. 2002) or Bärenstein/Vejprty on the German–Czech border (Holly 2002; Holly et al. 2003), or in the aftermath of the First and then again the Second World War, as was the case in Moschendorf/Pinkamindzent on the Austrian–Hungarian border (Wastl-Walter et al. 2003). Other borders also divide the same ethnolinguistic groups as is the case with Slovenians in Eisenkappel and Zelezna Kapla on the Austrian–Slovenian border and Gorizia/Nova Gorica on the Italian–Slovenian border. Here, Slovenians have majority status within Slovenia on one side of the border, and minority status within Austria and Italy respectively on the other side (Hipfl et al 2002 and 2003; Carli et al 2002 and 2003). Hungarians studied by Koscic and his team in the project have similar minority status in many of its adjacent states.[3] In the turbulent history of twentieth-century Europe, border communities such as these thus both exemplify and symbolise places of historical conflict and division.

The *EU Border Identities* project studied six such divided border communities along the former (south-)eastern border of the European Union, but included communities on the (by then dissolved) East–West German border.[4] In researching families from the respective *majority* societies on either side, we prioritised certain phenomena of transnational relations over others, namely those that were structured on the one hand through the close *spatial* contingency of border people but on the other hand – and apart from the German case – through sharp differences in national identity, history, language and culture. During the lifespan of these three-generation families, its members had experienced major sociopolitical shifts in their public lives, which had massive implications for everyday life and social relations. Ten years after German unification, the collapse of the Soviet Union and several years after other major political upheavals such as the collapse of Yugoslavia, and the division of Czechoslovakia, our research tapped into the identity formations of members of three generations shortly before EU enlargement in 2004 would embrace all of them within the new supranational frame of the European Union. Hence the purpose of our research was specifically to understand the extent to which the sociopolitical upheavals in the lives of family members, who were natives of their respective (and in the past often inimical) nation-states had affected their identities, and to what extent the prospect of a shared European future was salient with them. This we gauged through ethnographic interviews and subsequent fine-tuned discourse analysis, using highly charged photographs of clearly identifiable places or events in these communities during the three historical phases as triggers (Meinhof and Galasinski 2005: Chapter 5). Apart from a plethora of single- or co-authored articles, our work resulted in two joint key publications (Meinhof 2002; Meinhof 2003a). The first of these focused on key narratives on either side of the divided borders, and by key narratives we mean stories to which our informants returned time and time again, and which had such saliency that they seemed to be at the centre of the identity constructions and a source of in-grouping and out-grouping of the people on either side of the border. To give some examples only from those border regions which are once more touched upon by the project: in some cases, as for example in Baerenstein/Vejperty on the German–Czech border, key narratives were structured through the historical memories of the fascist period and its immediate post-Second World War effects (Holly 2002). In others, such as the adjacent communities of Moschendorf and Pinkamindzent on the Austrian–Hungarian border, key narratives revolved around anxieties and fears of a steady decline and its effects on the social fabric in culturally and economically marginalised villages where out-migration continued to reduce the population in a downward spiral (Wastl-Walter et al. 2002). For Germans on either side of the by then long-dissolved internal border – and somewhat ironically – it was a mutual concern with status and financial rewards attached to work which fuelled mutual suspicion and a sense of injustice on both sides (Armbruster and Meinhof 2002).[5] Hence key narratives looked at through the prism of local cross-border relations at specific borders were those where people were focusing on similar concerns yet using them as distancing devices against each other.

In our second edited collection we used a different lens for a comparative analysis, though we stayed with the same border communities and peoples' narratives. Rather than focusing on key stories *across* the national borders in adjacent communities we now analysed the similarities and differences *alongside* the borderline itself, comparing all the data we had collected through our photographic elicitation method with one another. This allowed us to recognise clusters of shared perceptions that united people alongside the eastern as against the western borderline with very similar patterns of in-group and out-group formations affecting either side. Hence there were similarities in the narrativisation of experiences between the older EU countries (Germany, Austria and Italy) as against the then non-EU countries of Poland, the Czech Republic, Hungary and Slovenia. The transnational stories that divided eastern from western communities arose from a double and mutually enforcing set of problematic circumstances: one arose from the fact that these borders represented the fault lines of historical and political upheaval – wars, redefinition of sociopolitical systems, large population shifts through flight, resettlement or expulsion. The other, and mapped upon the traumatic experiences from the past, was the contemporary socioeconomic inequality that existed between the richer communities on the western and the poorer communities on the eastern side (for detailed analysis see Holly et al., Wastl-Walter et al., Sussi et al., Galasinka and Galasinki – all published in Meinhof [2003a]). Thus, by 2003 our work pointed to an often deeply felt sense of rejection of and by the people of the respective nations on either side of their borders. For the youngest generation, this continued and even magnified the negative effects of 'out-grouping', and created a continuing vicious cycle whereby historical trauma and present-day social inequalities translated themselves into indifference at best, and dislike, rejection and even hatred at worst. Europe was rarely invoked as a unifying agent, nor did it signify the same geographical, cultural or political space for different informants (Armbruster et al. 2003; Meinhof and Galasinski 2005: Chapter 7). Our results thus foregrounded the difficulties which needed to be overcome in the field of human relations, especially in the light of ordinary people's rejection of well-meant and often substantial forms of top-down planning and assistance, including major national, transregional and EU-financed projects and investment. Our recommendations at the end of the project pointed to the lack of agency, and pervasive powerlessness experienced by the local people, and proposed that future research might investigate the ways in which a stronger involvement of bottom-up civil society agents might be able to overcome difference (see also the final report of *EU Border Identities* and a substantive bibliography of team members' work on the project at www.borderidentities.soton.ac.uk/publicat01.html).

This somewhat depressing result became the stimulus for changing the focus away from an imaginary of borders, which in 2003 seemed to reify rather than transcend national differences, with little evidence emerging of a super ordinate European identity, and an alarming overall situation where the youngest generations seemed more hostile or disaffected than the older ones (Meinhof 2004). Anecdotally sparked off by the incidental comment of one of my young informants in

Guben, who disliked Polish Gubin and its inhabitants but declared that the Polish capital city of Warsaw was 'almost as good as Berlin',[6] we turned to metropolitan cities as an alternative conceptual frame and empirical space in the search for a new Europe. Rather than conceptualising Europe as a club of nations framed by borders we felt that cities provided a better cognitive tool for imagining Europe. In this we also expanded from an optic on multigenerational majority populations with a long history of wars and conflict between them to one which now embraced the multicultural realities of twenty-first-century Europe, and from a geopolitically defined space to one of flows and networks.

1.2 Networks across city spaces

In researching and reflecting on networks and networking within and across metropolitan city spaces we prioritised different phenomena of transnational relations over those encountered with the border project. To start with, we were no longer looking at sharply divided spaces with clearly demarcated borders between nationally defined majority populations on either side of the divide, but with our focus on capital cities we now thematised the extensive cultural diversity of European societies. Secondly, we were looking at networking structures and strategies of and between people of all kinds of backgrounds. Thirdly, we were thematising the interchange or lack of it between cultural agents on the ground and those top-down policymakers who were formulating and regulating cultural politics in the cities. The *Changing City Spaces* project (2002–5) thus differed in its theme, target group and research questions from the Border Identities project, but was nevertheless building on the insights gained from it by challenging as well as complementing some of the key perspectives of our previous work on borders. To spell out these differences in more detail:

- Through the prism of metropolitan cities we deliberately aimed to challenge the nation-state paradigms and their institutionalisation across national borders. European metropolitan cities we argued, were spaces of negotiation and encounter between culturally diverse people, and in principle and praxis disruptive of the often monocultural imaginary of the nation-state.
- Through the prism of networks across capital cities rather than spatially conceived districts, we foregrounded translocal and transnational connections and flows and their effects. This challenged a community-based approach to specific groups and sites, and suggested

a multi-sited rather than a single-space approach (Marcus 1995, 2010; Hannerz 2003).[7]

- Through the prism of migrants in these cities, we deliberately steered away from the national optic on majority populations towards the translocal or transnational interconnections of people from highly diverse backgrounds, while a 'subject-centred ethnography' (Rice 2003) of following individual artists through very different life-contexts in the cities counteracted the risk of 'methodological nationalism' (Wimmer and Glick-Schiller 2003).
- Through the prism of migrant artists and cultural actors we focused on people who represented this alternative and more challenging vision of European culture by their own artistic and cultural practices.
- Finally, and connecting all the previous elements, a focus on cultural policy allowed us to engage with what during the 1990s could be seen as a 'cultural turn' in European discourses (Meinhof and Triandafyllidou 2006: 3), a concern with cultural policy at European level and with it the questions of what and who constitutes European culture. Migrant artists living and working in urban spaces and interconnecting translocally and transnationally across them provided an excellent optic for challenging any nationally driven vision of a Europe of indigenous majority populations.

The emphasis on capital cities, artistic networks, movements or 'flows' of people and goods suggests a transnational and to some extant cosmopolitan frame and could thus easily be taken for an innocent celebratory form of cosmopolitanism (Beck 2000), a risk of which we were well aware. As Pratt (2005) rightly points out, the metaphor of flow tends to naturalise inequality and power structures between the first and the third world, 'obliterate human agency and intentionality' and exemplify 'the official, legitimizing language of globalization [...] detached from any ethical dimension' (Pratt 2005: 278). However, in our emphasis on the multidirectional networking and 'flows' of migrant artists it was precisely their agency and their ways of representing cultural diversity bottom-up that went centre-stage. In this we were working much closer to the paradigm of what Featherstone et al. (2007: 386) have described as the 'spatialities of transnational networks', where networks are defined 'as the overlapping and contested material, cultural and political flows and circuits that bind different places together through differentiated relations of power'. In our work, the 'bottom-up' activities and often existential struggles of migrants living and working in and across different European cities were set in contrast and comparison to those policies of multiculturalism produced top-down in the ministries and public offices at the level of the city, the nation-state, and Europe. With *SeFoNe* we continued this concern with the correlation – or lack of it – between official policies and bottom-up initiatives of individuals, groups and associations. All chapters in this volume bear witness of this tension between the top-down and the bottom-up, between policy and practice, particularly observable in the complex and confusing discourses of integration. But by contrast to *Changing City Spaces*, in *SeFoNe* we were no longer restricted to big cities with their cosmopolitan appeal but were now taking note of the multicultural realities of provincial and cross-border regions. This is in recognition of the contemporary social reality of Europe where cultural diversity exists across all kinds of different localities with different rules and different kinds of boundaries – banlieues *and* city centres, metropolitan cities *and* provincial towns, urban *and* rural contexts.

1.3 Networks as social and transcultural capital

Another key idea which connects the concerns of *CCS* with those of *SeFoNe* is the notion that networking forms part of social capital (Bourdieu and Waquant 1992). Theories of social capital have recently gained special popularity among both scholars and policymakers (Baron et al. 2000; Dekker and Uslaner 2001; Edwards et al. 2001; Harper 2001; Field 2003; Halpern 2005). In *CCS* it was the networking of migrant artists within and across their own ethnic groups which constituted their social capital and which helped underpin their professional and economic survival in the new environment. Meinhof and Triandafyllidou (2206b: 200–22) have therefore included social capital in their conceptualisation of 'transcultural capital', which they see as a combination of three forms of capital, which migrants may use or acquire: social, cultural and economic. In *SeFoNe*, the zooming-in on specific networks, associations and groupings at grass-roots level, both locally and translocally, allowed us to investigate the grounds on which social capital is built and/or undermined. This comes out strongest in the chapter by Ellerbe-Dueck in this volume, where networks take on the role of safe spaces for black women which allow them to group and formulate resistance against a society that marginalises them, but is also – though less explicitly – present in all the other chapters as well. A networking focus thus brings new kinds of cultural mobility into the picture, by exploring the extent to which local lives are embedded, and perhaps enriched by translocal practices of belonging and cooperating.

Thus, with the new EU call – now under the 6th framework project – which thematised 'new borders, new neighbourhoods' in the new Europe, we were able to develop a new approach which would build on the insights of our preceding projects by interlacing concepts of borders, networks and social/transcultural capital in a new expanded framework that could go beyond the conceptual and empirical limitations of the work that preceded it. This third project took its cue from the EU's own terminology of neighbourhood, but as before with the capital city concept we used it as a conceptual metaphor and not just as a geopolitical description for the new post-accession border realities on Europe's new frontiers. Hence we conceived of neighbourhoods in a non-conventional way as applying to both geospatial and non-spatial vicinity, i.e. inclusive of 'translocal' transnational networks. At the same time we re-signified 'borders' to embrace not only the notion of borderlands between the EU and its neighbouring states (i.e. the borders between Hungary and its surrounding states, and between the two parts of Cyprus) but also that of psychosocial 'borders' in regions where old borders had ceased to exist (i.e. in the former borderlands of Upper Frankonia and Saxony in former Western and East Germany), or were configured differently as at the 'liquid' border of the Mediterranean Sea (Sicily).

1.4 Neighbourhoods and neighbouring

In adopting the concept of neighbourhood as a prism through which to investigate social relations and practices across different types of 'borders', we are dealing with both the material reality of people literally living next to one another as well as a symbolic reality of vicinity through social networking. Although neighbourhood is an integrative term, it does not have the same connotations of homogeneity, uniformity or sense of belonging as 'community' often has,[8] nor does it imply the shared imaginary of what Anderson has famously coined as 'imagined communities' (Anderson 1983). The advantage of a neighbourhood concept is that it offers a conceptual metaphor, an optic for studying relations of many different kinds and of very different orders of scale. Neighbourhoods can be differently composed and stratified, historically shifting, and in spite of 'urban assumptions' (Henderson and Thomas 2002: 20) they can be both rural and urban. They can be invoked for individuals or groups, even states, and the term's affective meaning can be quite neutral. A very brief selection of a few different usages of 'neighbourhoods' in popular and policy discourse makes very clear that being a neighbour in itself presupposes neither a state of personal friendship nor one of communal spirit: we have all read plenty of newspaper headlines about those *neighbours* from hell; an English proverb reminds us that 'good fences make good *neighbours*', and the German satirical writer and caricaturist Wilhelm Busch adds the observation, 'Es kann der Brävste nicht in Frieden leben, wenn es dem bösen Nachbarn nicht gefällt' (Even the best cannot live peacefully if the nasty *neighbour* does not like it). An intercultural association in Germany has *Neighbours becoming friends* ('Aus Nachbarn werden Freunde') as its slogan. Without the adjective 'good' preceding it, a neighbourhood could also mean hostility, dislike, or indifference towards those 'next door'.

Within European policy discourse and at the level of relations between states, the term neighbourhood appears not only in the 6th framework call for 'New Europe, new neighbours' under which *SeFoNe* was funded, but also in the European Neighbourhood Policy (ENP), to cater for global relations between the EU and non-EU members, especially those to the south and south-east around the Mediterranean–North Africa, Middle East and Turkey, and to non-EU states such as the Ukraine, Belarus and Albania in Eastern and South-eastern Europe. Here the purpose of the neighbourhood discourse is strategic, underpinning different initiatives in the sociopolitical and economic spheres (see also Delanty and Rumford 2005: 127).

Hence the concept of neighbourhood can cover very different scales of relations, from the level of suprastates and adjacent states down to that of individual people next door or in virtual communication networks with one another. 'Neighbourhood' and its derivative verb *neighbouring* offer a good conceptual vantage point for investigating those processes of Europeanisation and globalisation that have transformed old neighbourhoods, not only by turning former enemies or strangers separated by Cold War borders into new neighbours from the level of state politics to that of individual personal connections, but also by diversifying local neighbourhoods through processes of economic restructuring and migration. The neighbouring lens thus offers a focus on issues and concerns of ordinary people – members of different social and ethnic groups who are living in Europe in new and old 'borderlands' – in their everyday lives ***and*** in response to the shifting sociopolitical contexts set at local, regional, national and transnational policy level. Their new forms of cooperation and conflict in these settings, of moving towards or away from one another, is the theme of *SeFoNe* and of this volume.

1.5 Introducing *SeFoNe*[9]

As already mentioned, *SeFoNe* is an acronym, and it references a 6th Framework research project entitled *Searching for Neighbours* by trying to understand the dynamics of physical and mental borders in the new Europe. The chapters collected in this volume have all arisen from work within and across three strands: geopolitical borders, multicultural provincial regions and ethnic networks. They represent a further stage, and a very different though complementary perspective to the work that was started in 2000 with the *Border Identities* project and continued in 2002 with *Changing City Spaces*. The border regions studied in the first EU project through the prism of families in *divided* border towns along the German–Polish, German–Czech and Austrian–Hungarian borders by authors in this volume (Meinhof, Holly, Wastl-Walter, Váradi) and the former German border territory on the Frankonian, Thuringian and Saxonian border (Armbruster, Meinhof) had by 2004 all become internal spaces within the EU. All were signatories to the Schengen Treaty allowing free access across EU–internal borders and thus effectively 'de-bordered'. Yet in other ways, new borders have arisen that now bear the imprint not only of the remnants of historical reality of past divisions between majority populations of their native states (see Wastl-Walter and Váradi in this volume), but also the marks of new and far less visible signs of boundaries between majority and minority populations (see Carstensen-Egwuom and Holly; Dorsch; Licciardello and Damigella; Ellerbe-Dueck in this volume). What our work intends to underline is the myriad of initiatives at grass-roots, semi-official or official level which highlight the extent to which good neighbouring activities are evolving – bottom-up or top-down – to engage with the old and new realities of cultural diversities and criss-crossing borders within and across the expanding European Union. The underlying assumption of *SeFoNe* is that in the process of EU enlargement, the need for building good neighbourhoods across and within EU nation states is periodically challenged by 'nationalised' sociopolitical conflicts which at the same time encourage parties on the extreme Right. Hence, *SeFoNe* explores and compares models of 'translocal' neighbourhood, focusing on emerging discourses and good practices in three spheres of life in the new Europe:

- Physical 'borderlands' of the new EU: here we were researching the relations between people across four of the seven borders of Hungary which between them comprise all the different permutations possible between a new EU partner and its EU or non-EU neighbours (Wastl- Walter and Våradi; Erőss et al. in this volume). A further cross-border site in the newly expanded Europe is the so-called Cypriot 'Green Line' which, in spite of many advancements in the very recent past, is still highly divisive and remains a stumbling block for Turkey's entry to the EU (Demetriou et al. in this volume).

- Mental border experiences in multicultural provincial regions of the EU: here we were researching two regions in Germany – the former East German region of Saxony and the neighbouring West German region of Upper Franconia, with a special focus on the two towns of Chemnitz and Bayreuth (Carstensen-Egwuom and Holly; Dorsch, in this volume). Although without a national border between them since German unification in 1990, and without any EU border to the east since the accession of the Czech Republic and Poland to the EU in 2004, the presence of people from different nations in these regions retains on the one hand traces of the former divisions, borders, and East–West alignments (e.g. a large presence of Turkish migrants in Upper Franconia and the presence of Vietnamese migrants in Saxony) while at the same time new population movements have substantially increased the overall number of migrants from many different countries. The absence of any institutionalised border has not reduced the presence of mental borders – quite the opposite is the case – with xenophobia affecting especially the Eastern German region. It is this phenomenon of increased mental bordering in the absence of any visible political divisions – or what we describe as the dynamics between mental and physical borders – which was the focus of our work in these regions. Beyond that we were also investigating the region and town of Catania in Sicily, which again lacks an institutional border but has for centuries been a crossing point for East > West and South > North migration (Licciardello and Damigella in this volume).
- Transnational/translocal networks of Africans. In the third strand of our work we investigated different types of dispersed translocal networks of people originating from Africa. This perspective highlighted the network relations of individuals or groups beyond specific geographically bounded sites. The focus was on spatially dispersed people who form 'virtual neighbourhoods', and on the connections between social groups such as friends and family members that are upheld by their physical movements and flows across the European and non-European space, as well as internet and satellite phone connections. While maintaining the regional connections, in this strand

we investigated 'nodes' in networks determined by the movements and virtual interconnections of individuals or small groups across different localities that originate from or lead into the regions we were studying. Our emphasis here was an emphasis on migrants of African origin and their networks. Despite their historical and contemporary European presence, non-whites are frequently denied their 'belonging to' Europe, even if born here, and their presence is increasingly problematised and often posed as a threat to those who are deemed to belong. But in all the regions we studied, most notably in Sicily, migrants of African background have become part of the local social and economic fabric. Even remote regions and outposts of the EU can thus no longer be imagined as monocultural. This third strand provided a fresh and illuminating perspective on contemporary imaginings of the nation, the region, Europe and the EU. It ran parallel to a further study on transnational networks based on African-descended musicians – in a research project that grew from the *Changing City Spaces* results, entitled *TNMundi: Diaspora as Social and Cultural practice* (Meinhof and Kiwan 2006–10). This showed that the transnational networks of migrant musicians represent a powerful form of social capital, which can be strategically useful in sustaining the artists' transnational musical careers (Kiwan and Meinhof 2011; Meinhof 2009: 151 ff.). In a different but not unrelated vein, the chapter by Ellerbe-Dueck defines the networks of the Black Women European Council she studied as 'safe spaces' rendering support for action and strengthening the womens' capacity to have their voices heard.

1.6 Chapter summaries

In this final section of the chapter I would now like to concentrate on the central theme of neighbouring at grass-roots level as discussed by the various authors of this volume within the wider frame of the project's genealogy.

1.6.1 Neighbouring and networking

Chapters 2–4 all deal with neighbourhood practices between countries within the EU or between the EU and non-EU, and highlight very different relations from the political and institutional down to grass-roots and individual levels. In Cyprus, the subject of Chapter 2, Demetriou, Christou and Mavris suggest that neighbouring at the level of individuals and less formal civic society actions work better than those at the more formal civil society or governmental level. Whereas the former draw on largely local resources of identification through a shared village (Pyla), or a street (Ledra Street), more formal organisations and projects find it harder to overcome the divisions imposed by macropolitical structures. Taking as their case studies three spheres of interaction, the cohabiting of Greek and Turkish Cypriots in the bicommunal village of Pyla, formal civil society arts organisations in the North and the South of Cyprus, and various low-level initiatives to open Ledra Street in Nikosia, the authors show the contextual conditions under which low-level developments open up new prospects for collaboration. Good neighbouring seems to work through identifications at local level which – while not escaping the macropolitical divisions of the island – are nevertheless able to partially avoid and bypass them through personal action: from an individual level where Greek and Turkish Cypriots share food in Pyla, to resistance of influences perceived as outside interference, to a shared sense of opposition to respective state policies.

The possibility that identification with a cross-border locality at the smallest scale and a shared opposition to higher-level policies and developments can realign people differently, and thus cut across ethnic divisions and national interest is also present in Chapter 3. Wastl-Walter and Váradi take as their case study an environmental conflict on the Austrian–Hungarian border. Here the plans of an Austrian company to install a waste incinerator just inside the Austrian side of the border but close to the small Hungarian town of Szentgotthard has realigned people according to their support or opposition to this development. While, in the case of the more public representation of the region and the state, the division follows national lines (with the Austrian region and state supporting the development and the Hungarian side opposing it), at a more grass-roots level different allegiances are formed that cut across such national allegiances. Wastl-Walter and Váradi show the ways in which the significance of the state border weakens or disappears in these cross-border neighbourhoods when people – lay or expert – fear for their local environment and its safety. Within the de-bordered zones of the EU, shared interests and values thus create different lines of identification and opposition. The focus of Wastl-Walter and Váradi is on a border which has undergone a substantial transformation from the sharp division of the Iron Curtain until 1999 between West and East, to the indifferent side-by-side existence of two nation-states in the 1990s and early 2000 to the new post-2004 reality of united Europe. In this location the old EU united with the new EU in 2004.

By contrast, the remaining borders of Hungary have neighbours with whom until 1999 they shared a socialist past. Following the collapse of the Soviet Union, successive states of the former Warsaw Pact have applied for and been granted EU membership, leaving only the Ukraine, Croatia and Serbia as non-EU neighbouring states for Hungary. This position of Hungary as a Central European country bordering on states which comprise all possible formal relations with the EU makes Hungary's borderlands an almost unique setting for studying the different kinds of effects of shifting borders on populations on either side. Chapter 4 by Erőss, Filep, Koscis and Tátrai is based on their work across three of these post-communist borders. In all three borderlands the two world wars and subsequent peace treaties in the twentieth century entailed the loss of formerly Hungarian territory to its neighbours. As a result, the geopolitical boundaries no longer coincide with ethnolinguistic borders. In all three non-Hungarian border towns studied – in Komárno (Slovakia), Oradea (Romania), and Berehove (Ukraine) – ethnic Hungarians form majorities or substantial minorities. Ethnic Hungarians in these towns thus have minority status at national level, majority or sizeable minority status at local level, and share an ethnolinguistic identity with the Hungarian majority population on the respective Hungarian border or near-border towns of Komárom, Debrecen and Vásárosnamény. The chapter thus offers three distinctive settings to compare the possibilities and hindrances of inter- *as against* intra-ethnic neighbouring practices, of local cooperation and conflicts, put in relief against policies of perceived national interest.

All three chapters in the section on geopolitical border regions thus raise major issues of the different ways in which local cooperation between people on the ground is helped or hindered by policies at local, national and supranational level, and of the extent to which institutional interests are in support or contradiction of individual values and affiliations. But whereas in Chapters 2–4 it was the shifting and reconfiguring of national borders that created the frame for studying cross-border intra- and inter-ethnic relations, in the following it is the relation between diverse people originating from all over the world and who live in medium-sized provincial towns rather than on state borders that moves centre-stage. Neither Bayreuth in Upper Franconia, Chemnitz in Saxony, nor Catania in Sicily are border towns. However, through their position near the former intra-German border on the one hand, and as a port city on the Mediterranean Sea shared with Northern Africa on the other hand, they continue to leave their traces in the make-up of the migrant population. 'Neighbouring practices' in these multicultural regions are fractured through a discourse of 'immigration' and 'integration' at public level and its various uptakes and modifications by migrants themselves at grass-roots level. Especially in Germany, the debate about integration has replaced earlier highly controversial debates about Leitkultur and Multiculturalism (see also Kiwan and Meinhof 2006: 73–8). Integration is institutionalised in national and municipal integration plans and the creation of integration officers. The term is omnipresent in national and local media discourses and policies. However, in those areas where 'integration' is also reflected by migrants themselves, it is contested: some regard it as a demand to assimilate rather than an invitation for the construction of a common neighbourhood, others adapt and modify its meaning to claim an equal share for their own cultural capital. Among 'white' or 'indigenous' Germans active in 'integration' contexts, there are different discursive clusters around the use of the term integration, which range from the most uncritical uptake as a solution to all problems to a highly critical view or even rejection of the term as being too assimilationist. Chapters 5–8 offer case studies that throw a particular light on similar local and national practices of integration. Chapters 5–6 focus on the German contexts in the towns of Chemnitz and Bayreuth respectively.

Chapter 5 by Carstensen-Egwuom and Holly shows the ways in which recent public discourses of immigration in Germany are being appropriated and reshaped in migrants' experiential narratives, with some surprising results. Neither of the three individuals of Vietnamese, Jewish-Ukrainian and Afro-German origin use the lexicon of integration in quite the way public discourse would have it, and in their reconfigurations point to alternative perspectives on the everyday practices of communal living and cohabitation with the native German population, and in doing so, raise issues of personal identity. The Vietnamese informant turns integration from a process that he, as a migrant, is supposed to engage with into an event in which native Germans are invited to participate; the Jewish informant represses her Jewish identity in public so as not to be noticed as different, and rejects the special allowances made for Jews by her teacher because of Germany's horrendous crimes; and the African-German opts out of prevalent discourses of no-go zones so as to assert her own independence and personal freedom.

Whereas Chapter 5 homes in on individual practices of migrants, Chapter 6 by Dorsch takes as its subject a top-down municipal but nationally inspired event – the Intercultural Week. Aimed at furthering integration processes in the town of Bayreuth, the Week intends to showcase the different groups of people that make up Bayreuth's multicultural reality. Dorsch analyses the event that took place in 2007, as discussed in meetings preparing the follow-up event in 2008, and the reasons for its perceived failure. These highlight both a series of absences from this event by particular groups and the non-communication between those who participated. The chapter contextualises this failure of intercultural communication by pointing to specific historical, religious and social factors which influence the ways in which multiculturalism is conceived by public and private bodies in the town.

Chapter 7 by Licciardello and Danigella also focus on activities and practices aimed at integration of people from different backgrounds in Catania. To the sociolinguistic and anthropological perspective of the preceding two chapters they now add a sociopsychological framework where the perception of migrants about their life and life perspectives in the town is further contextualised through the authors' ethnographic observation in four different sites of interaction between majority and minority populations: a market, a community centre, an immigrant office and schools. The picture that emerges is not at all unified, showing a whole plethora of different kinds of evaluations, from the most positively valued to the most negative. The authors make a strong plea for action research and positive sociopolitical intervention based on needs as perceived and articulated by the immigrants themselves. The chapter's call for immigrant participation in all decision-making processes thus provides an interesting correlate to that by Dorsch, where the absence of migrants in the organisation of events in Bayreuth aimed at them emerged as one of the reasons for its failure.

It also provides an excellent link with the subsequent chapter by Ellerbe-Dueck who, in her position as a black female anthropologist, contributes an insider perspective on the role of black women in Germany and Austria, and pleads for more activist ethnography. Here the notion of neighbourhoods or neighbouring is realised through a focus on networking between people who are marginalised by their respective mainstream societies and, as a result of being victims of exclusion, discrimination and threats, are using networks as 'safe spaces' to interact with one another and make their voices heard. In the specific example of the Black European Womens' Council, Ellerbe-Dueck sees a particularly potent organisation to challenge the mental and symbolic borders that they have to face in their encounters with their white European co-citizens.

The final chapter by co-director of *SeFoNe* Heidi Armbruster offers a conclusion to the volume by revisiting the different case studies of the volume as evidence of the contradictions between what she calls the 'national and post-national dynamics of the European project'. *SeFoNe*'s endeavour to merge concerns of border studies with those of migration studies is the vantage point from which she discusses European integration issues. These equally revolve around external nation-state borders on the one hand and internal multicultural complexities on the other. Armbruster shows how these two domains are nevertheless largely treated as separate political, institutional and discursive issues in the EU. Her chapter critically analyses the different and mutually exclusive visions of Europe that answer to the motto 'unity in diversity'.

Finally, a last word about the conceptual terms and metaphors we are using, and on their significance for a linguistically aware Social Science. If the metaphor of borders prioritises division and boundaries, the metaphor of networks that of nodes of interconnections, and the metaphor of flows that of mobility and movement, then the metaphor of neighbourhoods evokes the sense of coexistence between people. But as several papers (and in particular the detailed linguistic analysis of Carstensen-Egwuom and Holly) have shown, it is their pragmatic uptake by the people involved which sets their context. Thus, one of the most prevalent keywords in the discussion about multicultural neighbourhoods – *integration* – needs a great deal of deconstructing if it is to be more than an empty formula. I would therefore like to conclude with an example from my own fieldwork in Bayreuth. One of my own informants there – Michael, who lives in the small town of Speichersdorf near Bayreuth, and who as a young activist was instrumental in turning a derelict chocolate factory into a youth-run skate park – provides quite involuntarily some interesting insights into the ways in which integration discourses are almost automatically premised on a problematic situation.

For this we need to understand two opposite contexts, which are also relevant to the chapter by Dorsch in this volume.

The village of Speichersdorf, is a small town of a few thousand inhabitants near Bayreuth, where around 600 so-called Germans from Russia were housed. Due to the prevalent 'ius sanguinis' which at the time offered German nationality and passports to all who could prove German ethnicity irrespective of other criteria such as knowledge of the German language, these 'Aussiedler' had arrived in large numbers in Germany after the collapse of the Soviet Union, and – as Dorsch also shows – were the source of a great deal of anxiety and a target for discrimination from local inhabitants. When talking about the problematic relations between these Germans from Russia and the 'indigenous' Speichersdorf residents, Michael uses the term integration as one of the aims to be achieved in this troublesome spot where the presence of such 'Russlanddeutsche' is in general perceived as a problem. He immediately thinks of the effort made by voluntary workers to do integration work ('Integrationsarbeit'), the problems this causes, and the progress being made by their commitment. However, when talking about the many young people of different backgrounds who come and use his skate parks first in the open air and later in the dedicated hall of the chocolate factory, there is a notable absence of integration discourse even when he describes some young people who do not fit in quite so readily.

> I: And are these children with a migration background?
> MK: Yes, they're there as well, but they make up only a small part, they find it a bit harder, to [pause] to get involved [lit: 'warmwerden'] with the sport or with the group [...] And [kids from] all social classes came along, who just wanted to have some fun, and from every part of the country [...] all of the sudden quite a lot of Russians came with their skateboards, who just wanted to have a go, that was great, somehow all that became quite ***normal.***[10]

The avoidance of the word to integrate 'sich integrieren' is particularly noticeable in the German original since Michael had already started the sentence with the reflexive pronoun of the verb '*sich* integrieren', but abandoned it after a brief pause and replaced it by 'warmwerden' – to get involved, to become friendly. Such a differentiated use of official integration discourse on the one hand, as against the assertion of 'normal' human mixing and interrelating on the other hand, allows an interesting insight. Whereas the Germans from Russia – the politically correct description – need to be 'integrated' into Speichersdorf, the Russians with their skateboards – a politically incorrect and rejected description for the 'Russlanddeutsche' – are just one of a bunch of kids who wanted to have some fun. One of the discursive clusters to look out for in this linguistic minefield is the presence of integration discourse as a problematising discourse for others, whereas its absence may well signal a neighbourhood where 'all became quite normal'. In the neighbourhoods emerging in the different spaces and places of European everyday life, a truly integrated one may just arguably be measured best by a high level of shared concerns, debates and activities of the people involved, and a total absence of integration rhetoric.

Notes

1. Armbruster, Holly, Varady and Wastl-Walter were members of the research teams for both the EU Border Discourse and the *SeFoNe* project. Armbruster furthermore was co-director of *SeFoNe*.
2. Kiwan was Meinhof's collaborator on *Changing City Spaces*, which later gave rise to a joint British–AHRC-funded project on *Diaspora as social and cultural practice. African networks across Europe and Africa*, 2006–10, which ran in parallel with *SeFoNe* (Kiwan and Meinhof 2011). The Malagasy musician and cultural consultant Zafimahaleo Rasolofondraosolo (aka Dama from the group Mahaleo) was advisor and cultural project curator on three projects: *Changing City Spaces*, and *TNMundi*.
3. In sharp contrast to the ethnolinguistic Austrian–Hungarian border studied by Wastl-Walter and her team in both the Border Discourse and the project (Wastl-Walter et al. 2003 and Wastl-Walter and Váradi in this volume), Komárno in Slovakia, Oradea in Romania, and Berehove in the western Ukraine all have sizeable Hungarian minority populations (see Erőss, Filep, Kocsis and Tátrai in this volume).
4. See Meinhof and Galasinski 2000; Armbruster and Meinhof 2002, 2005.
5. Memories of fascism were also at the heart of the communities studied on the Italian–Slovenian border (Carli et al 2002), while status and inequality questions appeared at the heart of the narratives on the German–Polish border (Galasinska et al. 2002).
6. Interview conducted by Meinhof in 2001 with young male in Guben.
7. Working within the framework of an EU project at the time still limited our focus to capital cities in Europe and neglected the non-European countries from which our informants originated. The insight that we needed to go beyond Europe if we wanted to get a fuller picture of transnational connections of migrants in Europe led to the *TNMundi* project (Meinhof and Kiwan 2006–10). *Diaspora as social and cultural practice: transnational musicians networks across Africa and Europe*. Running side by side with *SeFoNe*, this allowed an element of continuity and cross-fertilisation.
8. This does not mean that all work using the umbrella term community is by definition based on a model of homogeneity. Indeed, we ourselves employed the term when we wrote about cross-border communities that were deeply divided (see also the work conducted under the Transnational Communities project, directed by Vertovec).
9. *SeFoNe* constitutes a research consortium of six partner universities which can be accessed via our website. Since parts of this paper were taken from our original project proposal and the end of Year 1 report, I would like to acknowledge collaboration with the co-director of *SeFoNe* Dr Heidi Armbruster, as well as the work of the two research fellows associated with the project, Dr Hauke Dorsch and Dr Cassandra Ellerbe-Dueck.
10. Interview with Michael Kleber by Meinhof and Armbruster, Bayreuth, 2008. German original, full text:Interviewer: *Und das sind Kinder die migrantischen Hintergrund haben?*
    MK: auch auch sind auch mit dabei, machen aber nur einen kleinen Teil aus, die tun sich da immer schwer sich irgendwo ... mit dem Sport oder mit der Gruppe da irgendwo ***warmzuwerden****. Am Anfang wars schöner, muss ich sagen, wo wir die*

Schanz gebaut haben, des war einfach eine komplett neue Kinderspielplatzanlage in em Stadtteil, da kamen alle Schichten mit vorbei, die einfach mal Spass haben wollten und auch von jedem Landesteil, den man sich so vorstellen kann, auf einmal kamen auch viele Russen auf dem Skateboard, die haben das einfach mal ausprobiert, das war toll, des is irgendwo normal geworden.

References

Anderson, B. (1983). *Imagined Communities: Reflections on the Origin and Spread of Nationalism* (London: Verso).

Armbruster, H. and U. H. Meinhof (2002). 'Working Identities: Key Narratives in a Former Border Region in Germany', in U. H. Meinhof (ed.) *Living (with) Borders* (Aldershot, UK: Ashgate), pp. 15–32.

Armbruster, H. and U. H. Meinhof (2005). 'Storying East-German Pasts: Memory Discourses and Narratives of Readjustment on the German/Polish and Former German/German border', in J. Thornborrow and J. Coates (eds) *The Sociolinguistics of Narrative* (Amsterdam: John Benjamins), pp. 41–65.

Armbruster, H., C. Rollo and U. H. Meinhof (2003). 'Imagining Europe: Everyday Narratives in European Border Communities', *Journal of Ethnic and Migration Studies*, vol. 29, no. 5: pp. 885–99.

Bauböck, R. and T. Faist (eds) (2010). *Diaspora and Transnationalism: Concepts, Theories and Methods* (Amsterdam University Press).

Baron, S., J. Field and T. Schuller (2000). *Social Capital: Critical Perspectives* (Oxford University Press).

Beck, U. (2000). *What is Globalization?* (Cambridge: Polity Press).

Bourdieu, P. and L. D. Wacqant (1992). *An Invitation to Reflexive Sociology* (Chicago: Chicago University Press).

Carli, A., E. Sussi and M. Kaučič-Basa (2002). 'History and Stories: Identity Construction on the Italian-Slovenian Border', in U. H. Meinhof (ed.) *Living (with) Borders* (Aldershot: Ashgate), pp. 33–52.

Carli, A., Guardiano, Kaučič-Basa, E. Sussi, M. Tessarolo and M. Ussai (2003). 'Asserting Ethnic Identity and Power Through Language', *Journal of Ethnic and Migration Studies*, vol. 29, no. 5: pp. 865–84.

Dekker, P. and E. M. Uslaner (2001). *Social Capital and Participation in Everyday Life* (London and New York: Routledge).

Delanty, G. and C. Rumford (2005). *Rethinking Europe: Social Theory and the Implications of Europeanization* (London: Routledge).

Diez, T. (2006). 'The Paradoxes of Europe's Borders', *Contemporary European Politics*, vol. 1, no. 18: pp. 1–18.

Edwards, B. and M. W. Foley (2001). 'Civil Society and Social Capital: A Primer', in B. Edwards, M. W. Foley and M. Diani (eds) *Beyond Toequeville: Civil Society and the Social Capital Debate in Comparative Perspective* (Hanover and London: University Press of New England), pp. 1–16.

Featherstone, D., R. Phillips and J. Waters (2007). 'Spatialities of Transnational Networks', *Global Networks*, vol. 7, no. 4: pp. 383–91.

Field, J. (2003). *Social Capital* (London: Routledge).

Galasinska, A., C. Rollo, and U. H. Meinhof (2002). 'Urban Space and the Construction of Identity on the German–Polish Border', in U. H. Meinhof

(ed.) *Living (with) Borders: Identity Discourses on East-West Borders in Europe* (Aldershot: Ashgate), pp. 119–40.
Galasińska, A. and D. Galasiński (2003). 'Discursive Strategies for Coping with Sensitive Topics of the Other', *Journal of Ethnic and Migration Studies*, vol. 29, no. 5: pp. 849–63.
Halpern, D. (2005). *Social Capital* (Malden, MA: Polity).
Hannerz, U. (2003). 'Being There ... and There ... and There! Reflections on Multi-Sited Ethnography', *Ethnography*, vol. 4, no. 2: pp. 201–16.
Harper, R. (2001). *Social Capital: A Review of the Literature* (London: Social Analysis and Reporting Division, Office for National Statistics).
Henderson, P., and D. N. Thomas (2002). *Skills in Neighbourhood Work*, 3rd edn (London: Routledge).
Herrmann, R. K., T. Risse and M. B. Brewer (eds) *Transnational Identities: Becoming European in the EU* (Lanham, USA; Oxford, UK: Rowman and Littlefield).
Hipfl, B., A. Bister,, P. Strohmaier, and B. Busch (2002). 'Shifting Borders: Spatial Constructions of Identity in an Austrian/Slovenian Border Region', in U. H. Meinhof (ed.) *Living (with) Borders: Identity Discourses on East-West Borders in Europe*, (Aldershot: Ashgate), pp. 53–74.
Hipfl, B., A. Bister, and P. Strohmaier (2003). 'Youth Identities along the Eastern Border of the European Union', *Journal of Ethnic and Migration Studies*, vol. 29, no. 5: pp. 835–48.
Holly, W. (2002). 'Traces of German–Czech History in Biographical Interviews at the Border: Construction of Identities and the Year 1938 in Barenstein – Vejprty', in U. H. Meinhof (ed.) (2002) *Living (with) Borders: Identity Discourses on East-West Borders in Europe* (Aldershot: Ashgate), pp. 95–118.
Holly, W., J. Nekvapil, I. Scherm, and P. Tia (2003) 'Unequal Neighbours: Coping with Assymmetries', *Journal of Ethnic and Migration Studies*, vol. 29, no. 5: pp. 819–34.
Kiwan, N. and U. H. Meinhof (2006). 'Perspectives on Cultural Diversity: A Discourse Analytical Approach', in Meinhof, U. H and A. Triandafyllidou (eds) pp. 57–84.
Kiwan, N. and U. H. Meinhof (2011). *Cultural Globalization and Music* (Basingstoke, UK; New York, USA: Palgrave Macmillan).
Marcus, G. E. (1995). 'Ethnography in/of the World System: The Emergence of Multi-Sited Ethnography', *Annual Review of Anthropology*, vol. 24: pp. 95–117.
Marcus, G. E. (2010). *Ethnography through Thick and Thin* (Princeton University Press).
Meinhof, U. H. (ed.) (2002). Living (with) Borders (Aldershot, UK: Ashgate).
Meinhof, U. H. (ed.) (2003a). 'Bordering European Identities: Special Issue', *Journal of Ethnic and Migration Studies*, vol. 29, no. 5: pp. 781–899.
Meinhof, U. H. (2003b). 'Migrating Borders: An Introduction to European Identity Construction in Process', *Journal of Ethnic and Migration Studies*, vol. 29, no. 5: pp. 781–96.
Meinhof, U. H. (2004). 'Europe Viewed from Below: Agents, Victims and the Threat of the Other', in Herrmann, R. K., Risse, T. and M. B. Brewer (eds) *Transnational Identities: Becoming European in the EU* (Lanham, USA; Oxford, UK: Rowman and Littlefield), pp. 214–46.
Meinhof, U. H. (2009). 'Transnational flows, Networks and "Transcultural Capital": Reflections on Researching Migrant Networks Through Linguistic

Ethnography', in S. Slembrouck, J. Collins and M. Baynham (eds) *Globalization and Languages in Contact: Scale, Migration, and Communicative Practices,* (Continuum), pp. 148–69.

Meinhof, U. H. and D. Galasiński (2000). 'Photography, Memory and the Construction of Identities on the Former East-West German Border', *Discourse Studies*, vol. 2, no. 3: pp. 323–53.

Meinhof, U. H. and D. Galasiński, (2005). *The Language of Belonging* (Basingstoke: Palgrave Macmillan).

Meinhof, U. H. and A. Triandafyllidou (eds) (2006). *Transcultural Europe: Cultural Policy in a Changing Europe* (Basingstoke: Palgrave Macmillan).

Meinhof, U. H. and A. Triandafyllidou (2006). 'Beyond the Diaspora: Transnational Practices as Transcultural Capital', in U. H. Meinhof and A. Triandafyllidou (eds) *Transcultural Europe: Cultural Policy in a Changing Europe*, pp. 200–22.

Nugent, P. and A. I. Asiwaju (eds) (1996). *African Boundaries: Barriers, Conduits and Opportunitie* (London: Frances Pinter).

O'Dowd, L. (2002). 'The Changing significance of European Borders', *Regional and Federal Studies*, vol. 12, no. 4: pp. 13–36.

Pratt, M.-L. (2005). 'Why the Virgin of Zapopan went to Los Angeles: Reflections on Mobility and Globality', *in* J. Anderson and W. Rowe (eds) *Images of Power. Iconography, Culture and State in Latin America*, (Berghahn), pp. 271–90.

Rice, T. (2003). 'Time, Place, and Metaphor in Musical Experience and Ethnography', *Ethnomusicology*, vol. 47, no. 2: pp. 151–79.

Sassen, S. (1996) 'Analytical Borderlands: Race, Gender and Representation in the New City', in A. King (ed.) *Representing the City: Ethnicity, Capital and Culture in the 21st Century*, New York University Press, New York, pp. 183–202

Sassen S. (2001). *The Global City: New York, London, Tokyo* (Princeton University Press, New Jersey, USA).

Schuster, L. and J. Solomos (2002). 'Rights and Wrongs across European Borders: Migrants, Minorities and Citizenship', *Citizenship Studies*, vol. 6, no. 1: pp. 37–54.

Vertovec, S. and R. Cohen (eds) (2002). *Conceiving Cosmopolitanism: Theory, Context, and Practice* (Oxford: Oxford University Press).

Wastl-Walter, D., M. Vàradi and F. Veider (2002). 'Bordering Silence: Border Narratives from the Austro-Hungarian Border', in U. H. Meinhof (ed.) *Living (with) Borders: Identity Discourses on East-West Borders in Europe* (Aldershot: Ashgate), pp. 75–93.

Wastl-Walter, M. Doris, Vàradi and F. Veider (2003). 'Coping with Marginality: To Stay or to Go', *Journal of Ethnic and Migration Studies*, vol. 29, no. 5: pp. 797–817.

Wimmer, A. and N. Glick-Schiller, (2003). 'Methodological Nationalism, the Social Sciences, and the Study of Migration: An Essay in Historical Epistemology', *The International Migration Review*, vol. 37, no. 33: pp. 576–610.

2

Becoming Good Neighbours in Cyprus: Civic Action and the Relevance of the State

Olga Demetriou, Georgina Christou and John C. Mavris

2.1 Introduction

'Neighbourhood' is a concept that combines a range of 'top-down' and 'bottom-up' points of view. It implies a space of multiple inside/ outside boundaries, e.g. domestic, public, in- and out-groups, locality and state. At the same time, these boundaries are open to definition, negotiation and redefinition: neighbourhoods always border other neighbourhoods and are created within and across different neighbourhoods – one's 'neighbourhood' always places the self at the centre. Neighbourhoods are also made, remade and maintained by individuals, informal groups, organised civil society, local authorities, state structures, perhaps even international actions. Hence our preference for the term neighbouring. Neighbourhoods can be held together by cohesion, but can also be divided and riddled with conflict.[1] To study the processes of neighbouring, therefore, requires a bifocal attention to institutions and structures, as well as to individual spontaneous or mundane activities.

This chapter focuses specifically on this bifocal quality of studying neighbouring processes, and seeks to apply this analytic frame to the case of Cyprus. The chapter takes 'neighbouring' as the cluster of relationships formed across the island's 'ethnic divide', which is marked by the Green Line (see map 2.1).[2] While this specific divide is certainly not the only marker of 'neighbourhood' (linguistic, class and variously interpreted other 'cultural' divisions exist throughout the island and not least in urban centres, for example), it does provide an excellent starting point for exploring sets of other divides and relationships forming across them that use it as a key referent. Thus, for example, cross-cultural relations between locals and migrants on the two sides are in direct and indirect ways linked to the persistence of the ethnic conflict and are spatially concentrated on the area of the border in the capital, Nicosia.[3] In this sense, what one encounters most prominently when looking at the macro-social level in Cyprus is the persisting ethnopolitical conflict that has been 'frozen' for over three decades, and where a spuriously defined 'border' marks two very distinct areas. The study of 'neighbourhood' and 'neighbouring', in this context, is inevitably a study of changing relations between political and ethnic identities.[4] The institutions and structures to be studied here, therefore, have an ultimate reference back to the conflict and the diachronic political relations between the groups inhabiting the two sides of the dividing Green Line. Similarly, the actions of individuals and everyday processes also occur within this context of division. This context, it could be argued, is one of an uneasy habitus, whereby the division per se is seen as an aberration, yet daily life is organised on the basis of its existence.[5]

The chapter tries to show the ways in which the two situations of simultaneously exceptionalising and normalising the division are reconciled to create a normality of 'neighbourhood' on the ground that is fraught with unease. To do this, the chapter surveys 'neighbourhood' relations on two levels: that of policy and that of everyday life. On these two fronts the problems and successes of 'good neighbouring' are highlighted. A series of examples has been chosen by the authors to exemplify these, and the current chapter aims at presenting only a brief outline of the workings of each. On the policy level, we have taken the example of local policies regarding the administration of everyday life in the village of Pyla (see map 2.1). On the level of less formal ways of making neighbourhood, however, the examples are drawn from: (a) forms of cooperation in the artistic field; and (b) activism around the opening of crossing points in the Green Line. In these examples, the structural level of organising cooperation, which is driven by specific sets of objectives, is compared to the experiential level of individuals' assessments of the extent to which these objectives are achieved, or superseded by other priorities. In this sense, this second set of examples also seeks to foreground the complicated relationships involved in 'civil society' activities, which are shown to be far from representative of 'the everyday', as is often the assumption in particular strands of research.[6]

The methodology followed to obtain the data on which the analysis is based draws largely on critical discourse analysis of interview data, documentation and visuals, and follows a primarily anthropological perspective. The analysis thus concentrates on the interrelations between the different levels of organised or institutional discourse and action on the one hand, and the internalisation, reception and response to these

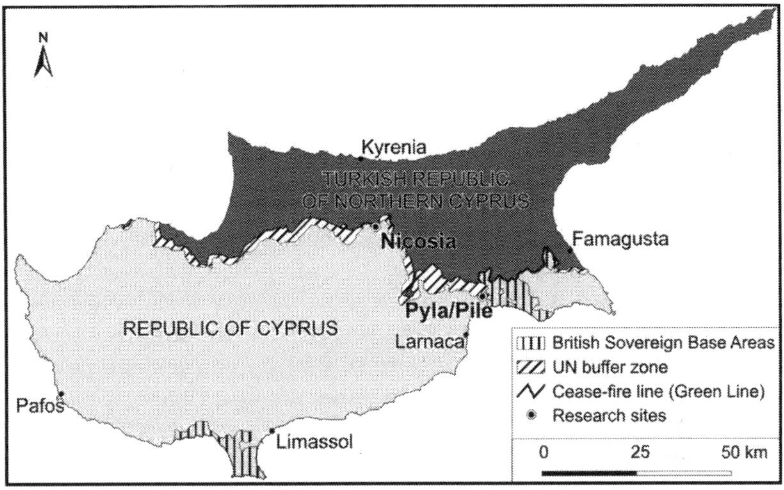

Map 2.1 Cyprus

on the level of individuals and everyday life on the other. In order to contextualise this better, a background section on the development of the conflict and historical attempts and failures to create 'neighbourhood' prefaces the presentation of the analysis.

2.2 Background

'Neighbourhood' in Cyprus is experienced through the prism of the island's division into a largely Greek-Cypriot 'south' and a largely Turkish-Cypriot 'north'. It is thus often the case that in political discourse the terms *i yítones mas* in Greek or *komşumuz* in Turkish are used to refer to coexistence with the other ethnic group. Yet, unlike the situation in Greece and Turkey, where this terminology has the same connotations, these references simultaneously entail an understanding of spatial division that is contested between the two sides. Thus, the reference to *yítones* in Cyprus entails an ideal of 'coexistence' and 'cohabitation' (*siníparxi* and *simvíosi* in Greek) at the very level of 'local neighbourhood', conforming to the discourse that before the division of 1974 Greek- and Turkish-Cypriots 'lived together well' in mixed villages and mixed urban neighbourhoods. Such coexistence then forms the basis upon which a future situation of an ideal solution is imagined as coexistence of two ethnocultural communities integrated into a common people, living in an undivided territory. However, the

Turkish use of *komşu* is premised on the notion of two groups/people living 'side by side', in spaces that are essentially 'one's own'; this then forms the basis of imagining a post-solution Cyprus in the frame of 'neighbourhood'-writ-large, between two essentially different regions.

Both of these notions have roots in the historical experience of the conflict. Thus, even though the North–South division in its current form did not exist prior to the war of 1974, studies have shown a gradual estrangement and territorial separation between the Greek- and Turkish-Cypriot communities throughout the twentieth century, which attended the onset of nationalism. Most graphically, Attalides has traced the 'unmixing' of 'neighbourhood' in the decline in numbers of mixed villages from 1881 to 1970 (1979: 89). This was amplified by the development of separate educational systems (Bryant 2004), the imbuing of ethnic separation in class-based movements (Katsiaounis 1996; Panayiotou 1999), and the rise of Helleno-centric and Turko-centric understandings of identity to hegemonic proportions (Mavratsas 1998; Peristianis 1995, 2006). This dichotomic separation of identity was finally inscribed in the Constitution of the Republic that emerged in 1960, at the end of the British colonial period, which required that all citizens belong to one of the two communities, including those members of religious groups that were neither Greek nor Turkish, i.e. Armenians, Maronites and Latins (Constantinou 2008). This transposition of division on the legal plane in turn permeated all structures of the state, with common institutions (e.g. police, civil service, parliament, courts) requiring strict representation on the basis of ethnocommunal belonging, while others remained completely distinct (e.g. education and civil matters came under the separate Greek and Turkish Communal Chambers). When this arrangement broke down in 1963, at a time of intercommunal violence, Turkish-Cypriots were no longer represented in these structures and relocated (or withdrew) into overpopulated enclaves. 'Neighbourhood' from then on acquired, in very material terms, a homogeneous ethnic character that solidified with the landing of Turkish troops in 1974 and the division that has since been marked by the Green Line. It is this division that today forms the premise on which experiences of 'neighbourhood' and the possibilities of neighbouring are based.

One of the core discourses that structure this experience of division in Cyprus is that of state recognition that relies heavily on interpretations of neighbouring relations within the legal domain. According to this discourse, the legitimacy of authorities on each side of the Green Line is disputed by the other. The Greek-Cypriot discourse thus underlines that the self-declared state of the Turkish Republic of Northern Cyprus (TRNC) in the North (which has remained unrecognised by the international community since its declaration in 1983) is illegal, and that the territory in question belongs to the Republic of Cyprus and has been under occupation by the Turkish army since 1974.[7] The Turkish-Cypriot discourse, however, maintains that the Republic of Cyprus is inherently a bicommunal Republic usurped by Greek-Cypriots who sought to dominate Turkish-Cypriots in 1963 and up to the point of intervention by the Turkish army in 1974. Within these conflictual poles, various moderate positions exist. However, the ultimate discursive frame within which relations are enacted is one that acknowledges the inability of one state to represent 'the other community'.[8] This structures relations at the level of institutions and organisations, but also at that of individuals and the mundane. The relevance of this 'neighbourhood-(un-)making' has come to the foreground since 2003, when crossing between the two sides of the Green Line, which had been near-impossible since 1974, was allowed. This chapter argues that what is at issue in the making of neighbourhood across the Cypriot Green Line today is the extent to which interactions and good neighbouring practices on the various levels examined can overcome the problems posed by this overarching discourse of conflict.

2.3 Integration at the local authority level: the example of Pyla/Pile

The village of Pyla/Pile, which is often used as a 'laboratory' to test the viability of bicommunal coexistence in media, academia and policy (Papadakis 1997) is a good place to begin this examination. It is an otherwise typical Cypriot village approximately 12 kilometres north of Larnaka Bay. It is, however, (in) famous as the only village to have retained its bicommunal composition post-1974 – making it a site in which its Greek- and Turkish-Cypriot inhabitants must constantly negotiate the common space they share. As such, Pyla functions both as an exception and a microcosm of the situation throughout the island, displaying many of the characteristics that define cross-border interaction at the various levels; from the state/institutional level down to everyday life.

Pyla is divided into three (albeit not clearly demarcated and, therefore, contested) zones of approximately equal size. The traditional centre of the village now lies squarely within the Buffer Zone[9] and, as such, comes under the supervision of the United Nations (UN). The authorities of the Republic of Cyprus and the TRNC may enter this area under special circumstances. Another third of the village lies within the territory controlled by the Republic of Cyprus. It extends to the developing coastline and is administered by the Pyla Village Council. A final third is designated as part of the British Sovereign Base Area (BSBA) of Dhekelia, and remains off-limits to most activity other than agriculture.[10] This sectioning of the village at the wider geographical level becomes problematic on account of the multifaceted power structures which exist within it: Greek-Cypriot community leadership; Turkish-Cypriot community leadership; United Nations Force in Cyprus (UNFICYP) command; BSBA authorities; as well as the respective wider authorities in the island, the TRNC and the Republic of Cyprus.

When the island gained its independence from the British in 1960, the associated Treaty of Establishment, signed at the time, installed two community leaders or mayors in Pyla, one Greek-Cypriot and one Turkish-Cypriot. As this persists, it also reflects the broader fact that, on the level of social organisation, Pyla is the only village that maintains key features of the legal bicommunalism inscribed in the 1960 constitution (another example includes having a Greek and Turkish school). However, even at this level, the village has been impacted by the communal separation of the 1960s and the formal division of 1974, in that its bicommunal leadership is disputed. While this setup continues in practice today, the Greek-Cypriot leadership sees the Turkish-Cypriot community leader as a purely nominal head, and all decisions regarding both the provision of services and the development of the village pass through the elected and official Greek-Cypriot community board and its head.

In practical terms, however, both mayors, as representatives of their communities, must co-sign projects which are put forward by the other; this ensures that both communities are heard and their interests taken into consideration. Usually, there is a great deal of overlap in the interests of each so that many decisions are reached swiftly and easily. Larger development plans, however, are hampered by this process. A comprehensive scheme to revamp Pyla's central square, for instance, was halted by the Turkish-Cypriot mayor on account of the need to demolish several older Turkish-Cypriot structures (uninhabited houses). However, a scheme to complete a specific road which linked Pyla with an area in the TRNC was halted by the Greek-Cypriot mayor, on account of it forming a passageway into occupied territory.

Nevertheless, there is the shared perception in the village that the two community boards cooperate and find solutions to mutual problems. The UN rarely steps in, and then only when the two parties cannot reach an agreement. In spite of this sustained cooperation and the stability this has afforded, both the Greek- and Turkish-Cypriot community leaders draw a distinction between Pyla as a unique example of cooperation and tolerance, and a view of Pyla as a model upon which all other Cypriot villages can be based. The Turkish-Cypriot leadership, for instance, often cites the ongoing division between the two communities outside the village, which has, inevitably, carried over into the village in the hearts and minds of its inhabitants. On this, the Greek-Cypriot leadership notably comments: 'Things are good, we do all get along. But it is not ideal, not like before [pre-1974]'. While Pyla is, therefore, often characterised as an enduring and functional example of bicommunal collaboration, it is not hailed as an ideal model of this. In this sense, several practical conflict points abound, exemplary among which is the controversy over the issue of taxes (water, electricity and property tax), which the Turkish-Cypriots have not paid to the village's Community Fund since 1963 (i.e. when the ethnic power-sharing arrangement instituted post-independence broke down).[11] Accordingly, the cost of maintaining services and implementing construction schemes is shouldered by the Greek-Cypriot local authority and the government of the Republic. More specifically, local development projects are financed through local taxation (20 per cent), while the remaining amount (80 per cent) is covered by the Republic (using interior funds, as well as, more recently, EU funds).

In effect, the UN military force in Cyprus, which has administrative control over the village, performs a mediating role between the Greek- and Turkish-Cypriot local communities. In accordance with a UN Mandate, the UN acts as a liaison between their respective Community Boards. The problematic aspect of this, according to many locals, is that while the Mandate was drawn up to correspond with the laws of the Republic of Cyprus, there is often a (perceived) marked distinction between theory and practice. This appears part of a wider conception, whereby each community views the UN force with a high degree of suspicion, interpreting its activities as, at the very least, unsympathetic. Villagers also sometimes view the UN's contribution as prejudicial, favouring the 'other side': 'They say they are impartial, but they often take "their" side' is a common mantra; often said in humour, but revealing a strain of bitterness.

While the general consensus is that at a time of uncertainty and given the particularities of Pyla the UN's arrival in the village was necessary, villagers remain divided on whether their continued stay throughout the years has been useful and/or warranted. For example, the functionality of UNFICYP is often contested: 'They are observers [...] you go to them, make your complaint, and they make a report – nothing else',[12] one Greek-Cypriot male villager explained. Many villagers (both Greek- and Turkish-Cypriot) go even further by denouncing the UN force as an unwelcome mainstay of foreign involvement in Cypriot affairs. Thus, according to one Turkish-Cypriot male villager: 'We are living together in harmony, aren't we? [But] they stay so that the English and Americans can have a say in the island.'[13] Yet, while the practical utility of the UN is regularly called into question and derogated, their symbolic function is oftentimes largely elevated: 'From the moment Turkish troops exist, the UN must inevitably exist too, because you don't know what tomorrow holds',[14] is one view articulated by a Greek-Cypriot resident.

Communication between the villagers takes place on an everyday basis, but interactions often seem restricted to an 'as and when' event, in that one's 'neighbours' are not consistently and consciously sought out. There are exceptions, with many overt instances of practices of sharing among Greek- and Turkish-Cypriot co-villagers. For example, one Greek-Cypriot woman explained: 'Whenever I bake something, I usually share it with my [Turkish-Cypriot] neighbour. And why not? I tend to bake a lot, and they are human too, aren't they? Do they not have mouths to eat?'[15] Speaking more generally, a Turkish-Cypriot woman remarked: 'If you ran out of coffee and you had a guest over, you would go to your [Greek-Cypriot] neighbour for some, no problem.'[16] Such neighbouring practices indicate a common thread of cooperation among villagers of each community, notwithstanding communal belonging.

Regarding communication on broader issues, however, particularly of an overtly political nature, there seems to be avoidance on both parts. A conscious effort is made, at both the official local authority level and the unofficial everyday level, to steer clear of highly politicised events and issues. This can be seen as part of a wider strategy of 'preserving the status quo'. The period leading up to and following the Annan Plan, for instance, was marked by a quiet tension, given that the majority of Greek-Cypriots had voted 'No' and the majority of Turkish-Cypriots had voted 'Yes'.[17] Nevertheless, no public dispute or discussion arose in the village: 'We avoid these things' and 'neither we nor they interfered', remain common responses of most Greek- and Turkish-Cypriot villagers to questions on this. In relating this non-communication, or silence, in the form of 'we' and 'they', however, villagers reveal that the division of Pyla into *Pyliotes* (Greek-Cypriot villagers) and *Pileliler* (Turkish-Cypriot villagers) is an important, if not defining, one.

Interestingly, though, this political alliance with respective 'states' is not unbreakable and, in fact, seems to be completely set aside when the status quo of the village is threatened. Thus, when the TRNC initiated a plan to funnel settlers from mainland Turkey into Pyla in 2005 (viewed by some villagers as an attempt to facilitate an additional shift in the Green Line), both communities reacted strongly against this. Through continual cajoling and appeals, the villagers cooperated in removing their new 'neighbours', whom they jointly regarded as outsiders, in order to safeguard 'internal' relations. A distinction between the longstanding 'Turks of Cyprus' (as the Turkish-Cypriots are often referred to) and the Turks of mainland Turkey was evidently at work in this effort. Curiously enough, this distinction carries as much weight among the Turkish-Cypriot villagers as it does among their Greek-Cypriot neighbours: 'They are not like us, cannot relate to us', Turkish-Cypriot villagers commonly say. Beyond the actual or perceived differences which may exist between these groups of 'Turks', *Pileliler* are still inextricably linked to the village of Pyla/Pile, as are the *Pyliotes*; adding a layer of identification which perhaps accounts for, or at least contributes to, the continued stability of the village: 'They don't feel Cyprus as their home [...] we, both Turkish-Cypriot and Greek-Cypriot members of this village, say that this land is ours.'[18]

Thus, Pyla presents an example of neighbourhood-making where the maintenance of delicate balances is paramount and where the preservation of local neighbourhood, even though at times strained by the political conflict at the state level, forms a major point of allegiance.

2.4 Building good neighbourhood via civil society action in Cyprus

At this point, it becomes important to consider the processes of building 'good neighbourhood' at the level of organised civil society groups. Since the 1990s, the United Nations Development Programme (UNDP) and the United States Agency for International Development (USAID) have been two of the most important funders and facilitators of initiatives aiming at the creation of 'good neighbourhood', understood as a trusting and peaceful relationship between the two communities. Gradually, and following Cyprus's accession to the EU, European funding was also used to strengthen this relationship at the level of civil society. During our fieldwork, particular attention has been given to initiatives organised by the European Mediterranean Arts Association (EMAA) and the Cyprus Chamber of Fine Arts (EKATE). The first is a non-governmental organisation (NGO) representing artists based in the North, while the other is based in the South. Both NGOs frequently organise art initiatives that seek to establish good and sustainable relationships among Greek- and Turkish-Cypriot artists. One such recent example was the Art Attack project, funded by UNDP-ACT (Action for Cooperation and Trust), which is overviewed here. Particular attention was also given to another recent project involving UNDP-ACT, the 'Restoration of Peristerona House' in the village of Peristerona. This building will function as the base of the Cultural Institute of the Morphou Bishopric and of a Bicommunal Committee on Cultural Affairs. The Morphou Bishopric has been a bishopric 'in exile' since 1974, following the takeover of the town of Morphou and most of the district by Turkish troops. The funding for the restoration was provided by both the bishopric and UNDP-ACT. Since the focus of analysis is on civic initiatives, considerable attention has been placed on the position that individuals and the state occupy in these, as well as to how perceptions regarding the role of each hinder efforts to create inclusive neighbourhoods.

One of the biggest challenges faced by UNDP is the issue of state recognition. As indicated by participants in these projects, as well as by experts who participated in the bicommunal movement of the 1990s, the fear (especially on the Greek-Cypriot side) of lending legitimacy to the authorities in the North, or providing any indication that the circumstances created in 1974 are being accepted as a fait accompli, posed many challenges to the organisers (Broome 2005). For example, joint art exhibitions and lectures in the North were hard to organise when it came to identifying spaces for exhibitions accepted by the Greek-Cypriot authorities. This is largely due to the unresolved issue of property, which forms the basis of Greek-Cypriot objections to the use of spaces whose Greek-Cypriot owners were displaced after 1974 and may have been used since by individuals or authorities in the North. As one interviewee put it:

> We must be very careful not to choose a place that belongs, or used to belong or still belongs to a Greek-Cypriot because of the situation [...] this is a big problem, I don't know how we are going to solve it. We had a discussion about the possibility that the winner is a settler [...] are we going to give him or her the prize?[19]

Another aspect on which the recognition issue impacts is the participation of Greek-Cypriot professionals in such activities. Thus, up until three to four years ago, such participation may not have been condoned by the bodies to which the professionals were affiliated, even if they attended in their individual capacities. This is one of the reasons that the UNDP has mostly worked with civil-society groups, they being easier to bring together and less fixated on the issue.

Despite these difficulties, the experience of people – including artists who attended joint exhibitions, as well as young people who participated in programmes such as the bicommunal summer camps – was that an understanding and changing in perception towards the other community was achieved; or, at the very least, negative stereotypical perceptions were effectively challenged.[20]

Nevertheless, one of the basic obstacles at the level of UNDP-funded civil-society initiatives seems to be the limited appreciation by the people in the two communities of the potential that civil action can have in reuniting the island. The reasons for this lack of appreciation are various and intersecting. First, there is a tendency, enforced by the media and politicians, to believe that the Cyprus issue can only be solved at the top level of political negotiations, and that it is therefore the sole responsibility (and right) of the state and political actors to work towards that goal. This kind of rhetoric affects civic action because it implies that civic initiatives cannot essentially contribute to the solution of the problem. Thus, actors striving to make a difference in this direction are effectively disempowered and their credibility undermined. This is reinforced by the widespread restriction of active citizenship to activism and affiliation with and within political parties (CIVICUS 2005; Vasilara and Piaton 2007). Furthermore, the adoption of political rhetoric by the people inhibits critical reflection and, thus, their potential to take action to solve the problem. This rhetoric is based on creating inextricable links between reunification and the reintegration of the two communities after the removal of the Turkish troops on the Greek-Cypriot side, or reunification and the day of recognition of the TRNC on the Turkish-Cypriot side; thus inhibiting the development of substantial relationships among Greek- and Turkish-Cypriots before these events come to pass. According to UNDP experience, this conceptualisation of civil society is what impedes bicommunal relationships moving from a superficial to a more substantial level.[21]

Moreover, one of the key – if not the most important – drawbacks in the case of UNDP projects is the level of impact that these projects have on Cypriot society at large. Interviewees, including both organisers of projects (civil-society actors) and UNDP personnel, emphasised the problems in the sustainability of the projects, as well as the failure to reach a wider public. This negative result is inextricably linked to the argument made above, that agency regarding the management of the 'national problem' is solely relegated to the high political level, thus excluding low-level politics from dealing with the issue. This exclusion is particularly strongly felt by personnel at UNDP, which at the level of public participation in bicommunal projects has been the premium international actor in bringing the two communities together.[22] Thus, the people who participate in such initiatives, at least in those pertaining to art, are usually the same relatively few individuals. As one interviewee put it, 'the people are being recycled a bit, this is the major problem of bicommunal [initiatives], that the participants are the same'. This is also the case for the type of organisations that apply for UNDP funding. It seems that a large part of the NGO community, at least in the South, is reluctant if not unwilling to participate in projects of a bicommunal nature, especially if their funding can be secured from other sources. Youth NGOs associated with political parties and the current government are not excluded from this reluctant NGO community, despite the fact that current governmental efforts on the part of the Republic of Cyprus appear to be geared towards the island's reunification and the pursuit of 'reconciliation and peaceful co-existence with the Turkish Cypriots'.[23]

This paradox, as well as the lack of top-down encouragement, is a crucial problem in fostering good neighbouring relationships at the ground level. These relationships, as one participant mentioned, appear to have stayed at the level of organised programmes/initiatives.[24] This translates into a lack of substantial interaction between participants of bicommunal programmes after the funding and the programme have come to an end. UNDP has, in this sense, also identified a need for more strategic planning regarding the channelling of funds aimed at achieving greater impact. Focus and funding are thus now directed towards creating strong networks among NGOs in the North and South, so as to sustain bicommunal initiatives and relationships among people and organisations on the ground. At the same time, there is also an expectation that the EU will acquire a more active role in the promotion and financial support of such activities, and 'also take responsibility for this issue in a very coherent way to strengthen these [bicommunal] relationships'.[25]

However, despite UNDP projects lacking wide and diverse public participation, strong personal and professional relationships developed among those people who had participated, especially at the level of members of civil-society groups. Regarding the initiatives examined here, what appeared to be recurrent and essential in creating good neighbourhood were the perceptions that participating civil actors shared in terms of the turbulent events of the past. For the main actors in the Peristerona project, the dissociation from official historical narratives regarding the conflict and the attribution of shared blame to both communities for the current division helped them to come to terms with past conflict and to envisage a common future. This was reinforced by the view shared by the organisers in art associations that 'true unity will come from the people, from the citizens'.[26] This view is quite contradictory to official political rhetoric, providing the impetus to move forward, as it also contributes to the abolition of the victim role promoted through official politico-historical narratives, which tends to cripple individual potential for change.

The agency of these civil actors towards change and unity was reinforced with the opening of the borders in 2003. This event gave them the opportunity to reimagine the border, this time as offering a potential for contact, purging a divisive past, and creating a different future. The initial enthusiasm that emanated from the opening of the border also affected the local people in Peristerona, which used to be a mixed village with a long history of peaceful coexistence among its Greek- and Turkish-Cypriot inhabitants. During the period after the opening of the borders in 2003, there was a great deal of interaction between Greek- and Turkish-Cypriot co-villagers, as well as between people in the wider area of Morphou. Cooperation grew at various levels, from religious affairs in terms of restoring and operating religious buildings, to the exchange of information on the fate of missing persons or families separated during the war. The period after the referendum in 2004, and the lack of encouragement by the government for such cooperation (at least on the Greek-Cypriot side), saw an essential reduction in this type of interaction. At the everyday level, the people of Peristerona express nostalgia about the days of coexistence in the village, yet this cannot translate into wider initiatives to strengthen the bonds at ground level. There are, however, a few Greek-Cypriot families, which maintain friendly ties with Turkish-Cypriot families from the village and meet on a regular basis.

These examples show that civil society has many challenges to face in Cyprus in terms of leading the way in the development of 'good neighbouring', i.e. substantial relationships among the people of the two communities. These challenges can be found at two levels: first, perceptions of civic action; and, second, funding resources. Top-down encouragement is needed in terms of both mentality and funding for such initiatives to grow stronger and develop to their full potential. For this reason, the role of the EU is now all the more important and necessary, in both funding and creating an organisational framework for such initiatives to work efficiently – especially as the UNDP-ACT mandate comes to an end in 2011.

2.5 Contact on the ground: The opening of Ledra Street

In comparison to such 'organised' civil society initiatives, less organised forms of civic action seem to have been more able to impact political changes on the ground, by taking advantage of revisions in the political discourse, following the election of a new government in 2008. A first spectacular example of such changes, in the period following the election of a new government in the South, was the opening of Ledra Street in April 2008. This came at the heels of high-level meetings between the leaders of the two sides, in which the implementation of a number of 'confidence-building measures' (CBMs) and the beginning of a new round of talks to solve the conflict were decided. Top on the CBM list this time was the opening of Ledra Street. However, in order to fully understand the relevance of this event to the making of neighbourhood, an analysis of 'grassroots' activities focusing on the goal of opening Ledra Street needs to be undertaken. In this sense, the top-level initiative in the specific case can be seen as a response to, and legitimisation of, ground-level action.

As the main shopping street of the old town centre, running north to south, Ledra Street was first divided with barbed wire segregating the capital's Greek and Turkish sector in 1958, and has been a symbol of the Cyprus conflict ever since. Its reopening thus became symbolic of an impending reunification of the whole island following the opening of checkpoints elsewhere in 2003. By implication, the failure to open it prior to April 2008 was also widely seen as emblematic of the problems impeding a solution and, thus, reunification. The Greek-Cypriot argument that it would not consent to the opening unless the area of the crossing point was demilitarised, for example, was firmly anchored in the discourse that 'the Cyprus problem is one of invasion and occupation' of the northern part of the island by Turkey.[27] The significance of the opening of Ledra Street to the creation of neighbourhood is, therefore, amplified by the existence of this symbolic loading, because it has meant that the street has become a focus of peace-seeking, civil-society lobbying efforts.

Before its opening in April 2008, arguments had been made for and against on both sides, with the debate being most fierce in the South. This is because in the North the shopping area that lies around the Street was not as popular as the corresponding area in the South and, therefore, local shopkeepers saw in the prospective opening the possibility of increasing their clientele. However, shopkeepers in the South seemed more divided between those who predicted a rise in touristic interest (both local and foreign) and, therefore, an overall rise in clientele on both sides, and those who felt that clients would be lost to the shops in the North, where 'prices are cheaper'. It is indicative of this polarisation that one Greek-Cypriot shopkeeper, whose shop was clearly suffering from lack of traffic because of its proximity to the border, expressed support for initiatives to open the crossing point, claiming that those shopkeepers who opposed them did not see that it would be beneficial for both sides.[28] After the opening, he appeared to have been proven right, with his shop now evidently more populated with clients (notably, on both occasions he insisted on not being recorded or named).[29] Indeed, following the opening, the traffic rose quickly and the area appears to have benefited not only from shopping-related activities but also from an increase in property prices. This further attests to the area slowly losing its 'borderland' feel of abandonment.

These actual changes on the ground, which are located mainly in the economic sphere, provide interesting comparisons with the discourses that had framed the question of opening Ledra Street before April 2008, and which were located largely in the political and symbolic sphere. For example, the activist group 'Committee for the Opening of the Checkpoints', which most vocally pushed for the opening of Ledra Street, focused its arguments on the prospect of achieving a solution through fostering good social relations between people on the two sides (i.e. fostering good neighbouring). The dismantling of the separation wall that stood at the end of the street symbolised, in this discourse, the tearing down of walls of 'hatred and intolerance' (*ta tíhi tou mísous ke tis misallodhoxías*). Events organised to underscore that message included the singing of songs associated with anti-fascism and peace, and the symbolic release of helium balloons into the air. Echoing this symbolism was the release of doves by the Greek- and Turkish-Cypriot leftist mayors of the town on the day when the crossing point was actually opened.

Yet, organisers appeared well-aware of the interconnections between the spheres of symbolism, politics and economics. Thus, they foresaw that the eventual opening of the street would financially benefit both sides, while at the same time they emphasised the significance of such economic benefits to the improvement of cross-border cooperation and social relations. Within their Marxist perspective, the meaning of social action is strengthened, not diluted, by economic concerns. It is for this reason that they made considerable efforts to meet with shopkeepers on both sides of Ledra Street prior to the formulation of the campaign, discussed concerns with them and elicited their support.[30]

Throughout the formation of this initiative, cooperation across the dividing line was of primary importance. Thus, the formative decisions around the campaign were taken jointly by activists on the two sides, and were based on a good understanding of 'the climate' on the other side. Greek-Cypriot members of the group were and continue to be frequent visitors to the North, as are the Turkish-Cypriot members. Indicative of the extent to which actions have been guided by this understanding was the organisation of campaigning events that aimed at locally specific problems, without being guided by a 'mirror' logic whereby anything that happens on one side must be mirrored on the other side. Thus, when a first 'scanning' of the terrain to elicit support showed that many Greek-Cypriot shopkeepers were in fact supportive of the opening but scared to say so, a joint march of Greek- and Turkish-Cypriot activists was organised on the South side only, calling on the Greek-Cypriot authorities to abandon their intransigent stance. The march attracted a small crowd and was not as successful as later events with the same aim. But for one Greek-Cypriot organiser, the most gratifying moment of the campaign was seeing one of his Turkish-Cypriot colleagues genuinely impressed with the turnout: 'and just to think that this person, who had a leading role in the demonstrations of 2002, when half the Turkish-Cypriot population was in the streets, was impressed by this!'[31] The significance of this quotation is that it shows that the power that pervades activist efforts like this one is not exhausted by the ability to amass support. It most saliently inheres in the ability to articulate a critique of structures. Thus, the importance of the march at that point was not that it was well attended, but that it showed Turkish-Cypriots, who had successfully overthrown a nationalist leadership in 2003, that Greek-Cypriots were also willing to take to the streets and criticise their own government.

Another important event in the campaign was a gathering at the (then closed) checkpoint, which drew the attention of an extreme nationalist organisation, members of which marched in counter-protest against the activists. The failure of the nationalist crowd to hinder the peace activists, and their withdrawal without substantially affecting the event, was read as proof of the insubstantial nature of nationalist discourse. At the same time, the government's failure to criticise the counter-demonstrators and their later statements, equating both crowds by reference to 'two groups of extremists', was taken as tacit approval of the working of such nationalist groups, and as an indication of how crucial a blow to nationalist discourse the opening of Ledra Street would eventually be.

With Ledra Street thus far looking like a 'success story', the efforts of the group are now concentrated on calling for further crossing points to open. In essence, then, what these less organised civic initiatives demonstrate is the importance of mounting a substantial critique of state policy, at the heart of which lies a critique of nationalist ideology.

2.6 Conclusion

The division of Cyprus on consecutively the cultural, political, and territorial levels has entailed its own dynamics of neighbouring, which have been subject to diachronic changes. These changes have gained increased momentum since the island's accession to the EU in 2004, which brought increased migration, new initiatives for resolution of the political problem, and a range of new policies relating to multiculturalism and exclusion.

The Cyprus case study presented in this chapter has sought to situate these recent changes within the larger frame of the diachronic prominence of the ethnopolitical conflict in political and daily local life, and to examine the extent to which discourses and practices of neighbouring have acquired a more inclusive character as a result. By moving between different levels, from the governmental (and international) to the individual, and by paying particular attention to civic initiatives, we have sought to provide a rounded perspective on the possibilities and obstacles to good neighbourhood-making. The making of 'good neighbourhood' is thus shown to be ultimately circumscribed by understanding of the 'public sphere' and the space occupied by the state in it. Nevertheless, this process is a dynamic one and, therefore, the boundaries between civic and state power are always in negotiation.

Notes

1. In social science literature, the concept of 'neighbourhood' has been mostly elaborated in urban studies and geography. For recent reviews, see Forrest and Kearns (2001); Kallus and Law-Yone (2000); Kearns and Parkinson (2001); Martin (2003); Lupton and Power (2004); Volker et al. (2007).
2. On the interpretations of 'division' marked by the Green Line, see Demetriou (2007); Navaro-Yashin (2003, 2005); Papadakis (2005); and Papadakis et al. (2006).
3. See, for example, Demetriou (2009).
4. In this respect, anthropological studies of such processes of change in border areas offer perhaps the best comparisons. An indicative sample is Armbruster et al. (2003); Bridger and Pine (1998); Bringa (1996); Donnan and Wilson (1999).
5. This situation has been explored elsewhere (Demetriou 2007b).
6. This view persists within political science literature on Cyprus, and despite scores of critiques on simplistic views of 'civil society' (Agathangelou 1997: 45–94; Fraser 1990; Hann and Dunn 1996; Navaro-Yasin 2003: 130–7).
7. This discourse is largely based on UN resolutions confirming the illegality of the declaration of independence by the TRNC.
8. It is interesting to note that this commonly used phrase overshadows the existence of groups beyond the bicommunal understandings of coexistence in Cyprus (Constantinou 2008).
9. This was not always the case and, in fact, the Green Line did not initially impact the village. A gradual re-shifting of the ceasefire line southwards, however, on four separate occasions, brought Pyla directly within the Buffer Zone.

10. The Treaty of Establishment gave Great Britain the right to retain two sovereign bases on the island; one of which is Dhekelia, in the south-east, the other Akrotiri, in the south.
11. Paradoxically, in recent years, Turkish-Cypriot villagers have begun paying certain taxes to the TRNC. The only utility which Turkish-Cypriot villagers have paid for in the Republic of Cyprus is their phone bill, which is offered through CYTA, the Cyprus Telecommunications Authority (the state provider of telecommunications services in the Republic).
12. Interview: Pyla Village Community Board, 2006. All Pyla interviews were initially conducted in 2006. Follow-up interviews in the village included the original informants and took place as part of the *SeFoNe* Project, 2007–10.
13. Interview: Pyla, private household, 2006.
14. Interview: Pyla Village Community Board, 2006.
15. Interview: Pyla, private household, 2006.
16. Interview: Pyla, private household, 2006.
17. Voting results in Pyla largely mirrored the island-wide Greek- to Turkish-Cypriot yes/no average. The referendum, it should be noted, took place simultaneously on both parts of the island in April 2004. Voters were asked to endorse a UN-brokered plan for 'a comprehensive settlement to the Cyprus problem', widely referred to as 'The Annan Plan' after the then UN Secretary General. Since it was rejected by the majority of the Greek-Cypriot voters, it was officially declared 'null and void'; yet its provisions are still a subject of public debate.
18. Interview: Pyla, private household, 2006.
19. Interview, member of the European Mediterranean Arts Association (EMAA), Nicosia, 28/11/2007. In this quotation, the interviewee refers to the UNDP project Art Attack and the island-wide competition that was organised as part of the project. Following the competition, an island-wide exhibition of the chosen art works was organised.
20. The ongoing Cyprus Youth Dialogue Project, again funded by UNDP-ACT, brought together 24 young Greek- and Turkish-Cypriots to engage in dialogue on the common problems they face. According to several of them, an important part of this dialogue was the effective challenging/changing of their perception of the 'other'.
21. Interview, UNDP's personnel, Buffer Zone, 08/09/2008.
22. Low Greek-Cypriot participation in such projects is also considered to be a result of the ways the previous government sought to discredit people involved in these kinds of activities: accusing them of bribery by foreign actors and interests in order to vote in favour of the Annan Plan in the referendum of 24/04/2004. For further information, see Drousiotis (2005).
23. Press and Information Office – Republic of Cyprus (2008).
24. Interview, Manager of the Cultural Institute of the Morphou Bishopric, Nicosia, 12/03/2008.
25. Interview, UNDP's personnel, Buffer Zone, 08/09/2008.
26. Interview, president of the Board of the Cyprus Chamber of Fine Arts, Nicosia, 06/08/2008.
27. An analysis of this and other impediments has been undertaken elsewhere (Demetriou 2007a).

28. Interview, Nicosia, 19/12/2007.
29. Interviews, Nicosia, 19/12/2007 and 18/4/2008.
30. Series of interviews, member of the Committee for the Opening of the Checkpoints, December 2007–January 2010.
31. Interview, Nicosia, 09/02/2008.

References

Agathangelou, A. M. (1997). *The Cypriot 'Ethnic' Conflict in the Production of Global Power* (Syracuse, NY: Syracuse University).

Armbruster, H., C. Rollo and U. H. Meinhof (2003). 'Imagining Europe: Everyday Narratives in European Border Communities', *Journal of Ethnic and Migration Studies*, vol. 29, no. 5: pp. 885–99.

Attalides, M. (1979). *Cyprus, Nationalism and International Politics* (London: Macmillan Press).

Bridger, S. and F. Pine (eds) (1998). *Surviving Post-Socialism: Local Strategies and Regional Responses in Eastern Europe and the former Soviet Union* (London: Routledge).

Bringa, T. (1996). *Being Muslim the Bosnian Way: Identity and Community in a Central Bosnian Village* (Princeton: Princeton University Press).

Broome, B. J. (2005). *Building Bridges across the Green Line: A Guide to Intercultural Communication in Cyprus* (Nicosia: United Nations Development Programme (UNDP)).

Bryant, R. (2004). *Imagining the Modern: The Cultures of Nationalism in Cyprus* (London: I. B. Tauris).

CIVICUS (2005). Civil Society Index Report for Cyprus: An Assessement of Civil Society in Cyprus: A Map for the Future. Conducted by the Management Centre of the Mediterranean in collaboration with Intercollege (available at http://www.civicus.org, accessed June 2010).

Constantinou, C. (2008). 'On the Cypriot States of Exception', *International Political Sociology*, vol. 2, no. 2: pp. 145–64.

Demetriou, O. (2007a). 'Freedom Square: The Unspoken Reunification of a Divided City', *Hagar International Social Science Review*, vol. 7, no. 1: pp. 55–78.

Demetriou, O. (2007b). 'To Cross or not to Cross? Subjectivization and the Absent State in Cyprus', *Journal of the Royal Anthropological Institute*, vol. 13, no. 4: pp. 987–1005.

Demetriou, O. (2009). *Migrant Cities: Nicosia South* (Nicosia: British Council).

Donnan, H. and T. M. Wilson (1999). *Borders: Frontiers of Identity, Nation and State* (Oxford: Berg).

Drousiotis, M. (2005). *The Construction of Reality and the Mass Media in Cyprus*, http://www.makarios.ws/cgibin/hweb?-A=980and-V=perireousa, accessed June 2010.

Forrest, R., and A. Kearns (2001). 'Social Cohesion, Social Capital and the Neighbourhood', *Urban Studies*, vol. 38, no. 12: pp. 2125–43.

Fraser, N. (1990). 'Rethinking the Public Sphere: A Contribution to the Critique of Actually Existing Democracy', *Social Text*, vol. 25, no. 26: pp. 56–80.

Hann, C. M. and E. Dunn (eds) (1996). *Civil Society: Challenging Western Models* (London: Routledge).

Kallus, R. and H. Law-Yone (2000). 'What is a Neighbourhood? The Structure and Function of an Idea', *Environmental Planning B: Planning and Design*, vol. 27, no. 6: pp. 815–26.

Katsiaounis, R. (1996). *Labour, Society and Politics in Cyprus during the Second Half of the Nineteen Century* (Nicosia: Cyprus Research Centre).

Kearns, A. and M. Parkinson (2001). 'The Significance of Neighbourhood', *Urban Studies*, vol. 38, no. 22: pp. 2103–10.

Lupton, R. and A. Power (2002). 'Social Exclusion and Neighbhourhoods', in J. Hills, J. Le Grand and D. Piachaud (eds). *Understanding Social Exclusion* (Oxford: Oxford University Press), pp. 118–40.

Martin, D. G. (2003). '"Place-Framing" as Place-Making: Constituting a Neighborhood for Organizing and Activism', *Annals of the Association of American Geographers*, vol ICIII, no. III: pp. 730–50.

Mavratsas, C. V. (1998). 'Greek-Cypriot Political Culture and the Prospect of European Union Membership: A Worst-Case Scenario', *The Cyprus Review*, 10: pp. 67–76.

Navaro-Yashin, Y. (2003). '"Life is Dead Here": Sensing the Political in "No Man's Land"', *Anthropological Theory*, vol. 3, no. 1: pp. 107–25.

Navaro-Yashin, Y. (2005) 'Confinement and the Imagination: Sovereignty and Subjectivity in a Quasi-State,' in T. Blom Hansen and F. Steputtat (eds), *Sovereign Bodies: Citizens, Migrants and States in the Postcolonial World* (Princeton: Princeton University Press), pp. 103–119.

Panayiotou, A. (1999). *Island Radicals: The Emergence and Consolidation of the Cypriot Left, 1920–60* (Santa Cruz, CA: University of California).

Papadakis, Y. (1997). 'Pyla: A Mixed Borderline Village under UN Supervision in Cyprus', *International Journal on Minority and Group Rights*, vol. 4, no. 3–4: pp. 353–72.

Papadakis, Y. (2005). *Echoes from the Dead Zone: Across the Cyprus Divide* (London: I. B. Tauris).

Papadakis, Y., N. Peristianis and G. Welz (2006). 'Modernity, History and Conflict in Divided Cyprus: An Overview', in Y. Papadakis, N. Peristianis and G. Welz (eds). *Divided Cyprus: Modernity, History, and an Island in Conflict* (Bloomington: Indiana University Press), pp. 1–29.

Peristianis, N. (2006). 'The Rise of the Left and of the Intra-Ethnic Cleavage', in H. Faustmann and N. Peristianis (eds). *Britain in Cyprus: Colonialism and Post-Colonialism, 1878–2006* (Mannheim and Möhnesee: Bibliopolis), pp. 233–68.

Press and Information Office – Republic of Cyprus, Cyprus Problem: Recent Developments (2008). *Demetris Christofias: New President of the Republic*, http://www.moi.gov.cy/moi/pio/pio.nsf/developments_en/developments_en?opendocument#14, accessed September 2010.

Vasilara, M. and Piaton, G. (2007). 'The Role of Civil Society in Cyprus', *The Cyprus Review*, 19 (1): pp. 107–21.

Volker, B., H. Flap and S. Lindenberg (2007). 'When Are Neighbourhoods Communities? Community in Dutch Neighbourhoods', *European Sociological Review*, vol. 23, no. 1: pp. 99–114.

3

Austrian–Hungarian Environmental Conflict: Struggling for Political Participation in the Borderland

Doris Wastl-Walter and Monika Mária Váradi

The Austrian–Hungarian–Slovenian triple border area, which has traditionally been characterised by good neighbourhood relations, has become the scene of a serious environmental conflict in recent years. This conflict has evolved in the triple border area, but it is Hungarian and Austrian settlements, particularly the small Hungarian town of Szentgotthárd, which are involved in it (see map 3.1). The conflict was precipitated by an Austrian company planning to install a large-capacity waste incinerator next to the border near Szentgotthárd, which the inhabitants there are striving to prevent. The conflict has not been deleterious for traditional neighbourhood relations, but it has rearranged former political coalitions along various interests and values, resulting in the emergence of new cross-border and multigenerational networks. In the discourses formed about the conflict, 'neighbourhood' appears emphatically as a category that is simultaneously embedded in local, national and EU contexts.

3.1 Borders and neighbourhood relations

Until the Second World War, Szentgotthárd was the centre of the surrounding Hungarian, Austrian and Slovenian villages located on the inner periphery of the Austro-Hungarian monarchy. Following the redrawing of the border in Trianon after the First World War, the town lost a significant part of its labour and agricultural markets, and the villages, then on the other side of the border, lost their centre and became the outer periphery of the new states (see Beluszky 2005). In this area, the Trianon border followed the ethnic and linguistic border so that cross-border relations were not burdened by undigested national, ethnic and territorial grievances and conflicts. The border remained traversable until the

Map 3.1 The triple-border area

Iron Curtain was erected after the Second World War, which hermetically sealed off the Hungarian side and Szentgotthárd not only from 'hostile' Austria, but also from the inner parts of Hungary (see Seger and Beluszky 1993; Wastl-Walter et al. 2003b; Wastl-Walter and Váradi 2004).

The 1980s were a revival period for cross-border neighbourhood relations. Since then the cross-border connections of individuals, non-governmental organisations (NGOs), institutions and settlements have gradually broadened and transformed in the course of geopolitical changes, the gradual border openings, the collapse of the socialist bloc and the frameworks and opportunities offered by European integration (Baumgartner et al. 2002; Wastl-Walter et al. 2003a, 2003c).

Connections were first developed by sports clubs and cultural associations. On the political level, cooperation became institutionalised when Szentgotthárd received town status in 1983. Life along the Austrian–Hungarian border was reanimated: children from Heiligenkreuz and Szentgotthárd became acquainted with one another and their languages in summer camps; choirs gave mutual village concerts; and football teams played friendly matches. In 1988, after lengthy preparation, the joint youth orchestra called the 'Raabtaler Jungendorchester' comprising pupils and teachers of the music schools of Szentgotthárd and Austrian Jennersdorf was established and is still operating today. In 1987, the settlements involved managed to have Szentgotthárd join the Heiligenkreuz–Jennersdorf sewage works. The sewage of the town has since been treated there. Everyday life also changed with the collapse of the Iron Curtain in 1989: Austrian shopping tourism started flourishing and Hungarian employees appeared on the legal and illegal Austrian labour markets.

Cross-border relations have also been shaped by the expanding European Union, with its development policies and resources, by educational institutions, NGOs and bi- and multilateral cooperative projects for national parks. Noteworthy here is the cross-border, fully equipped Szentgotthárd-Heiligenkreuz Industrial Park (IP), a unique development in Europe established in 1997 with support from PHARE CBC and Interreg II.[1]

In the first three years, the property rights of the 65-hectare IP were shared almost equally between the Hungarian and Austrian parties. In 2000 a capital boost was necessary for further development, but Szentgotthárd's government could not contribute. Then Wirtschaftsservice Burgenland Aktiengesellschaft (WIBAG) – which is entirely owned by Burgenland, one of the nine Austrian federal states – became the majority owner of the IP shares. This led to a stark financial and political imbalance between the two partners, as Szentgotthárd, owning only 8.7 per cent of the shares, could represent its interests concerning the IP's marketing and investment uses only to that extent.[2]

The IP remained an EU investment representing good neighbourly relations until the installation plan of the incinerator became public. In light of the conflictual developments since, the former Mayor of Szentgotthárd emphasised to us that it had been a mistake not to settle on a joint regulation about the investment policies for the IP: 'Nobody thought of this, since relations were so good' (Interview with Mr K.B., former Mayor, Szentgotthárd, 05.12.2007).

3.2 Environmental conflict and neighbourhood

3.2.1 Important stages of the conflict

In May 2006, the Burgenländische Erdgasversorgung-AG (BEGAS)[3] held a project presentation in the Heiligenkreuz IP, to which neither the leadership of Szentgotthárd nor the Hungarian manager employed by the IP were invited, though the latter accidentally attended the presentation. It turned out that BEGAS, in agreement with Lenzing Fibers GmbH (cellulose production), the largest firm on the Austrian side of the IP, was planning to install an incinerator with an annual capacity to burn 250,000 tons of sludge, plastic and wood residue, in order to provide low-cost energy for the IP firms, particularly for Lenzing.

News of the investment plan – which by then had appeared on the BEGAS website – and the alleged phrase 'and we will convince the Hungarians' in the upper corner of one slide during the presentation, immediately reached the leadership of Szentgotthárd. Reaction was swift and firm. The representative body of Szentgotthárd passed a resolution in May declaring that it did not agree with a project incongruous with the interests of the town's inhabitants and the region's development plans. The local government set out on a political and diplomatic mission, seeking national and European members of parliament, and initiating negotiations with ministries. Meanwhile, the town's NGOs became active. The first demonstration took place in June 2006, and a long series of protests started with a roadblock at the Rábafüzes–Heiligenkreuz border station.[4]

In July 2006, the leaders of BEGAS responded by inviting the mayors of the neighbouring Austrian villages and Szentgotthárd to a trip to Vienna, where they were taken on a tour of the city's waste incinerators in order to be shown that the technology to be applied was up-to-date, environmentally friendly and safe for human health. The Hungarian participants were not convinced.

In February 2007, the Mayor of Szentgotthárd replaced the Hungarian national banner with a black flag of mourning in the Friendship of Peoples Memorial Park built along the former Iron Curtain, to express that 'we are mourning friendship!' (Mr T. V., Mayor, Szentgotthárd, 17.03.2007, see [www.danke.szentgotthard.hu]). In March, at a special seminar about environmental issues held for over 1,000 pupils of the town, the 'Danke Nein!' movement was launched, which replaced the black flag with one bearing the legend 'Danke Nein!'. It is still flying there (see Photo 3.1). In the spring of 2007, the largest demonstration to date took place. A sharp-tongued correspondence between the Austrian Ambassador and the Mayor of Szentgotthárd was published in the press, and the Hungarian Parliament passed a declaration in support of the town. Meanwhile, committed citizens founded Pro Natura St Gotthard (PRONAS), Hungarian, Austrian and Slovenian Green NGOs initiated cooperation, and the Austrian BürgerInitiative Gegen AbfallSchweinerei (BIGAS) or 'citizens movement against waste rascality', (a play on words ridiculing the company acronym BEGAS) was launched.

In January 2008, the investor published an 'environmental impact assessment study'. Since the incinerator is to be constructed next to the border and its environmental impacts will affect Hungary, the Hungarian state must be involved in the licensing procedure in accordance with the Espoo Convention of the UN.[5] The convention grants consultation but no veto rights to the government. Austrian legislation also made possible an involvement in the project licensing procedure. It stipulates that anyone living in the vicinity of the project could submit their views about the planned investment. Moreover, individual inhabitants of the neighbouring settlements (including Szentgotthárd) who could prove that the investment caused them financial or moral harm could register as clients, as could Hungarian environmental organisations. Client status is important, because it provides the rights of participation and appeal in the licensing procedure.

Public consultation for the environmental impact assessment study ended in March 2008. But protest continued and 5605 petitions from both Austria and Hungary were submitted to the licensing authority. While the consultation procedure for the environmental impact assessment study was in progress, Szentgotthárd organised a referendum 'for the protection of our health and environment' for 6 April 2008, which included a question regarding the rejection of the incinerator. The local, non-binding referendum drew a high voter turnout (59.27 per cent), and 98 per cent of the voters rejected the installation of the incinerator. In 2008 a fissure appeared in the previous wall of support when the representatives of three small settlements in Austria (Mogersdorf, Weichselbaum, Eltendorf) adopted a resolution against the incinerator. The circle of protesters widened. A hundred Hungarian and Austrian doctors protested against the investment because of its damaging effects on human health, and after the publication of the environmental impact assessment study, the managers of nearby Austrian spas expressed their disapproval of the investment for reasons of feared environmental damage.

On 12 December 2008, the municipal councils of Szentgotthárd and Mogersdorf, the Austrian Green Party, and five Slovenian Green parties together with PRONAS and BIGAS signed a joint petition expressing their objection to the planned incinerator and sent it to the European Parliament. Immediately afterwards, the town of Szentgotthárd launched a witty protest action: Hungarian citizens could object to the incinerator on bilingual postcards addressed to the Austrian investor and the leaders of the federal state of Burgenland. Nevertheless, the Burgenland State Office provided a licence to build the incinerator in February 2009, arguing that it was in tune with the environmental impact study. At the time of writing in spring 2010, the Austrian environment protection authority (Umweltsenat) has not yet decided on the investment project and the protest of the people of Szentgotthárd continues.

3.2.2 The asymmetries of conflict management

As soon as the news about the incinerator project was published, it grew into a major local issue but also had national, transnational and European-Union level ramifications in Hungary. The strategy of PRONAS, the NGO in Szentgotthárd opposing the project, was not only to approach Hungarian authorities but to directly call upon Austrian actors, be they environmental authorities, ministries or political parties. This strategy encouraged the concerned parties to react directly. In addition to coverage on the PRONAS website, there was broad national media coverage on the process of the conflict and PRONAS activities, including the nearly 50 smaller and larger demonstrations organised since 2006. The ceaseless public presence of the organisation and the tirelessly produced letters and petitions forced the Hungarian government and representatives of political parties to acknowledge the environmental conflict along the border. Members of the Hungarian and European Parliaments, environment ministers, and Hungary's President and Prime Minister expressed their opposition at every possible occasion and criticised the 'intolerable and cynical' attitude of the Austrian authorities.

The incinerator controversy was brought up at the joint Austrian–Hungarian government session on 29 November 2007 in Budapest, where the Hungarian Prime Minister asked the Austrian Chancellor to consider building the incinerator at another site, given the concerns and objections of those living on the Hungarian side of the border. The Austrian Chancellor assured his Hungarian colleague that international treaties and Austrian laws had been observed in the licensing procedure and the opinion of those affected had been considered. He also proclaimed that the incinerator was an economic not a political issue.

The Chancellor's opinion is shared by Austrian experts and politicians supporting the project, who stress its economic and technological benefits. On the Austrian side its political effects remained minimal.

For example, the investment hardly figured in the location election campaigns in Burgenland in autumn 2007. Only the representatives of the small opposition parties in Burgenland's parliament and local governments (the Freiheitliche Partei Österreichs (FPÖ) and the Green Party) expressed their opposition to the building of the incinerator and their support for Hungarian protests. The investor and the politicians supporting the incinerator claim that the protest is an expression of cantankerousness and hostility against much needed regional development.

The investor BEGAS has also created its own publicity. As of June 2007, an employee of the project management located in the information office in the IP is responsible for communication with the local inhabitants. Anyone interested can walk in to make enquiries during working hours. The office provides detailed information on the investment and the current status of the environmental impact assessment study, and responds to concerns which are framed as questions on a separate website. Of course, these answers point in one direction only, arguing in favour of the project.[6]

3.2.3 Continuity and change in cross-border neighbourliness

Environmental conflicts have not transformed the well-developed cross-border relations of individuals, cultural and sports organisations, institutions and economic actors. However, the patterns of political cooperation and coalitions have changed. Previously, the relations of the leadership of Heiligenkreuz and Szentgotthárd were based on jovial friendship. In the wake of the conflict, though, the Mayor of Szentgotthárd suspended official relations with the Mayor and the representative body of the neighbouring town. At the same time, he entered into closer cooperation with the local government in neighbouring Austrian Mogersdorf, which opposed the project. The new coalition choreography spectacularly appeared during the events around Hungary's accession to Schengen. While Szentgotthárd held official celebrations with Mogersdorf, Hungarian, Austrian and Slovenian Green NGOs organised another protest at the border section along Heiligenkreuz, in the Peoples' Friendship Memorial Park. These Green organisations have transformed the content and character of cross-border neighbourhood relations and discourses about the border to the greatest extent. Hungarian civilians protesting against the installation of the incinerator formed relations with neighbouring Austrian and Slovenian Greens, and a cross-border network of Greens, environmental organisations, individuals and experts swiftly formed. Establishing the network itself became a joint learning process. In order to effectively stand up against environmental pollution, participants needed to acquire new knowledge and skills in the fields of environmental protection, waste management, national and EU legislation, the organisation of public actions and effective public presentation. This network is flexible, as shown by the mobilisation of regional doctors against the incinerator. Today Hungarian civilians also participate in Austrian and Slovenian environmental demonstrations, even if their own localities are not directly affected by the issue. Along with the formation of the Green network, new and not necessarily locally based actors have become involved in shaping neighbourhood relations.

More importantly, however, the conflict has redrawn the borders and modified their meanings. The controversial project is linked to the local geography of a national border. However, opposition to and support for the incinerator have formed additional links creating a new, global and virtual border that includes a zone where values, development concepts and policies, and visions of the future collide. Whereas the national border has lost its significance the immaterial new border connects and divides along the lines of worldviews, values, interests and commitments. A politician from the Green Party and leader of BIGAS comments:

> We have participated in each other's actions, and we formed a cross-border initiative, which we can call trilateral as it includes Slovenia as well. Apart from the negative thing that is planned here, I consider this positive. I grew up next to the border and I always looked in just one direction, never towards the East. We don't know the language and it's a pity there were no connections. So I think it is a very positive thing that we are working together here, and finally looking at the other side, too. We have things in common. After all, we form one region, no matter which country we live in.
>
> (Ms Ch. B., Green politician and leader of BIGAS, Mogersdorf, 30.01.2008)

Supporters of the project expect the significance of national borders to recede in economic terms, a promise they see realised with the incinerator. According to the former Mayor of Heiligenkreuz:

> Private and economic relations go their own way, because there only reality matters. And I am convinced that Hungarian economic experts will probably be very pleased if the whole thing goes on developing as it seems to be now.
>
> (Mr F. M., former Mayor, Heiligenkreuz, 29.01.2008)

3.3 Parallel worlds and discourses

The discourses supporting and opposing the incinerator run side by side. There is little dialogue between them, since they present different worldviews, values, facts and beliefs (see Szijártó 2008). All are permeated by intense emotions even though these may be hidden under numbers and statistics. The stakes are high for all parties involved as they see major concerns implicated in this conflict, reaching from the future security of human life, to safety and mutual trust.

3.3.1 The scripts of development

Frequently, these discourses seem irreconcilable as do the interests of those who express them. On the Austrian side, strong economic interests are linked to the planned investment. However, the Austrian opponents highlight that there is also a political dimension to the project, most strikingly expressed in the fact that the state of Burgenland is both an owner of the investor firm and the state authority that is to license the project. The investment – of about €115 million – aims at providing cheap and environment-friendly energy (electricity and heat) for the Heiligenkreuz factory of Lenzing Fiber GmbH, which produces cellulose pulp with an extremely high energy demand. At stake, according to the representatives of BEGAS and its branch RVH Heiligenkreuz, and the supporters of the project, is whether the company can remain in the IP, expand its production and increase the number of its employees. Thus, the immediate stake is a factory of significant capacity and capital to preserve 180 jobs. Among long-term economic interests the production of cheap and sustainable energy is a priority, which may also be attractive for start-up businesses. Cheap energy is greatly needed for the current and future companies to remain competitive in the global market. The investor envisages the establishment of an energy park, where the energy produced by bio-mass, bio-gas plants, and the incinerator will replace the present energy resources whose prices continually rise.

Opponents argue for increasing the economic potential of tourism. Szentgotthárd opened a spa in autumn 2006 and its inhabitants argue that if the incinerator is built, the town and spa will lose their touristic attraction. They fear that 'it is not the sunset but the incinerator's smoking chimneys that will be seen' from the hotel currently being constructed. Austrian opponents see Green tourism as key to the development of the villages of southern Burgenland, the conservation of the Naturpark Raab, and the expansion of the organic food industry that has begun to cater for the spa tourism in the area. The opponents view the incinerator as an inevitable setback for these developments in tourism, and challenge the view that it will provide significant employment. Their estimates indicate that the project endangers 6,000 jobs in tourism and its related sectors, which largely surpass the number of new jobs to be provided by the incinerator. This criticism turned vocal especially when it emerged that instead of the previously announced 100 new jobs the new incinerator would provide only 40.

The opponents – and some economists – have also expressed their concerns about further investments in the IP. They argue that there is a real threat that industries which require a large amount of cheap energy, such as chemical factories – will be attracted to the IP, which will generate an expansion of the incinerator and increase environmental pollution. According to the published plans, such an expansion would be feasible. Behind the opposing economic arguments are contrasting conceptual differences about desirable development paths: 'classic' industry versus the 'industry' of ecological and health tourism based on the values of environmental protection.

3.3.2 Topographies

The discussion also reveals asymmetric notions of developed West/North vs underdeveloped East/South. According to politicians supporting the investment, the energy park and the incinerator are necessary because they will improve the chances of the structurally disadvantaged southern Burgenland catching up with the developing central regions of the country and with the more developed northern Burgenland. The opponents turn this argument around and stress that the project endangers the values offered by an unspoilt natural environment and tranquil rural region. They argue that these have remained intact due to the region's longstanding peripheral position and form the basis for a genuine, sustainable development of tourism. They see the conflict as a typical power struggle between a waste-producing centre and a waste-regenerating periphery. A politician from the Green Party and leader of BIGAS comments:

> A woman said this to me when we were collecting signatures: 'Maybe it sounds disgusting but I put the trash out in the farthest corner in my garden. This is why they put this [the incinerator] in Burgenland here, in Heiligenkreuz and not Eisenstadt [the capital of the province].' So here within Burgenland we are on the periphery. Though Lenzing has its factory here, I doubt that in the northern part of Burgenland the installation of such a project would be started and completed.
>
> (Ms Ch. B., Green politician and leader of BIGAS, Mogersdorf, 30.01.2008)

On the Austrian side in Burgenland, contrasting North and South refers not only to the differences in development, but also to the asymmetry of power relations. While decisions are made in Eisenstadt, the centre of the province situated in the North, the consequences must be borne by the South. Hungarian opponents look from East to West. At the press conference following the first roadblock, a member of the Szentgotthárd municipal leadership said:

> On the other side of the hills, the Austrians run four or five spas, they drive around in posh cars and there is wealth. For Szentgotthárd to achieve this, its only opportunity lies in the development of tourism. We would also like expensive cars and wealth, but this is thwarted by the incinerator which is allegedly environment-friendly. If this is really so, they should install it next to one of the popular ski resorts in Austria!
> ([www.szentgotthard.hu], accessed 14.06.2006)

These sentences reveal not only anger but a more general frustration about having to interact with the western neighbour on terms over which Hungarians have no control. The opposition argument also includes contrasting small and large, weak and strong. One of the grievances of Szentgotthárd's inhabitants is that the incinerator chimney will be higher (90 m) than the tower of their baroque cathedral (60 m). This church, the town emblem and third largest baroque church in Hungary, attracts the eye from afar and is a point of orientation. The chimney will be in the IP, but besides spouting smoke, it is feared that it will radically transform the traditional spatial and religious symbolic order.

Both in public and personal discussions, it was frequently and emphatically voiced that Szentgotthárd's protest was not aimed at Austrians or Austria but at the investor company and the economic and political forces supporting it. Hungarians also frequently felt that they were part of a conflict between unequal parties. 'To combat a hundred million Euros is a huge challenge, but we have no other choice,' said a local representative in 2006. Later, referring to the referendum of April 2008, the Mayor of Szentgotthárd declared:

> The fight against the incinerator has been that of David and Goliath from the start but, like David, we also have faith in ultimate victory.
> ([www.webgotthard.hu], accessed 31.03.2008)

These opposition discourses in particular place the specific local issue in a broader, national, cross-border and symbolic topography. At the same time, they mark the opponents as small but fearless, drawing strength from a higher truth and moral superiority. The interpretations permeating the oppositional discourse have also dramatically appeared in one of the award-winning pictures of the town's environmental drawing contest called 'This space here is ours!' as can be seen in Photo 3.2.

3.3.3 Information, knowledge and trust

The key objection to the incinerator is that it endangers the natural environment and people's health. The investor counters this at every event by claiming that the project does not hold risks for people or the natural environment. Nevertheless, sharp differences can be found in the use of language which is permeated by the ideological conflict. The investors' 'thermal residue-recycling plant' is the opponents' 'waste incinerator'. The motto on the website of RVH Heiligenkreuz is 'we recycle in a clean manner' (*wir verwerten sauber*). The seemingly neutral language of technology and bureaucratic rationality used by the investors is opposed to the everyday emotion-laden and 'frank' language of the opponents. Thus, for instance, documents published by the supporters promise a 'hi-tech waste processing factory', in which a 'modern flue-gas filter' ensures that no harmful materials are released into the air; an 'excellent model project' based on 'the best available and tested technologies', thanks to which 'pure and reasonably priced' electricity and thermal energy will be produced ([www.sauber-verwerten.at]). In contrasting language, opponents claim: 'Where there is waste, there is stench, rats, infections and diseases' (Interview with Mr B.L., representative, Szentgotthárd, 03.12.2007).

The linguistic expressions of the conflict also reveal that it revolves around assertions and counter-assertions in which claims to scientific expertise and knowledge represent a crucial factor in the struggle for legitimacy. One of the central 'scientific' questions in the debate between opponents and supporters focuses on air pollution. The environmental activists claim that the prevailing winds would blow the smoke from the incinerator's chimney towards Hungary, and that the emissions would cause considerable health risks locally and further afield. The investor, however, stresses that: the most modern technology available would be applied; emission levels would conform to stricter environmental regulations than those prescribed by the EU; emission of toxic material would be constantly measured; and the existing air quality would even improve after the installation of the incinerator. The opponents, in turn, claim that: incineration is a 'prehistoric technology'; it could not guarantee complete safety; filters could break down; only a fragment of the released toxic material would be measured; and the entire process could not be fully traced and checked. In addition, the concern has been raised that the amount of waste to be processed would require its long-distance transportation to the site, in itself environmentally problematic. In response, the investor has emphasised that the impact assessment study and nameable experts have confirmed that the factory would not be harmful to the environment and that the BEGAS operation already has a proven track record in showing 'high responsibility towards the environment and people'.

In this struggle over superior expertise, information and knowledge, the unequal balance between the two opposing parties has become clear, revealing a dynamic that is familiar in environmental conflicts. The investor and the experts participating in the design and realisation of the project have claimed scientific expertise and its implied authority, and contrasted this with the opponents' lack of competence and understanding.

In the course of the consultation and licensing procedure that should assess the environmental impact of the incinerator, the NGOs were simply unable to commission a scientific study that would have strengthened their voice. They resorted to forms of activist dissent that were financially feasible and included many voices. During the consultation procedure, they sent petitions to the government of Burgenland, thus hoping to protract the procedure. To facilitate the protest and large-scale participation, activists composed the petitions in advance, which were then signed by individual opponents. These petitions contained general objections – stressing the perceived risks to the environment, health, workplaces and value of nearby real estate – rather than scientific statistics and survey data. After reviewing the petitions, BEGAS promptly announced in a press release that 99 per cent of the petitions were duplications of the same text:

> One petition would have been enough; it would have saved a lot of paper and bureaucratic work. Basically these petitions are not grounded in expertise and they contain mostly emotional declarations, which are discredited in the environmental impact assessment. We expected more professional competence.
>
> ([www.sauber-verwerten.at], accessed 15 11 2008. Presse)

The press release stated that only 55 petitions containing credible expertise had been submitted to the bureau. In the public discourse of BEGAS and RVH Heiligenkreuz, the dichotomies dominate: reliable, accurate facts vs distortions; expert claims vs emotional statements; sound information vs 'horror' stories. This discursive strategy serves to mark out the positions of the project's supporters and opponents. The knowledge and expertise represented by the company employees and experts legitimise the expedience, cogency and safety of the project. Those unable to muster similar scientifically legitimated knowledge, expertise and authority in support of their arguments seem to demonstrate their professional incompetence and thus become discredited participants in the debate. As a result they appear to strengthen the position and truth of the investor. As the manager of BEGAS states:

> There are people who don't understand but this must be because many don't understand technology, they don't have expertise.
> (Mr S., manager BEGAS, Businesspark, Heiligenkreuz, 24.01.2008)

The considerable power of expertise and knowledge and of how it is charged, distributed and legitimated in this conflict has itself emerged as a contentious question. Clearly there has been a tendency by the investor side to devalue the knowledge and expertise people assumed locally through their challenge to what should be built on their doorstep. The engineer employed by the investor, for example, blamed NGOs and some 'irresponsible' politicians for playing with local people's fears instead of allowing open space for 'objective' information. Behind this argument lies the assumption that support for or opposition to the incinerator basically depends on appropriate technical information, which allows people to make rational decisions and dispels their fears. It also suggests that environmental concern in itself is an illegitimate response.

Clearly this did not convince as people distrusted the politics of information. Sharing information became one of the central issues in the conflict and the discourses about the incinerator. The Hungarian accounts started with the 'original sin', that happened when the concerned Hungarian stakeholders were not invited to the meeting where the plans were first announced.[7] Since then, appropriate and trustworthy information as well as the ability or inability to communicate have been recurring themes in the public debates and personal discussions. Both parties insist on their point of view. While the investors claim that the company has done its best to provide accurate information, opponents say that the company only provided information after protests pressured it to do so.[8]

The mutual, recurring accusations point ultimately to the question of trust, and to who believes whom, what and why. Distrust is structural and its walls impenetrable. Supporters and opponents profess with deep and passionate conviction that the other party manipulates, lies, and cannot be trusted.

3.4 What is the added value of the EU?

In March 2007, PRONAS wrote an open letter to the inhabitants of Heiligenkreuz and distributed it in mail boxes. The letter addressed the inhabitants of Heiligenkreuz as 'our dear neighbours', and asked them to support the people of Szentgotthárd:

> Although it is incredible, the EU does not even regulate its own ethical principles, even though ordinary people on both sides of the border realise that we shouldn't put our trash on our neighbour's doorstep! [See photo 3.3.]

In Hungary, we talked to politicians and experts holding the minority view that the Austrian investor would ensure the safety of the incinerator. However, actors on the Hungarian side uniformly believed that the Austrian investor and the politicians supporting the project offended the principles and rules of good neighbourhood. Single-handedly planning an incinerator, snubbing the protest of the Hungarian neighbours and treating them generally as inferiors were seen as challenges to amicable relations. The postcard campaign launched in December 2008 from Szentgotthárd, addressing the Austrian investor and government, put it this way:

> Austrians are nice people, we are good neighbours, sometimes we surprise each other, but we cannot accept all kinds of gifts. [See Photo 3.4.]

Respecting one's neighbour is an unwritten rule not only at the level of daily coexistence but also (at least in theory) in the EU. Hungarian discourses embed the issue of neighbourhood in an EU context. They argue that Austria, paradoxically renowned for its clean, environmentally conscious image, light-heartedly inflicts on its neighbour what it does not tolerate at home.[9] From the start of the conflict Hungarian politicians have stressed that Austria deliberately undermined their good neighbourly relations. The local and national discourses which oppose the project treat good neighbourhood as an endangered value. In Szentgotthárd, some believe that the Austrian party might eventually withdraw from the plan because it may not want to risk the traditionally good relations between the two countries. This seems a futile hope.

Both Austria and Hungary are member states of the EU, and the conflict also assumed an EU dimension. The Hungarian party, as noted above, took the case to the European Parliament, while the Austrians preferred to consider the incinerator an internal affair and a purely economic issue. However, in the conflictual debate the European Union frequently appears as a referential frame and an entity prescribing and sanctioning norms and rules. The Austrian experts and politicians supporting the project did not talk about shared neighbourhood but pointed to the waste management directives of the EU. The manager of BEGAS stated:

> I see it as a real problem that the Hungarian party does not accept reality. Anyone who deals with the EU just a little should know that depositing waste will sooner or later be banned in Hungary too [...] The EU prescribes, and this is how it already is in Austria, that we cannot deposit waste but we must incinerate. And incineration is so high-tech nowadays that Szentgotthárd would do a great favour to the purity of the air if instead of heating from home it used central heating [provided by the incinerator] so that the air becomes a bit cleaner.
>
> (Mr S., manager BEGAS, Businesspark, Heiligenkreuz, 24.01.2008)

Thus, by installing the incinerator, the investor does nothing less than deliver what is required by EU standards, like a model pupil. The Hungarians appear as wayward and unable to realise the latest EU-sanctioned environmental protection measure.

In the Hungarian discourses, professional arguments also emerge in the form of references to one of the most important EU policies. The principle of proximity declares that waste must be eliminated at a place nearest its origin, but this principle will be violated since the overwhelming amount of waste will have to be transported to its destination. More importantly, Hungarian discourses project the EU as a sort of political authority which should guarantee equal rights for the citizens of its member states. Since the plan for the incinerator first became public, Hungarian actors have stressed at every opportunity that they expect to participate in the project's licensing procedure as equals and on a par with Austrians. They have argued that their opinions should be heard if the project of the neighbouring country directly affects them or even puts them at risk. At the demonstrations the activists demanded veto rights, as they considered the possibilities offered by the Espoo Convention insufficient. Expectations and demands have been addressed partly to Austria and partly to the EU. While neighbouring Austria 'floods us with its trash' – so the accusation goes – it does not consider the Hungarians as equals, thereby violating what should be a balanced partnership between two EU member states. As a representative of Szentgotthárd put it:

> Even today, they think we are second-rate EU citizens. They think so because – Austrians are very kind, friendly people – now I am talking about the political and economic elite. Among others, I went in person to Kismarton [Eisenstadt] with Péter Olajos, who is a member of the environmental committee of the European Parliament, we wanted to hand over a petition, and the cleaning lady was waiting for us at the reception, and we had great difficulty getting in the office, where a fifth-rate or twentieth-rate bureaucrat took the petition. From a member of the European Parliament!
>
> (Mr B.L., representative, Szentgotthárd, 3.12.2007)

The experience of second-rate EU membership is a constant element in the Hungarian narratives. If Austria treats Hungary and Hungarians as second-rate EU neighbours, they are determined to prove to the EU that they are not inferior to the countries that joined earlier. The Mayor of Szentgotthárd saw an important aim of the referendum of April 2008 to 'also declare to the EU that we are enlightened, conscious European citizens, whose opinion cannot be disregarded' ([www.webgotthard.hu], accessed 31.3.2008).

In this conflict, the Hungarian party frequently portrays the EU as a forum of unquestionable authority, which can be expected to act as an arbiter of justice that rises above the particular interests of its member states. Placing the interpretation and handling of the conflict in an EU frame may be questionable. The planning and licensing of the incinerator have followed procedures which are in accordance with international treaties and national legal regulations. This was the opinion expressed by Stavros Dimas, EC commissioner responsible for the environment, when he replied to the question of MEP Péter Olajos:

> The Commission is presently unaware of any breaches of the Community legislation due to the planned operation of the installation concerned [...] [member states] are not obliged to send information concerning planning and development issues of such installations to the Commission [...] It is clear, however, that in all cases, the Austrian

authorities are responsible for ensuring that the requirements of the relevant EC environmental legislation on the assessment of the effects of certain public and private projects on the environment will have to be respected. The Commission cannot at this stage provide any additional comments, without more specific information.

([www.europarl.europa.eu/sides/getAllAnswers.do?reference=P-2008-5609andlanguage=EN], accessed 12.10.2009)

The investors and supporters of the project wish to enforce their right within the space defined by legislation, while the opponents want to enforce theirs by pushing the boundaries of this space. However, while it is clear that endorsed waste management regulations are to be followed by all EU members – even if the interpretation of these regulations is occasionally ambiguous – there are no regulations for cases in which environmental conflicts arise and transcend the national borders between two EU member states. Moreover, the incinerator can be regarded as a project complying with current environmental standards sanctioned by EU directives, and as an economic investment of some value. However, it directly affects a few thousand local citizens who see it as risky and therefore oppose it, but have little chance of stopping it. Evidently, the conflict has revealed that the right to participate in decision making is inequitable. On the one hand, there is a strong Austrian economic interest group, deeply embedded in existing power relations and enjoying the support of both regional and national politics. On the other hand, there are Hungarian and Austrian citizens with little economic and political clout, small NGOs, and local politicians or politicians of Green parties in weak political positions. The Hungarian political elite supports the opponents of the incinerator in vain, because it cannot effectively represent and enforce interests at the national and EU levels. The present structures, institutions and regulations favour the existing economic and formally legal context. The only option for the opponents is to create a precedent and push the incinerator project as a pre-eminent political issue into the political arena at EU-level.[10] If this attempt fails, the EU as a superior moral forum will remain a merely symbolic force in the unequal struggle for the right of political participation.

3.5 Conclusion: Lessons to be learnt

The environmental conflict in this Austrian–Hungarian border area indicates that borders do not disappear in a Europe that is still in the process of integration. Nevertheless, a border that used to represent little contact across ethnic and linguistic divisions (see Wastl-Walter et al. 1993) has become a lively contact zone with many different relationships connecting people in both cooperation and conflict (Váradi and Wastl-Walter 2009). Social and spatial neighbourhood can mean both friendliness and disputes. The cross-border conflict presented here suggests that there is a strong need for mediation and conflict resolution. So far, the two opponents have framed the issue in different ways: the proponents see the planned investment as a purely economic issue and significant contribution to further (industrial) regional development, while the opponents frame it as a predominantly ecological issue and threat to regional (tourist) development. The line between the two groups does not follow a national or ethnic division. This shows that the state border is strong as far as the defence of the interests of national affairs is concerned, but its significance recedes when citizens, experts and NGOs on both sides object to an investment project that affects their lives. While former mental borders might have been overcome, new ones have come into being which separate or connect people along spheres of interest, policies, values and beliefs, irrespective of the state they live in.

This also applies to the second dividing line: while the investors and proponents of the project insist that the licensing procedure for the incinerator has complied with existing democratic rules and requirements, and that environmental standards will be safeguarded, the opponents see themselves excluded from the decision-making process and propose ethical values about good neighbourhood. In their discourses of dissent, neighbourhood simultaneously emerges as a threatened value undermining the working relationship between people living on either side of the border, as a norm regulating everyday coexistence, and as a political claim for more equality and democratic participation.

Third, the conflict is also an unresolved issue of scale: the locally rooted conflict has been taken to the regional and national levels, where a resolution could not be found, so it has been taken to the European level. The EU appears in the debate as a normative, regulatory or sanctioning institution, as well as an arbiter of justice which is not guided by particular national interests. However, it seems that besides the creation and control of policies and regulations, the EU does not have the means to mediate in an environmental conflict crossing the borders of two neighbouring member states.

Photo 3.1 Flag posted by activists on the Hungarian side of the border facing the Industrial Park. It announces Danke nein! (no thank you!) in German

Photo 3.2 Winning entry to the drawing competition that was organized in Szentgotthárd. The motto of the competition was 'This space here is ours'

Photo 3.3 'Neighbour Don't Burn your Waste Here' (bilingual board at Austrian border crossing)

Photo 3.4 'The air of Heiligenkreuz'. Postcard sent to politicians in the Austrian Burgenland

Notes

1. Austria had been an EU member state for two years by then, and Burgenland as a preferential development area had received significant resources for development. Hungary joined the EU in 2004.
2. Evidently, the Hungarian representative of the IP and the local government of Szentgotthárd negotiate and make decisions on their own with investors planning projects on the Hungarian side. However, the value of the territory for both sides, for example, is determined by WIBAG.
3. The limited liability company providing Burgenland's electricity has consisted of three independent organisational units since 2002. BEGAS founded RVH Heiligenkreuz GmbH, the organisation responsible for the management of the incinerator project. The shareholders of BEGAS are the state and local governments of Burgenland. See: [www.begas.at] and [www.sauber-verwerten.at].
4. Szentgotthárd and Pro Natura St Gotthard (PRONAS), the NGO dedicated to solving environmental conflicts, have insisted on the daily documentation of events from the start. These documents and the analysis of articles published in the media form an important part of our research. See the websites [www.szentgotthard.hu], [www.danke.szentgotthard.hu] and [www.pronas.hu].
5. The Convention became operative in 1997.
6. See the website [www.sauber-verwerten.at]. In an effort to create counter publicities PRONAS regularly presents articles and reports in the Austrian media. They are accessible in chronological order on the website of the

NGO. On the website of RVH Heiligenkreuz, the press releases of the investor are presented. The Austrian Greens' and BIGAS's position papers, articles and reports on the various actions and demonstrations are available at [www.buergeraktiv.at].

7. The Austrian Greens also accused the investor of informing the public only after it had established the facts.
8. From reports about information meetings held by the company and citizens in Burgenland villages, it was apparent that each party could mobilise its own audience (stakeholders and supporters). The 'enemy' usually arrived uninvited, which again indicates that parallel publicities were operating side by side.
9. 'If we were doing the same, the Austrian army would already be lined up along the border,' says a town leader categorically (Mr B.L., representative, Szentgotthárd, 3.12.2007). Several people, including the Hungarian President, noted that when the opening of a lignite mine was planned in Torony, Hungary, five kilometres from the Austrian border, Austrians – Greens but even the Governor of Burgenland himself – protested alongside Hungarian opponents. 'Now we don't see the same solidarity and we miss it very much,' the President added in his proclamation on his visit to Szentgotthárd. The lignite mine was not opened.
10. This is supported by the fact that on 17 June 2008 – to a great extent as a result of Hungarian protest and pressure – the European Parliament adopted the report 'Environmental quality norms regarding waters' by Anna Laperouzze. This report is also called 'Lex Rába' and could lead to the improvement of the quality of border-crossing waters, provided the regulation is also adopted by the Council of Europe and the Council of Environment Ministers.

References

Baumgartner, G., E. Kovács and A. Vári (2002). *Entfernte Nachbarn: Jánossomorja und Andau 1990–2000* (Budapest: László Teleki Stiftung).

Beluszky, P. (2005). *Őrség-Vendvidék-Felső-Rába-Völgy: Szentgotthárd és környéke* (Budapest-Pécs: Dialóg Campus).

Seger, M. and P. Beluszky (eds) (1993). *Bruchlinie Eiserner Vorhang* (Wien: Böhlau).

Szijártó, Zs (2008). *A hely hatalma: lokális szcénák-globális folyamatok* (Budapest: Gondolat Kiadó).

Váradi, M. M. and D. Wastl-Walter (2009). 'A szomszédság színe és fonákja: határok, konfliktusok, diskurzusok', *Regio*, vol. 20, no. 1, pp. 85–116.

Wastl-Walter, D., M. Váradi and K. Kocsis (1993). 'Leben im Dorf an der Grenze', in Seger, M. and P. Beluszky (eds). *Bruchlinie Eiserner Vorhang* (Wien: Böhlau), pp. 225–64.

Wastl-Walter, D., F. Veider and M. M. Váradi (2003a). 'Eine Grenze verschwindet ... Neue Chancen durch die EU-Erweiterung? Das Beispiel der Mikroregion Moschendorf/Pinkamindszent, *Jahrbuch des Föderalismus*, Band 4: Föderalismus, Subsidiarität und Regionen in Europa (Baden-Baden: Nomos Verlagsgesellschaft), pp. 394–406.

Wastl-Walter, D., M. M. Váradi and F. Veider (2003b). 'Coping with Marginality: To Stay or to Go', in U. H. Meinhof (ed.). Bordering European Identities: Special

Issue on Borders, *Journal of Ethnic and Migration Studies*, September, vol. 29, no. 5, pp. 797–817.

Wastl-Walter, D., M. M. Váradi et F. Veider (2003c). 'L'élargissement de l'Union Européenne: voisinages anciens – nouvelles opportunités dans l'Union Européenne? L'exemple de la micro-région Moschendorf (Autriche) / Pinkamindszent (Hongrie)', *Revue Géographique de l'Est*, 4, (Tome XLIII), pp. 185–94.

Wastl-Walter, D. and M. M. Váradi (2004). 'Ruptures in the Austro-Hungarian Border Region', in V. K. Pavlakovich, B. Morehouse and D. Wastl-Walter (eds). *Challenged Borderlands: Transcending Political and Cultural Boundaries* (Aldershot: Ashgate), pp. 175–92.

4

On Linkages and Barriers: The Dynamics of Neighbourhood along the State Borders of Hungary since EU Enlargement

Ágnes Erőss, Béla Filep, Károly Kocsis and Patrik Tátrai

By contrast to the Hungarian–Austrian border discussed in Chapter 3 (the only 'eastern' one Hungary has), the borders between Hungary and its neighbours Slovakia, Ukraine and Romania discussed here relate to 'Eastern' – i.e. post-communist – neighbours. The eastern expansion of the EU has brought these countries into the new, shared neighbourhood of the EU and generated a process of Western integration. EU accession of Hungary and Slovakia in 2004, their incorporation into the Schengen zone at the end of 2007, and EU membership for Romania in 2007 have brought about major changes in the cross-border relations of this region. This has had implications for policies and neighbourhood relations at the transnational, national and local levels, but has also affected people's everyday life in the border regions.

Another contrast to the previous chapter lies in the composition of cross-border populations. Whereas the Austrian–Hungarian border communities have a sharp divide between the respective Hungarian and Austrian populations, the three cross-border sites discussed in this chapter are all characterised by ethnic, linguistic, cultural or religious diversity. Important for the discussion here, they all have sizeable Hungarian populations which form the majority population not only in the towns on the Hungarian side, but – in the case of Komarno and to a lesser extent Berehove – also on the Slovak and Ukrainian sides of the border. Hence, this chapter deals with a very different setting from the ones discussed in the previous two chapters, namely the neighbouring relations between people of the same ethnic background but within different contexts of statehood. The sites in question are the Danubian town(s) of Komárno (Slovakia) and Komárom (Hungary), the border towns of Oradea in Romania, and Berehove in the western Ukraine (see Map 4.1).

By analysing data from interviews, media discourses, and participant observation, we examine the effects of the more recent geopolitical shifts on cross-border as well as inter-ethnic neighbourhoods. Our research focused on how everyday inter-ethnic relations have been modified by the changing permeability of borders and the role of the EU in this process. Comparing three sites will demonstrate the importance of location in considering these larger transformations, and also the way in which historical relationships and contemporary alliances may contradict one another in complex ways, fuelling local tension.

4.1 A short history of Hungary's 'eastern' borders

Hungary's present-day borders date back to the end of the First World War, when the multi-ethnic Hungarian Kingdom, as a part of the Austro-Hungarian Empire, was dismembered. As a result of the Treaty of Trianon in 1920, the Hungarian Kingdom lost two-thirds of its territory. One third of the ethnic Hungarian population found itself outside the motherland, in sometimes highly concentrated clusters next to the new borders in the then newly established neighbouring countries of Czechoslovakia, the Kingdom of Serbs, Croats and Slovenes and the enlarged Romania. This historical fact is common to all three research sites: the neighbouring cities of Komárno/Révkomárom, Berehove/Beregszász and Oradea/Nagyvárad.

The Trianon dictate made it basically impossible to (re)build new relations between Hungary and its (new) neighbours in the interwar period. One issue determined the foreign affairs between the countries concerned: the 'revision' of the Treaty, which Hungary's neighbours clearly opposed. Hungary wished its former territories with their sizeable Hungarian populations in the successor states to be returned, which prompted the neighbouring countries to establish a political alliance against Hungary. Trianon also caused major economic problems, because the treaty divided formerly integrated regions. The new realities also affected the permeability of the borders, whose crossing was made difficult by bureaucratic rules (Baranyi 2006: 104–5).

On the eve of the Second World War, with the support of Germany and Italy, Hungary received back some territories inhabited mostly by Hungarians. These comprised a territory from Czechoslovakia returned in 1938, which included Komárno and Berehove, and from Romania one that included Oradea which was returned in 1940. This short Hungarian rule lasted until 1944. After the Second World War, Hungary lost the re-annexed territories once more, but Transcarpathia (including

Berehove) was now integrated into the Soviet Union and not returned to Czechoslovakia. Czechoslovakia as well as Romania and Hungary formed part of the communist bloc, and their internal and external affairs, including cross-border relations, were largely controlled by the Soviet Union, thus reducing the possibility of open conflicts.

During the socialist era, the state borders functioned as barriers. The borders were closed to most ordinary people, tied in to tedious crossing procedures and demarcated by few crossing points. All three borders under study separated socialist neighbours, but their permeability was different. The strictest closure was enforced at the Soviet border to the Socialist Republic of Ukraine, while Komárno/Révkomárom and Komárom enjoyed a more open atmosphere. However, the level of permeability always depended on the political relations of the day (Baranyi 2006: 105).

The geopolitical situation of the region has changed again after the collapse of communism. Czechoslovakia and the Soviet Union collapsed; Komárno became part of the newly founded Slovakia in 1993, while Berehove has been part of Ukraine since 1991. After the political transformation, Slovakia, Hungary and Romania have oriented themselves towards a Euro-Atlantic integration, while Ukraine has looked for its own post-Soviet way of negotiating East and West. Due to this new geopolitical situation, relations with ex-socialist neighbours have had to be rebuilt and re-evaluated, both in the light of their approach to 'minority issues' and their strong drive towards EU integration.

After 1990, the permeability of Hungary's 'Eastern' borders has developed with significant differences between the Slovak, Ukrainian and Romanian border zones. At the beginning of the twenty-first century, the border regimes in Romania and, even more so, Ukraine were still relatively strict (Ilieş 2005: 182). With the EU accession of Hungary and Slovakia in 2004, the different directions of development and the different neighbourhood strategies became increasingly perceptible. Up until that time most of Hungary's 'Eastern' borders were external borders of the European Union. With the EU accession of Romania in 2007, the only 'EU externals' left among Hungary's neighbours are the Ukraine, Serbia and Croatia. However, even if the permeability of the border with Romania has increased, the entry of Hungary into the Schengen area at the end of 2007 changed the picture again. The border with Ukraine, Serbia and Croatia became 'stronger' and, in the case of Ukraine, which has no EU membership perspective, strict measures of control were introduced. It is this situation, which provides the central context to our chapter.

4.2 Research sites

The research sites have been selected in order to compare the local effects of the three different degrees of EU accession in Hungary's 'Eastern' border zones. Starting with the Slovak–Hungarian border zone, the twin town of Komárno/Komárom was selected. In this case, two new EU members meet. In the northeastern border region Berehove was chosen in order to demonstrate the separation of a grown neighbourhood by a new EU border. The neighbourhood between two relatively recent EU members is represented by Oradea in Romania, which entered the EU three years after Hungary and Slovakia (see map 4.1).

In addition to their different patterns of relation to the EU, these border regions are also characterised by varying historically grown patterns of cross-border connections and (trans-)local inter-ethnic coexistence. The latter includes ethnic and political tensions which closely correlate with the nature and history of the state borders. These political borders do not coincide with ethnolinguistic boundaries, and so maintain 'ethnic issues' independently of political regimes. To understand the ongoing processes and cross-border relations in the Eastern regions of the EU, the characteristics of the present borders and the ethnic landscapes they traverse need to be examined.

All towns under study had predominant Hungarian populations before the First World War. The first shift happened following the change in

Map 4.1 The Hungarian borders

state power in 1920, when the local Hungarian majority became an ethnic minority. Fearing Hungarian revisionism and irredentism, the successor states looked at Hungarian border communities with suspicion. Trying to avoid the possibility of border changes, they made attempts to modify the ethnic structure of the border zone by enforcing population resettlement and statistical manipulation. By the end of the 1930s, ethnic Hungarians represented only half of the local population in the research sites (see Table 4.1).

The Vienna Awards arbitrated by the fascist governments of Germany and Italy modified the borders in 1938–40. This resulted in renewed reciprocal migrations and made the ethnic structure of the research sites more homogenously Hungarian again. During the Second World War and the Holocaust, a significant part of the population died and the Jewish communities perished.[1] This changed the ethnic composition again.

The postwar communist regimes proclaimed a new ideology emphasising internationalism and equality independent of ethnicity, and used new instruments to modify the existing conditions. One of these 'modernization acts' was the state-controlled mass resettlement in the framework of socialist urbanisation, which directed a large proportion of the rural population into urban centres. In culturally diverse regions, there was a second, undeclared aim of the urbanisation: to change the existing ethnic structure in favour of the state-constituting nations (Slovaks, Romanians and Ukrainians). Although the official ideology of communism was internationalism, relations between neighbouring countries remained stale and the discrimination of ethnic minorities continued. While the extent of the suppression of minorities was different in the countries in question, they all banned activities of ethnicity-based minority associations, cultural or educational institutions. The worst situation evolved in Romania, where a more tolerant period up until the 1960s was followed by the nationalist communism of the Ceauşescu Regime.

The worsening of the economic situation in the Soviet Union and Romania and the increasing oppression of minorities especially in Romania resulted in the migration of many Hungarians from Berehove and Oradea to Hungary from the mid-1980s onwards. As a consequence, by the time of the political transformations between 1989 and 1991, the Hungarians represented a significant minority in Oradea, while still forming the majority ethnic group in Komárno and Berehove.

Table 4.2 indicates the schematic spatial positions of each research site considering its position in relation to the ethnic and state borders and the ethnic composition in each site. As can be seen, Komárom/Komárno is divided by the state border, the Danube, separating Hungarians,

Table 4.1 Ethnic composition of the research sites, 1880–2001 (%)

	KOMÁRNO				**BEREHOVE**						**ORADEA**			
Year	Total	Hungarian	Slovak	German	Total	Hungarian	Ruthenian, Ukrainian	Russian	Jewish	Roma	Total	Hungarian	Romanian	Jewish
1880	*13,901*	*91.5*	*1.9*	*5.5*	*7,695*	*94.8*	*2.9*	...	...	...	*34,231*	*87.4*	*6.3*	...
1890	*13,952*	*93.5*	*1.7*	*3.7*	*9,028*	*95.7*	*2.6*	...	...	...	*42,042*	*89.5*	*6.1*	...
1900	*21,022*	*86.2*	*6.5*	*5.9*	*10,810*	*97.4*	*1.4*	...	...	...	*54,109*	*89.6*	*6.4*	...
1910	*23,051*	*89.5*	*3.3*	*5.4*	*14,470*	*96.4*	*1.6*	...	...	...	*68,960*	*91.3*	*5.5*	...
1920	19,075	78.2	12.7	3.8	15,376	60.9	10.8	0.0	19.2	0.0	73,025	62.2	11.8	24.6
1930	22,761	61.3	24.4	4.5	20,897	51.3	10.0	0.0	18.3	1.3	88,830	53.7	26.3	16.7
1941	*23,410*	*95.9*	*1.5*	*1.4*	*21,540*	*91.8*	*4.3*	*0.0*	*2.9*	*0.0*	*98,621*	*92.1*	*5.2*	*1.3*
1960	25,640	55.5	43.9	0.0	...	...	...	...	...	...	98,950	59.0	36.0	3.6
1970	28,376	61.7	37.2	0.0	24,700	...	...	...	...	...	122,534	51.4	46.1	1.2
1980	32,520	61.6	36.6	0.0	27,810	56.7	32.5	7.8	1.0	0.0	170,531	44.1	53.9	0.5
1990	37,346	63.6	34.0	0.0	29,221	51.8	35.0	7.6	0.0	3.3	222,741	33.3	64.8	0.1
2001	37,366	60.1	34.7	0.1	26,050	49.1	37.8	5.5	0.0	6.5	206,614	28.2	70.7	0.0
2001	*37,366*	*63.6*	*31.0*	*0.1*	*26,050*	*55.9*	*37.3*	*6.4*	*0.0*	*0.0*	*206,614*	*27.6*	*70.3*	*0.1*

Notes: italic figures = according to mother tongue; ... = no data.
Source: 1880–1910, 1941: Hungarian census data; 1920–30: Czechoslovak and Romanian census data; 1960–90: Czechoslovak, Soviet and Romanian census data; 2001: Slovak, Ukrainian and Romanian census data.

Table 4.2 Ethnic and state borders in the research sites

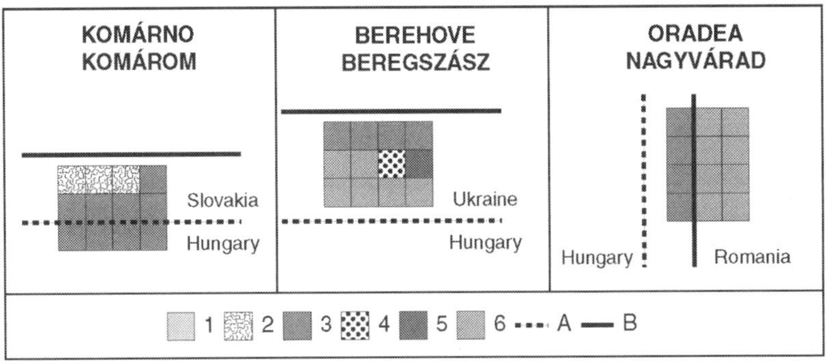

Notes: 1 = Hungarian; 2 = Slovak; 3 = Ukrainian; 4 = Roma; 5 = Russian; 6 = Romanian; A = state border; B = ethnic border.
Source: Slovak, Ukrainian and Romanian census data.

while the Slovaks form the local minority in the northern (Slovakian) side of the Danube. Berehove is situated between the state border and the ethnic border, and has quite a mixed population dominated by Hungarians. Contrastingly, the ethnic border runs through Oradea and the local ethnic majority here is Romanian. Although local ethnic diversity makes for three different situations, the ethnic majority dominates neighbourhood relations in political terms. This fact explains why we need to distinguish between local political power and ethnic and political configurations at the national level. But it is also important to emphasise that the local political and inter-ethnic relations cannot be discussed without taking into account the broader regional, national and European context in which they are embedded.

4.3 The Hungarian–Slovakian border: Komárno/ Révkomárom (SK) – Komárom (H)

Komárom (Komorn in German) was an historically and strategically important town within the Hungarian Kingdom, situated midway between Budapest and Pozsony/Pressburg (today's Bratislava). Komárom has been famous for its fortress system, and characterised by its links across the River Danube. Its historical centre has been established on the northern (left) part of the river since the eleventh century; in 1896, the village of Újszőny on the southern (right) bank was incorporated and made Komárom a cross-river town such as Budapest, Prague, Görlitz, Paris and many others. While the two settlements were already highly interconnected before, the official unification marked a dominant position of the historical part of Komárom. The Treaty of Trianon in 1920 divided the town and allocated the historical core to Czechoslovakia (now Komárno in Slovak, Révkomárom in Hungarian), while the southern part remained within Hungary. This was the beginning of enhanced growth and development on the southern bank, since all the important institutions had remained on the Czechoslovak side. At that time the population of Komárno was to a great extent Hungarian (see table above). Between 1938 and 1945 the two sides were reunited as a part of Hungary, but were divided again after the war in compliance with the Trianon border (Hevesi and Kocsis 2003: 101–2).

This status has been retained until today. Komárno in Slovakia and Komárom in Hungary are two administratively independent towns at the Hungarian–Slovakian state border separated by the Danube. However, symbolically it has not lost its unity, as expressed in a common slogan 'one town, two countries' (Sikos and Tiner 2007). This slogan has especially gained importance since the EU entry of both countries in 2004 and their Schengen entry in 2007, even though mainly Hungarians on both sides use it.The two towns are currently connected by both a bridge for motor vehicles (Erzsébet bridge, since 1892) and by the only Danubian railway bridge (since 1910) between Hungary and Slovakia.

Komárno/Révkomárom in Slovakia has approximately 37,000 inhabitants and was ethnically Hungarian until 1945. Thereafter 9,000 Hungarians were resettled and replaced by Slovaks. Today, the population consists of 63.6 per cent Hungarians, 31 per cent Slovaks and 1.3 per cent Roma. Komárom in Hungary has a population of approximately 20,000 inhabitants and is homogeneous ethnic Hungarian. Komárno/Révkomárom (SK) is known for its cultural and historical heritage, hosting a big theatre and a concert hall. Furthermore, it hosts the only Hungarian university in Slovakia (Selye János University since 2004), making it the only town in Slovakia where Hungarians can study in Hungarian from kindergarten to university, even though not all subjects are taught. Komárom (H), by contrast, is characterised by its economic strength. It has attracted several multinational companies, which contribute to its larger economic clout. *Nokia*, the biggest employer provides work for up to 20,000 people from both sides of the border.

4.4 Cooperation and competition across the state border and the EU-Schengen effect

The collapse of the communist regimes in Hungary and Czechoslovakia in 1989 and the EU accession of Hungary and Slovakia in 2004 first enabled and ultimately led to intensified cooperation between the two sides. As mentioned above, this cross-state-border neighbourhood and mutual attraction can be explained by two main factors: history, which gave rise to Hungarian 'ethnic solidarity', and proximity. Komárom and Komárno/Révkomárom organise, for instance, several joint cultural events throughout the year. The best known is the 'Komárom Days' cross-border cultural festival, which takes place every spring on both sides of the river. This highly popular event includes concerts, dance performances, podium discussions, fairs and sports competitions. There is a cross-border race that was already held in communist times, and every year the two towns' 'strongest men' compete in a tug-of-war on the Erzsébet bridge that connects the two city centres. Both cities participate in the organisation of the Komárom Days and stage performances. The fact that in 2010 this cultural festival took place for the 19th time suggests its sustainable success. Throughout the year, the two music academies and cultural centres of Komárom (H) and Komárno/Révkomárom (SK) are in close contact. Moreover, both cities have recently filed a joint application for the inclusion of their unique fortress complex in the UNESCO Cultural World Heritage List.

In the educational sphere, we discovered institutionalised cross-border cooperation as well as informal activities. It is, for instance, possible for parents to send their children to schools on the respective other side of the border. This holds true also for higher education. Even though it is mostly universities in Hungary that are popular among the Hungarians in Slovakia, a certain attraction also works the other way around: the Selye János University in Komárno/Révkomárom has received students from Hungary since its establishment in 2004. It even maintains a special preparatory grammar school in Komárom.

The local authorities exchange information on a regular basis and have developed common projects. In addition to the UNESCO application, the two planning departments have also closely cooperated and successfully completed the plans for a new Danube bridge connecting the industrial parks on both sides. For this project both towns had to take into consideration the city planning of the respective other. While it is an investment both municipalities are eager to realise, several instances during the research showed that the local (and sometimes regional) administrations are constrained by national legal frameworks, which makes cooperation and the coordination of responsibilities nearly impossible.

An important factor that facilitates successful cross-border cooperation lies in the fact that on both sides of the border the majority of the population is Hungarian. Old Komárom was a 'Hungarian' town and has remained one in the Hungarian population's mind. A degree of ethnic solidarity and the common language bind people together. The language competency has been an advantage for finding a job on the Hungarian side. Most of the 5.000 Slovak citizens who used to work in the industrial park in Komárom were ethnic Hungarians. It is also mostly Hungarians who participate in cross-border everyday life. Slovaks are far less interested in institutional cooperation due to 'old fears' (a possible reunification of the towns), as a Slovak representative in Komárno/Révkomárom stated in 2008. The EU and Schengen entry seem not to have changed this. However, the attractiveness of shopping has also made Slovaks cross the border more regularly. They visit the new *Tesco* supermarket on the Hungarian side, for instance, where the labelling is bilingual and Euros are accepted.

Apart from these cooperative structures and activities, the socio-economic gap and, partly, cultural difference separating both sides have also prompted patterns of competition and challenges to good neighbourliness. The industrial park (IP) in Komárom has undoubtedly improved the economic strength of the entire region, and generated many job opportunities for Slovak citizens. There are cross-border employee bus transfers organised by the IP companies. However, the economic investment has strengthened mainly Komárom (H) and left behind Komárno/Révkomárom (SK), whose own industrial park has attracted fewer investors.

There have been intense disputes across the two cities about how to improve the state of the old historical city of Komárno/Révkomárom (SK). While some support the creation of similar facilities for both sides of the border, a position mainly taken by the Slovakian side, others support cross-border complementarity in fulfilling certain functions. Tourism, for instance, is a sector in which local representatives in Komárno/Révkomárom would see a potential, however mostly with similar offers as on the Hungarian side. Komárom, though, is not interested in sharing its more lucrative facilities such as the thermal bath.

Our research revealed that issues of economic competition clearly challenged the often celebrated cross-border 'solidarity', making both sides appear to be merely fair-weather friends. With regard to the competition of the industrial parks, a local expert who was involved in the establishment of the IP in Komárom pointed at the problems, which the establishment of a park with companies of a similar industrial sector and demand for labour would face. In his opinion, Komárno (SK) should rather develop heavy industry, such as the shipyard. In 2007, he also saw a problem in finding the required labour force, since the regional cross-border labour market was exhausted by *Nokia* and its suppliers in the industrial park in Komárom. This changed with the economic crisis, when many people lost their jobs, especially the low-skilled contract workers. Even though a significant part of the latter were from outside the (cross-border) region, the crisis confronted both local administrations with an increasing unemployment rate in their municipalities.

4.5 Interethnic relations in the post-EU admission era: A failure of EU integration?

Even though Hungary and Slovakia signed a basic treaty in 1995, declaring the mutual recognition of the borders and the territorial integrity of both states, interstate and inter-ethnic relations were very tense in the 1990s. Only the Dzurinda Government in Slovakia from 1998 to 2006 brought some easing of tension, both in the relations between Hungary and Slovakia, and between Slovaks and Hungarians within Slovakia. In the light of Slovakia's entry into the EU, the Hungarian political party was a coalition partner in the government. However, the euphoria of the EU accession proved ephemeral, and the relations reverted to a state reminiscent of the 1990s when the autocrat Vladimír Meciar was in office. With the change of government in Slovakia to a left-wing, populist and nationalist coalition under Prime Minister Robert Fico, a former Communist Party member, the situation between Hungarians and Slovaks within Slovakia and across the border increasingly worsened. Since its inauguration in 2006, the government has led an anti-Hungarian and anti-Roma campaign. Hungarians and Slovaks have divided views of history and national symbols. At the same time one can observe a constant ethnic bargaining for democratic representation and minority rights for Hungarians in Slovakia. The Hungarian institutions are clearly discriminated against by the state, and different state policies have also hindered cohesion within the country, for instance in the education sector. While the Slovak language is compulsory in the education system, Slovaks have neither obligation nor opportunity to learn Hungarian at public schools.

The inter-ethnic conflict reached its temporary culmination in summer 2009. First, the Slovak parliament adopted a controversial Language Law that made the use of Slovak obligatory in all official and public-service communications. The law also includes fines of up to €5,000 for violations, a requirement for the Slovak language to be used first at cultural events, even if only minorities are present, and rules that stipulate that memorials and plaques must not have minority language inscriptions that are larger than the Slovak inscription. In August 2009, the Slovak government barred Hungary's then-President from entering the territory of Slovakia in order to inaugurate a statue in Komárno. The fact that the statue represented St Stephan, the founder of the Hungarian Kingdom in 1000, was regarded by the Slovaks as a provocation. It was the first time in EU history that a state official had been refused entry to another EU country, and that this occurred despite the fact that both countries are members of the Schengen area. The EU has not intervened in the new Slovak language policy, and declared the second dispute to be a bilateral issue between Slovakia and Hungary.

In spite of these conflicts, our observations in Komárno/ Révkomárom and the insights gained through many interviews have revealed a picture of peaceful coexistence between Hungarians and Slovaks. Everyday life proceeds without open conflicts, intermarriages and ethnically mixed circles of friends are not exceptional, and the majority of the population on the Slovak side is quasi-bilingual. Some restaurants are frequented by both groups, Hungarians attend Slovak schools, some Slovaks go to Hungarian schools, and while the two secondary schools have different languages of instruction they share a cafeteria. Hungarians and Slovaks work together, especially in the local administration; there is a bilingual weekly newspaper and a local TV station, both with an ethnically mixed editorial office; and sports clubs are also mixed. At least at the local level, the different churches cooperate from time to time in holding ecumenical events. At the same time, there are institutions and places that remain ethnically separate. Hungarians and Slovaks have their own cultural associations (Matica Slovenska, Csemadok), and many schools, dance groups, theatre groups, musical bands, clubs, bars and small cultural events are frequented by 'nationals' only.

Occasional conflicts erupt, such as the one that evolved around the erection of the statue of the Saints Cyril and Methodius, when the local government (with a Hungarian majority) objected to the site the Slovaks had chosen for it.

In observing the work of the Komárno/Révkomárom municipality, we gained the overall impression that in spite of its ethnic mix both sides often subtly but determinedly tried to protect their 'nation' – the Slovaks in the position of the minority in town, the Hungarians in the position of the minority in Slovakia. The director of the local Matica Slovenska (MS) branch explained in 2007 that in Komárno MS is of greater importance to Slovaks than in homogenous Slovak municipalities in the North of the country, where it would probably not be needed to 'protect, preserve and strengthen' people's Slovak identity.

Clearly, EU accession, which could be considered the most significant recent geopolitical event in the region, has not done much to improve inter-ethnic relations at the political level. Some politicians within Slovakia, both Hungarians and Slovaks, have made attempts to improve this. They have organised common protests against nationalism and discrimination, and established a new party in July 2009 named Híd-Most, the Hungarian word *híd* and the Slovakian word *most* mean 'bridge'. It consists of both ethnic Hungarians and Slovaks – with no satisfying improvement so far. The major change with the opening of the borders lies in the increasing cross-border contact. However, it is questionable, whether shopping and work on the Hungarian side have really decreased still entrenched ethnic perceptions of the border.

4.6 The Hungarian–Romanian border: Oradea/Nagyvárad

Today, Oradea (*Nagyvárad* in Hungarian) is situated at the centre of the western frontier zone of Romania. The city lies at the crossroads of the Great Hungarian Plain and the hills neighbouring the Romanian Western Carpathians. This north–south geographical line is crossed east–west by the valley of the River Crişul Repede in the centre of Oradea, only 14 km away from the present Hungarian–Romanian state border. Due to its geographical location, the city is one of the most important international traffic junctions and one of the most prosperous cities of Romania. Oradea is located 255 km from the Hungarian capital Budapest and 600 km from the Romanian capital Bucharest. Since the late seventeenth century, Oradea has been situated close to the Hungarian–Romanian ethnolinguistic border, and in the centre of the ethnically mixed county Bihor (*Bihar*).

Oradea has approximately 207,000 inhabitants; it is the eleventh largest city in Romania. It was predominantly Hungarian until the First World War and became ethnically mixed under Romanian rule. Since about 1973, the majority ethnic group is Romanian (see Table 4.1). Oradea's economic situation and its inhabitants' everyday life have been greatly influenced by the closeness to the border. In the last 20 years, geopolitical changes modified the permeability of the border and the ways of dealing with it. Recently, the European Union has generated the most significant changes. Since about 2000, the financial support of the EU, the EU membership perspective and the internal democratic transformation of Romania have all resulted in improving relations between Romania and Hungary and in providing better economic opportunities in the border zone. The physical state border has become more traversable, giving rise to cross-border activities.

Before the EU entry of Romania in 2007, many hopes and expectations were placed on future EU membership. As in other post-socialist countries, individuals and politicians alike expected a rise in the standard of living, more economic development, a way out of unemployment, and the simplification of travel within the EU. With the EU entry of Romania, the border between Romania and Hungary became an internal border of the EU. Consequently, border-crossings and the contact between the two sides became easier and customs offices were dismantled. This led to a higher-than-expected growth in trade.

Cross-border activities exist on two levels: a formal one, between different institutions in the two countries, and an informal one, between individuals on both sides of the border. The most important frame of the institutionalised cross-border cooperation is the Hajdú-Bihar–Bihor Euroregion established in 2003. In addition, the two county seats, Debrecen and Oradea maintain their own forms of collaboration. The Euroregion has a common fund, it applied for Phare CBC funds and later for Interreg. EU support for cross-border cooperation between 2007 and 2013 has reached €272 million for the whole Hungarian–Romanian border zone, and represents a decisive factor in the cooperation of the two regions. The main field of cooperation is economic (e.g. development of infrastructure and tourism), but cultural and educational forms of cooperation are also significant (e.g. cooperation between the theatres, museums and philharmonics, and the universities of Oradea and Debrecen). Besides cooperation, one can also observe competition between the two similarly sized cities, particularly in cases where there is a clash of interests such as when both sides wish to determine the location of a new airport.

The institutional framework of cooperation hardly touches the cross-border activities of individuals. People's everyday cross-border movements depend mostly on their economic situation, as they adjust to the economic development in the city and the increased permeability of the border.

During the economically hardest period of transition in the 1990s, thousands of people decided to search for work abroad. Romanians left mainly for Italy and Spain, while Hungarians more easily found seasonal work in agriculture in the neighbouring Hungarian regions or in Central Hungary or Germany. From the early 2000s onwards, more and more people saw the possibility of improving their economic situations back home. Those who worked abroad sent remittances that were invested in property, which in turn developed the construction industry. Due to foreign investment (mainly in light industry), Oradea's economic position much improved in the last decade, offering more job opportunities locally. As a consequence, unemployment decreased to around 2 per cent.

The opening of the border in 2007 made it possible for inhabitants of the border zone to profit from an easier border-crossing procedure. As the property prices on the Hungarian side of the border were about half of those in Oradea, many Romanians moved to Hungary while still working in Oradea. However, this process broadly followed ethnically determined settlement structures. While Hungarians benefit from a shared language on the other side of the border, Romanians moved mainly to villages in Hungary where the population is of Romanian origin (e.g. in Bedő). Between 2001 and 2006, about 3,500 Romanian citizens bought property in Hungary (Michalkó 2010: 98–9).

The Hungarian side of the border has retained its peripheral character, still reflecting the fact that Oradea was historically the administrative and economic centre in the region. With salary levels in Romania catching up with those in Hungary, more and more Hungarian citizens work in Oradea. They mostly take up labour in the construction industry, replacing local employees who themselves have moved out to work at the construction sites of the North Transylvanian highway.

There are other important components of individual cross-border traffic. For example, Hungarian children from Romania attend schools and universities in Hungary, Romanian patients are attracted to the comparatively higher standard of medical facilities in Hungary, and cross-border shopping tourism has grown into a considerable phenomenon (Szabó 2004: 292).

These activities are clearly the result of Romania's EU entry and opening of the border, and have started to restore Oradea's traditional role as an urban centre for the neighbouring Hungarian territories that were cut off by the state border in 1919 and 1944. Unfortunately, these newly formed connections are still hampered by the lack of a comprehensive cross-border public transport system.

4.7 'The conflict is above us, not among us': Inter-ethnic relations in Oradea

The geopolitical changes of the last 20 years have caused changing everyday relations in both the economic sphere and ethnic politics. Following the political transformation, EU integration, and supported by political party Democratic Alliance of Hungarians of Romania (Uniunea Democrată Maghiară din România/Romániai Magyar Demokrata Szövetség – UDMR/RMDSZ),[2] the discussion of inter-ethnic issues was no longer a taboo. Nationalism emerged as a new force, even though it has not reached the type of violence that has been seen in Central Transylvania.[3]

In Oradea, almost every interviewee stated that there were no problems between Romanians and Hungarians at the personal level. In any case, none of the ethnic groups can be considered homogenous but are internally stratified according to their social and economic status, their age structure, time of immigration during socialist urbanisation programmes or political affiliation. Neighbourhoods are culturally highly diverse. Everyday relations are friendly, in streets and markets both Romanian and Hungarian are audible and usable, and people respect one another's religious and national holidays. Cooperation can be observed at workplaces, most of which are mixed as the role of the ethnic enterprise is relatively small (see Brubaker et al. 2006: 109–18).

Most interviewees blamed politicians for ethnic tensions. At the local level this could mean that Hungarians raised collective cultural and political claims, but the city council dominated by Romanians opposed them. This has resulted in power struggles, which typically erupt around highly symbolic issues such as the mounting of bilingual street signs. Thus, for instance, Hungarians have challenged the Romanian administration's refusal to introduce bilingual street signs against a rule that normally obliges them to do so (Veress 2006: 39). Although most Romanians accept this requirement, the street signs are still monolingual. Another point of contention is the privileged role of the state-supported Orthodox Church, which has been able to build several new churches and has received back many properties from the state. Conflicts at the workplace sometimes turn into ethnic conflicts, which attract media attention. For example, during our research, the Hungarian Director of the Oradea State Philharmonic Orchestra was suspected of discriminating against Romanian employees, to which he answered that he had employed Hungarian musicians because of their professional competence. On another occasion, a literary assembly was held in the Library of Bihor County, where writers from Hungary also participated. Following this, the Romanian Director of the library was accused by the President of the County Council and the local press of organising anti-Romanian events.

Mostly, though, problems tend to arise because of national rather than local policies. For example, like in the Slovak case outlined above, educational policies of the national government also challenge the position of minority languages in Oradea. Minorities have to accept that the Romanian language is the sole language of instruction at school. National policies also influence relations on the ground, easily observable before elections when the 'ethnic card' tends to be played and politicians of both sides exploit sentiments based on existing stereotypes and the fear of the 'other'.

These national political tensions also manifest themselves at the local level in Oradea (for similar tensions in Cluj-Napoca see Brubaker et al. 2006). They are caused by the unequal power relations and the ethnic hierarchy that positions Romanians at the top, followed by Hungarians and the Roma at the bottom. This can result in ethnocentrism or in ethnic segregation. An important sign of this deeply buried tension is what could be described as 'parallelism', which can be seen in the coexistence of parallel discourses and societies in the city. Parallel institutional structures, networks and mental maps of the city prevail, taking root in the different perceptions of 'national' histories and the perceived difference in culture, language and education. At the same time, the barriers that exist between the communities more widely do not exclude genuine links between people, which include mixed marriages, friendships and close workplace relations. As many interviewees explained, the conflict is ignited top-down rather than bottom-up, or, in the words of a young student, 'the conflict is above us, not among us' (Interview, 24.4.2010).

During the EU integration process, there was pressure on Romania to harmonise its legal system and minority rights with those of the EU. Minorities in particular had placed high hopes and expectations on EU membership. They had anticipated more rights and less discrimination. However, after EU entry, these expectations proved illusory. The minority rights issue seemed to drop from the agenda as the aspiration of becoming an EU member-state prevailed. There is no doubt that Romania's EU accession had many – mostly economic – advantages for many Romanian citizens of all ethnic origins. Nonetheless, the country has continued to press ahead in forming a homogenous nation-state that is based on an assimilationist approach to cultural and ethnic diversity. In many ways, this reminds of a similar trend in Slovakia as seen in the section above.

4.8 Hungarian–Ukrainian Border: Berehove/Beregszász (Ukraine)

Berehove/Beregszász is located at the westernmost periphery of Ukraine in the county of Transcarpathia. It is located only 6 km from the

Hungarian–Ukrainian state border, yet 315 km from the Hungarian capital Budapest and 770 km from Kiev, the Ukrainian capital. It lies between the Berehove hills which belong to the volcanic range of the Carpathians and the Great Hungarian Plain which intersects principal international traffic corridors. This advantageous geographical location has enabled Berehove to become a prosperous merchant town. It used to be the administrative seat of the former Hungarian Bereg County (until 1919 and between 1938 and 1944). During the Czechoslovak (1919–38) and Soviet (1945–91) period, Berehove drifted to a peripheral position and maintained this status within Ukraine. In addition, Berehove (with approximately 26,000 inhabitants) is the intellectual, educational and cultural centre of the Hungarian population in Transcarpathia, and the only town in Transcarpathia and Ukraine where the Hungarian population is the (relative) majority (49.1 per cent). The second largest ethnic group is Ukrainian (37.8 per cent). The Roma constitute 6.5 per cent of the total population while 5.5 per cent are Russians who mostly moved here during the Socialist Regime.

From the moment the border was established, its role has been important in the local population's everyday life. From the interviews conducted with inhabitants, two characteristics can be derived concerning the effects of the geopolitical changes both for cross-border and inter-ethnic relations. First, there is a clear temporal dynamic with two separable periods: before Hungary's EU accession in 2004 and the period following it. Second, this shift has had different, sometimes contradictory effects at three levels of local society: the personal, the communal and the official-institutional.

4.9 Changes in cross-border relations: From linkage to barrier

The collapse of the socialist regimes was followed by a drastic economic depression, which was particularly serious in the peripheral Ukrainian–Hungarian border zone (Baranyi 2007: 138). Lacking opportunities for work and income, the mostly illegal border traffic became the main source of subsistence for many. Smuggling, 'one-day trade' and undocumented work became a useful income-generating strategy (Kiss 2000: 188; Baranyi 2007: 152; Balcsók and Dancs 2003: 54–6; Dancs 2005: 106). The most popular goods that left Ukraine were petrol, diesel, cigarettes and alcohol. These were traded for electronics, clothes and food items from Hungary. While the 'golden era' of smuggling was between 1994 and 1997, the black-market share in cross-border trade still accounted for more than 30 per cent of all trade in 2002 (Dancs and Koncz 2004: 132). Hungary attracted a cheap workforce into seasonal agricultural labour and the construction industry. Our interviewees in Berehove/Beregszász repeatedly emphasised that the economic crisis had been so drastic that even public functionaries had gone without payment for months, and resorted to the illegal cross-border trade in order to generate income. All were involved, independently of ethnicity.

As a result, the everyday orientation of locals turned towards Hungary, and the former barrier clearly became an economic lifeline for many. These economic personal networks often transformed into ethnically mixed friendships, cross-border marriages and general social networking encompassing entire communities. For Hungarians in Berehove/Beregszász this meant even more. After 40 years of separation during the communist era, formerly split families could meet again. As the financial situation worsened in Ukraine, thousands left Transcarpathia and Berehove to settle in the nearest towns and villages of Hungary or to enter Hungarian educational institutions. Many of them did not return. According to statistical data, nearly 5,000 Hungarians left Transcarpathia in the 1990s; however, local estimates report figures of 25,000–30,000 (Molnár 2005: 278). To illustrate the rate of resettlement, one interviewee claimed that Vásárosnamény, the closest town in Hungary, was known as 'little Beregszász' throughout the 1990s.

The revival of cross-border relations was perceptible at the official level as well, but its importance remained limited due to the different political orientations and interests of the two countries.[4] The opening of four more border crossing points was considered the most important issue for the locals in the 1990s. At the local level, twin town cooperations have been established, mostly in the fields of culture, sports and education. Hungarian charity and religious associations opened offices and organised activities in Berehove/Beregszász. Most of these aimed at supporting the Hungarian minority beyond the border, which – in changing intensity– is still an element of governmental policy in Hungary.

In 2004, political shifts in both countries greatly impacted on cross-border relations. In May, Hungary entered the EU, which resulted in a new and much stricter border regime (Dancs 2005: 102–8; Dancs and Raffay 2007: 423). It put a stop to the established goods traffic and made the newly established family and social links much more difficult to maintain. Meanwhile the financial and economic crisis in Hungary became apparent which resulted in decreasing job and business opportunities in the region. This gave rise to a new alienation from Hungary and the 'West' more widely. As one interviewee pointed out, the 'Orange Revolution' (October–December 2004) gave birth to a 'new' Ukraine, and fostered the image of a state that has the capacity to change and is committed to follow a Western orientation (Interview, 22.10.2007). This was initially followed by impressive economic development that contributed to the perception that Ukraine could become a place where people could make a living. The border crossing problems only intensified after the Schengen regime was put into force in December 2007. Schengen visas involve much bureaucratic effort and are expensive for locals. Although the EU accepted the local border traffic regulation, which includes easier access for those who live within a 50 km zone from the border, this does not match people's needs. Apart from financial and bureaucratic difficulties, both Hungarians and Ukrainians complained about difficult border crossing procedures, expressed in slow and sometimes humiliating customs controls. For them, they reflected what they regarded as the rebirth of an insurmountable barrier on their doorstep that involved both a physical and mental separation from the other side.

While the EU has launched numerous cross-border projects in order to compensate the negative effects of the Schengen closure, and while the aim of institutionally supported cultural and environmental cooperation has been maintained, experts in the field of regional development have stressed that long delays at the border impede de facto activity on the ground. It remains to be seen if new economic and institutional initiatives can reverse this effect.

4.10 Inter-ethnic relations and changing geopolitical orientations

So far, inter-ethnic neighbourhood relations in Berehove are amicable. However, the power relations between ethnic groups and their local positions have changed in compliance with the geopolitical shifts in Ukraine and Hungary. The coexistence of culturally diverse communities has had a long tradition in Berehove, despite the challenges posed by frequent shifts in political regimes and the ethnic tensions they gave rise to.

During Berehove's first decade within the independent Ukraine, the need to sustain economic livelihoods generated a connective link among ethnic groups. In the 1990s, when cross-border illegal business was wide-spread, the personal connections in Hungary and the knowledge of Hungarian proved to be a precious advantage. As it was primarily the Hungarians who had family connections and circles of friends on the other side of the border, Hungarians could take on a mediating role in business links with Ukrainians. In general, the local Hungarian community gained an advantageous position in the inter-ethnic fabric of power. They represented the majority of the population, dominated the local government, and started to emphasise Berehove's Hungarian identity by putting up statues and commemorative tablets, all referring to the history of the 'motherland'. The financial support from Hungarian governmental institutions, NGOs and churches played an important role in the maintenance of social or educational institutions, in a situation where the Ukrainian state could not guarantee their sustainability. Although the target group of these activities was the Hungarians, they reached many citizens independently of their ethnicity.

The geopolitical shift that started in 2004 has changed these power relations. The Ukraine born in the 'Orange Revolution' seemed to be a dynamic, economically developing country in contrast with Hungary's fall into a deep economic and political depression. Furthermore, the EU's Schengen policies hampered the personal relations with the western neighbour. Increasingly people recognised that as the channels towards Hungary narrowed, Ukrainian developments might provide new opportunities and the Hungarians in particular began to see them. In addition, the value and importance of the Ukrainian language has increased; something which many Hungarians now regard as the biggest challenge. The older generation only learned Russian, and those who started school after 1991 did not have a good chance to acquire a good command of Ukrainian, as language teaching remained underprofessionalised. As a consequence of the pre-Schengen era, most local Ukrainians can speak – or at least understand – Hungarian, so there has not been a direct need for Hungarians to study Ukrainian. According to a survey, only 25 per cent of Transcarpathian young Hungarian students can speak Ukrainian well enough (Molnár 2004: 103).

The Ukrainian government wished to strengthen the position of the language as part of the nation-building process, and modified the educational legislation in 2007 and 2008. This included the strengthening of Ukrainian throughout the education system. While nobody argues against the need for learning the official state language, the Hungarian community has launched protests against the methods by which this is enforced which it perceives as a sign of strengthening nationalism.

The Hungarian community itself has been divided over these issues. While one group reckons that the way to success is to enrol their children in Ukrainian schools, others hold that the preservation of their ethnic identity requires that children learn Ukrainian at Hungarian schools. Not just the assimilatory tendencies in education, but the permanent political and economical crisis in Ukraine might lead to a new shift in people's everyday strategies and orientation. Western Europe and Russia are predicted to influence possible directions in the future.

To sum up, three features of cross-border and interethnic relations in Berehove need to be highlighted. First, the local relations have always been significantly influenced by geopolitical and internal political developments. Second, the cross-border and interethnic relations are formed in close connection, and mutually influence each other. And third, the Hungarians have been strong practitioners of cross-border relations, motivated by what they consider an ethnic and cultural fellowship with Hungary.

4.11 Conclusions

The EU entry of Slovakia, Hungary and Romania, and the Schengen entry of Slovakia and Hungary have had different effects on the everyday life of people in the three border regions examined. The opening of the borders between Slovakia and Hungary and Hungary and Romania have undoubtedly facilitated the range and scope of cross-border exchange, and with it the creation of a neighbourhood that is marked by the free movement of people, goods, capital and services, the frequent exchange of information, the establishment of institutional partnerships or the building of friendships. Especially in economic terms, the geopolitical changes have opened doors for cooperation. However, the same developments have also generated translocal forms of competition between border regions and municipalities, the labour force and service providers. At the same time, this internal opening within the EU has negatively affected the Hungarian–Ukrainian border region, making the border crossing much harder for Ukrainian citizens. This has transformed the symbolic meaning of the border from a linkage to a barrier, and it has changed people's economic orientation towards the Ukraine and away from a closer orientation to Hungary.

Our analysis has revealed that the building of good cross-border neighbourliness is a dynamic process, a constant negotiation of political, economic and social aims and ambitions that offers many opportunities, but also confronts authorities, organisations and individuals with competitive situations. While the Hungarian minority has generally proved to be a 'mediator' of cross-border cooperation and partnership in all research sites, the Hungarian minority as a socio-economic (f)actor might also increase the sense of competition, as the example of Komárno and Komárom has shown.

Our work has shown that while ties between cross-border Hungarians have been strengthened, inter-ethnic tensions are by no means a thing of the past. On the contrary, EU integration has progressed in parallel with exacerbations of old or new ethnic conflicts in some areas. The relations between Hungarians and Slovaks (both in Slovakia and at the inter-state level) have reached an historical low point in recent years, while the relations between Hungarians and Romanians have somewhat stabilised. The inter-state relations between Hungary and Ukraine are dependent on the EU policy towards its external neighbour, yet Hungarian minority issues have suffered as a consequence of the region's peripheral location and political disputes inside multi-ethnic Ukraine.

It is this manifold and dynamic – at once improving and deteriorating – picture of inter-ethnic relations in all three contexts that makes the cross-border regions at Hungary's state borders intriguing examples for investigation. Moreover, they show that geopolitical changes (EU and Schengen) or initiatives (European Neighbourhood Policy) widely perceived as positive are no guarantee for building good neighbourliness locally. Problems may arise even within an extended European Union and in its self-proclaimed vicinity. Because we often find conflicts and best practice working hand in hand, there is a need to closely observe the developing dynamics in the region, for both researchers and EU policymakers.

Notes

1. In 1941, 2,743 Jews lived in unified Komárom. Only about 500 of them survived the Holocaust, most of whom left the town after the socialist turn. Oradea's Jewish community numbered 21,333 in 1941; by the end of the war only 3500 of them lived in the town. Later, many emigrated to Israel and Western countries. In 1941, 5856 Jews lived in Berehove. When Transcarpathia was joined to the Soviet Union, the few survivors first moved to Hungary and Czechoslovakia and later mainly to Israel (Braham 2007).
2. UDMR/RMDSZ was part of the coalition government of Romania between 1996 and 2000, 2004 and 2008, and since 2009. In Oradea they are an opposition party.
3. In March 1990, violent clashes erupted between Romanians and Hungarians in Târgu Mureş/Marosvásárhely. The incident lasted three days; eight people died and several hundred were injured. It was the first violent ethnic conflict in Eastern Europe since the fall of communism in 1989 (see Andersen 2005: 1–2).
4. After the collapse of the Socialist Regime, Hungary unequivocally sought an orientation towards Western Europe and the European Union. Ukraine searched for its place between West (EU) and East (Russia).

References

Andersen, C. M. (2005). *Resurgent Romanian Nationalism: In the Wake of the Interethnic Clashes in Târgu Mureş March 1990* (Prague: Anglo-American College).

Balcsók, I. and L. Dancs (2003). 'Munkaerőpiaci kapcsolatok az Északkelet-Alföldön, különös tekintettel a magyar-ukrán határ mentére / Relations in labour market in the Northeastern Alföld, especially along the Hungarian-Romanian border', *Alföldi Tanulmányok,* vol. 19, pp. 51–65.

Baranyi, B. (2006). 'Short-term Impacts of Enlargement in the Romanian and Hugarian Border Crossing', *Regio,* vol. 9, pp. 100–29.

Baranyi, B. (2007). 'A magyar-ukrán határmenti együttműködés új kihívásai / Facing new challanges in the Hungarian-Romanian cross-border co-operation', *Pro Minoritate,* vol. 15, no. 2: pp. 138–70.

Braham, R. L. (ed.) (2007). *A magyarországi holokauszt földrajzi enciklopédiája I. / The Geographical Encyclopedia of the Holocaust in Hungary I* (Budapest: Park Könyvkiadó).

Brubaker, R., M. Feischmidt, J. Fox and L. Grancea (2006). *Nationalist Politics and Everyday Ethnicity in a Transylvanian Town* (Princeton and Oxford: Princeton University Press).

Dancs, L. and Z. Raffay (2007). 'New Aspects of Cross-Border Relations in the Light of a Prominence Survey in the Hungarian-Ukrainian Border Region', in G. Szónokyné Ancsin (ed.) *Határok és eurorégiók* (Szeged: SZTE TTK Gazdaság – és Társadalomföldrajzi Tanszék), pp. 421–5.

Dancs, L. (2005). 'Lehetőségek és veszélyek a magyar-ukrán határ menti periférián / Opportunities and Risks Along the Periphery of the Hungarian-Ukrainian Border', in E. Nagy and G. Nagy (eds). *Az Európai Unió bővítésének kihívásai – régiók a keleti periférián,* (Békéscsaba: Nagyalföld Alapítvány), pp. 104–8.

Dancs, L. and G. Koncz (2004). 'A magyar-ukrán határ menti térség lakosságának alkalmazkodóképessége – a felzárkózás humánfeltételei / Adaptability of the Inhabitants of the Hungarian–Ukrainian Border Zone', in I. Süli-Zakar (ed.) *Határon átnyúló kapcsolatok, humán erőforrások,* (Debrecen: Kossuth Egyetemi Kiadó), pp. 128–34.

Hevesi, A. and K. Kocsis (2003). *A magyar-szlovák határvidék földrajza / The Geography of the Hungarian-Slovakian Borderland* (Dunaszerdahely: Lilium Aurum).

Ilieş, A. (2005). 'The Peculiarities of the Human Mobility frame in the Romanian–Hungarian and Romanian–Ukrainean Border Area', *BELGEO,* no. 1–2: 175–83.

Kiss, J. P. (2000). 'Illúziók nélkül: A határátkelőhelyek szerepe a határ menti kapcsolatok alakulásában az ukrán, a román és a szerb határszakaszon az 1990-es években / Without illusions: The Role of Border Crossing Points Forming Cross-Border Relations in the Ukrainian, Romanian, Serbian Border Zone after 1990', *Tér és Társadalom,* vol. 14, no. 1: pp. 179–92.

Michalkó, G. (2010). *Boldogító utazás / Felicific travelling* (Budapest: MTA Földrajztudományi Kutatóintézet).

Molnár, D. I. (2004). 'Migrational Attitudes of Transcarpathian Hungarian Youth in 2004', in I. Süli-Zakar (ed.) *Cross-border Co-operations – Schengen Challanges* (Debrecen: Kossuth Egyetemi Kiadó), pp. 101–5.

Molnár, D. I. (2005). 'Migrációs tendenciák Ukrajnában a függetleneség kivívását követően / Migration Tendencies in Ukraine after Independence', in I. Süli-Zakar (ed.) *Tájak – Régiók – Települések* (Debrecen: Didakt), pp. 274–8.

Sikos, T. T. and T. Tiner (2007). *Egy város – két ország. Komárom – Komárno / One Town – Two Countries: Komárom – Komárno* (Komárno: Selye János Egyetem Kutatóintézete).

Szabó, Gy. (2004). 'A határ menti kapcsolatok lakossági szemszögből a magyar-román határ mentén / Cross-border Connections From the Point of View of the Inhabitants at the Hungarian-Romanian Border Zone', in G. Kiss, J. Csoba and I. Czibere (eds) *Idővonat: Tanulmányok a társadalomtudományok köréből* (Debrecen: Kossuth Egyetemi Kiadó), pp. 281–99.

Veress, E. (2006). 'Nyelvhasználati jogok a román közigazgatásban / Language Use Rights in Romania's Administration', *Romániai Magyar Jogtudományi Közlöny*, vol. 4, no. 2: pp. 35–41.

5

Integration, Post-Holocaust Identities and No-Go Areas: Public Discourse and the Everyday Experience of Exclusion in a German Region

Inken Carstensen-Egwuom and Werner Holly

Despite the obvious fact that Germany has become a new home to many immigrants and that 'foreigners' have been a common topic of public discourse throughout the past 50 years (Bukow 2007: 29; also Ruhrmann/Kollmer 1987; Jung 1997; Klein 1995; Niehr and Böke 2000; Thomas 2003; Wengeler 2003), politicians long denied its status as an *Einwanderungsland*, or country of immigration. Since the introduction of the Immigration Act or *Zuwanderungsgesetz* in 2005, public policies and programmes appear to have adopted a more realistic perspective on immigration. In particular, the 'national integration plan' (*Nationaler Integrationsplan* [NIP]), which was drafted in collaboration with various immigrant organisations (IOs), has been a first step towards a policy discourse that focuses on communication *with* and not *about* immigrants (Beauftragte der Bundesregierung für Migration, Flüchtlinge und Integration 2007: 4). The NIP states:

> In view of demographic change and growing worldwide competition for the best minds, we must continue to utilise future immigration specifically for the economic and social interests of Germany. For this purpose, a long-term integration policy is urgently required.
>
> (Ibid.: 12).[1]

This policy paper thus emphasises common interests and a shared responsibility for the future economic success of society. According to the NIP, immigration is one of the core issues involved in promoting Germany's best interests in the future. A new dialogue with immigrants has been institutionalised via so-called 'integration summits'

(*Integrationsgipfel*). However, policy initiatives and public media discourses do not always capture the everyday reality of immigrants or meet their individual needs.

Meißner and Ruhrmann (2000: 9–11) show that the media discourse about immigrants is mostly structured in relation to negative events. Linguistic studies have demonstrated that the effects of global migration are usually presented by using the semantics of alarm and danger. In this field, processes of change are frequently introduced as fateful catastrophes rather than as calculable challenges that can be actively managed. Furthermore, according to Yildiz (1999: 57) and Bukow (2007: 29), a huge discrepancy can be detected between public discourse regarding immigration and the experiences of those people who live with diversity on an everyday basis. Their research, however, has primarily been conducted in large cities of western Germany. With our focus on Chemnitz, we look at a potentially very different situation in eastern Germany.

Our research examined what people in Chemnitz experience on the ground, how they speak about their individual experiences, and how all this relates to public policy and the media discourse. We conducted 28 open, in-depth interviews[2] with people who have migration histories, people who are actively involved in immigration-related NGOs, and employees of government bodies that deal with immigration issues. We chose a non-standardised approach to interviewing and employed a detailed linguistic analysis to obtain a good grasp of the underlying or hidden issues that would be lost in a standardised question-answer scheme or in a content analysis. A linguistic analysis of formulations, associations and implications, as well as argumentative, explicative and narrative strategies, hedges, interruptions, corrections and self-corrections can shed light on otherwise hidden elements and structures (Jäger 1996: 23). The linguistic analysis of people's utterances and their interaction with the researcher is complemented with an analysis of the social and historical context (ibid.: 19).

Below we will show how people from different immigration backgrounds appropriate, challenge and modify public discourse on immigration in manifold ways. In three case studies, we discuss the major subjects that dominate the German debate and that frequently emerge in interview narratives: first, we examine 'integration', which is a key term in the current immigration policy debate; second, we consider the subject of identity formation in the social context of a German school; and third, we explore the topic of 'no-go areas', a term which has taken on a crucial role in the debate about racism in Germany. We begin with a few remarks on the historical and sociopolitical context of our research area, and place a special focus on the past and present experiences of migration and diversity.

5.1 From Chemintz to Karl-Marx-Stadt and back again: History, economy and cultural diversity

Our focus is on the situation of immigrants and their realities in Chemnitz (see map 5.1). With 242,900 inhabitants in 2007, Chemnitz follows Leipzig and Dresden as the third largest city in the federal state of Saxony in the south of eastern Germany. In the past, Chemnitz has been a major industrial centre. Nineteenth-century industrialisation led to immense growth in the town and region. After the Second World War, the city – as Karl-Marx-Stadt – retained its status as an industrial centre in the German Democratic Republic (GDR). After the fall of the Berlin Wall though, Chemnitz suffered severe deindustrialisation and lost approximately 20 per cent of its inhabitants between 1991 and 2002 (Stadt Chemnitz 2002: 13). More recently, however, this trend has started to subside (Stadt Chemnitz 2008a: 12–14). The transformation of the economic base towards a small-scale, specialised industrial

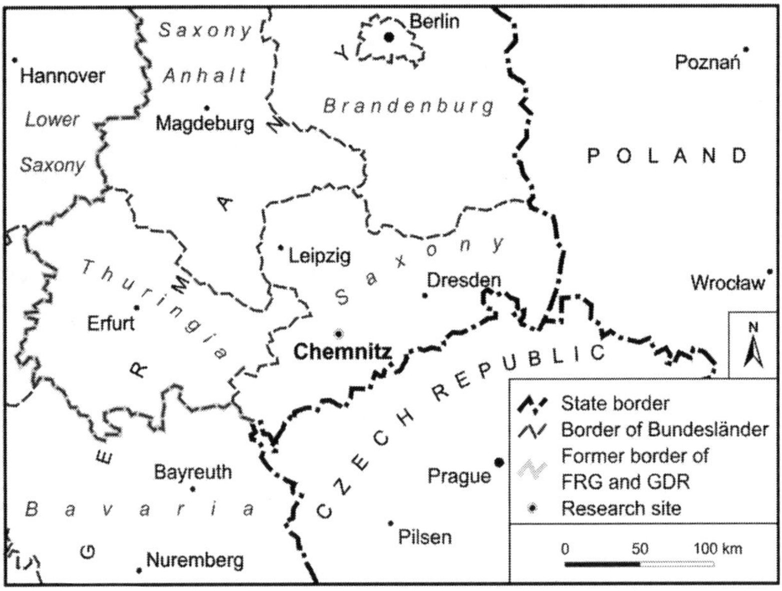

Map 5.1 Chemnitz in the German region of Saxony

structure has gained momentum and the current global economic crisis has not yet had disastrous effects on the local economy.

Chemnitz's GDR history, followed by subsequent border shifts and larger geopolitical changes, had repercussions on the composition and history of the region's immigrant population. Compared to western German cities of the same size, there are relatively few immigrants in Chemnitz: according to the registry office, foreign citizens comprised slightly less than 3 per cent of the population at the end of 2007 (Stadt Chemnitz 2008a: 18). Even though the number of foreign citizens does not directly reflect the number of 'people with a migration background', as they are officially called, the size of the latter group in Chemnitz is estimated to be not much higher than five to eight per cent of the population. This relatively small number of immigrants in eastern Germany is also reflected in the public discourse on migration and integration. Weiss puts it drastically:

> In the German debate about immigration and migration, it appears as though the eastern German states do not exist. By regarding only the small quantity of immigration, the special quality of immigration is thus overlooked.
>
> (Weiss 2007: 119).[3]

What Weiss refers to as 'the special quality of immigration' deserves closer examination. First of all, the countries of origin of the immigrants differ from those in the West. In the East, most immigrants come from Vietnam, the Russian Federation and Ukraine, whereas the largest groups of immigrants in western Germany come from Turkey and Italy (Sächsischer Landtag 2008: 49).

As mentioned above, this difference in the composition of the immigrant population in the new *Länder* is largely shaped by historical influences. The presence of immigrants from Vietnam – as well as from Cuba, Mozambique and Angola, albeit in far lower numbers – can be traced back to former communist alliances. Most of the immigrants from these countries came to the GDR on the basis of bilateral agreements between the governments of their home countries and the government of the GDR. The GDR contracted foreign labour because of a massive shortfall in the industrial workforce at the end of the 1970s. By 1989, approximately 59,000 Vietnamese, 15,100 Mozambicans, 8,300 Cubans and 1,300 Angolans were employed as so-called 'contract labourers' (*Vertragsarbeiter*) (Weiss 2007: 120–1). In addition, up until 1988, the GDR hosted as many as 42,000 foreign students, who also came primarily from socialist countries or movements (Weiss 2007: 120). However, only a fraction of them remained in Germany after the demise of the GDR in 1989/90 because of the breakdown of the eastern German economy, subsequent strong efforts by the German government to repatriate the remaining contract labourers, and a general sense of insecurity about the future.

In addition, three large-scale migration phenomena have affected both the western and eastern German regions in the years since unification: (a) the influx of 'ethnic Germans' (*Aussiedler* and, since 1993, *Spätaussiedler*) from former socialist countries, especially the Russian Federation, Kazakhstan, Uzbekistan, Tajikistan and South-eastern Europe (e.g. Romania); (b) immigration of so-called Jewish contingent refugees (*Kontingentflüchtlinge*) from Russia and neighbouring states, especially Ukraine; (c) an initial increase and subsequent noticeable decline of asylum seekers, following the passing of the 'safe third country' rule (*Drittstaatenregelung*) in the European Union in July 1993.

These three groups are allocated to the different German regions according to a fixed percentage. Thus, they do not come to stay in eastern Germany by choice (Glaser 2006: 56). Furthermore, difficulties on the job market have led to a high rate of relocation among immigrants in eastern Germany. This impedes the development of stable immigrant associations and strong networks.

The composition of foreign citizens in Chemnitz reflects the situation described above. Because ethnic Germans from Russia usually obtain a German passport upon entry into the territory of the Federal Republic of Germany (FRG), they are not included in statistics on foreign residents. However, their dependents as well as Jewish immigrants usually retain their former passports from the Soviet Union. Thus Ukrainians, with approximately 1,200 persons, Vietnamese, with approximately 800, and people from the Russian Federation, numbering approximately 750, are the three largest groups of foreigners in Chemnitz.

Overall, the migration history of the new *Länder* is considerably briefer than that of western Germany. The first generation began to arrive only during the late 1970s. Thus, the interval between their initial arrival and the recognition of Germany as a 'country of immigration' was considerably shorter. Furthermore, a growing concern about the lack of a skilled workforce due to severe out-migration and a fall in birth rates after 1990 has increased the official recognition of immigrants as an asset for the local economy in eastern Germany. Integration policies in Chemnitz include the Integration Network (*Integrationsnetzwerk*), which brings together all organisations dealing with immigration issues and the

Foreigners Advisory Council (*Ausländerbeirat*), which is appointed by the city council every four years, interacts directly with the city council and helps to strengthen the voice of the immigrant residents.

5.2 Case studies: Integration, identities and 'no-go areas'

The following three case studies employ a linguistic analysis of the interview data. Due to space constraints, we can only present a small selection from our research corpus. However, this cross-section will give some insights into the situation in Chemnitz as it shows that the problems which people experience and articulate are always connected to larger political or public discourses.

We propose that public discourse on immigration has an impact on how people talk about their own experiences and their views on living together as neighbours. In doing so, however, they are not merely passive objects who are manipulated by the media discourse (Keppler 1993: 113; Holly et al. 2001). Instead they actively engage with its contents and key concepts as they appropriate, challenge, and reinterpret publicly circulating information and knowledge in order to make it correspond more closely to their day-to-day experiences.

5.2.1 Integration and its daily usage

In recent years 'integration' has become the key concept in the German immigration discourse. Its use has become ubiquitous, especially among all those engaged with immigration and the situation of immigrants in Germany. By using the concept of *integration*, people avoid debates about *Leitkultur* or 'dominant culture' (considered too Right-leaning) or *multiculturalism* (the Leftist alternative), and promote a path beyond the perceived risks of *parallel societies*. Moreover, the political demand for 'integration' usually serves to criticise those who are considered unwilling or unable to blend in with mainstream society. The following is the official definition of 'integration' provided by the Federal Government:

> Integration is a long-term process. It's [*sic*] aim is to include everyone in society who lives in Germany on a permanent and legal basis. Immigrants should have the opportunity to participate fully in all areas of society on an equal standing. Their responsibility is to learn German and to respect and abide by the constitution and its laws.
>
> (www.integration-in-deutschland.de)

When taking a closer look at the 'national integration plan', a picture of immigrant integration emerges that is dominated by the principal themes of the media discourse:

- language skills and education;
- participation in the labour market through paid employment or self-employment
- knowledge of, and respect for, the rights and duties immigrants hold as residents of the country.

Integration problems are acknowledged in particular in situations where there is a lack of language skills or educational qualifications, and where unemployment is high (Beauftragte der Bundesregierung für Migration, Flüchtlinge und Integration 2007: 1). The most significant policy initiatives are the so-called 'integration courses'. These include German classes and an orientation course in German geography, history, culture and the political system. In addition, at different regional levels (city, county, state and federal, in part also EU-financed), NGOs, immigrant organisations and institutions can undertake so-called integration projects and apply for funding from the authorities.

5.2.1.1 Integration in Chemnitz: Everyday practice

Some of the interview partners that we met over the course of the field research were quite proficient at dealing with the 'integration' authorities and the 'integration project grants' they make available. One of these semi-professional 'integration organisers' is Hong[4], a member of the Vietnamese Association in Chemnitz.

In general, the public in Chemnitz frequently overlooks the Vietnamese who seem at once remarkably visible and invisible. Many locals hardly notice them despite their readily identifiable outward appearance. When asked about local groups of immigrants, residents often only mention the Vietnamese at the bottom of their list. This is remarkable, since most Vietnamese are self-employed, managing stores or working in the food and restaurant industry. Thus, they are in constant contact with native residents, yet seem scarcely to be noticed as individuals.

Hong himself is a business advisor who assists many Vietnamese business owners with bookkeeping and tax issues. Thus, as a professional he assumes the position of a middleman between German institutions and Vietnamese business owners. Remarkably, Hong readily uses buzzwords and formulations from official discourse in a professional manner in his talk, whereas his German generally sounds quite broken. The excerpt analysed below is taken from the middle of the interview where he outlines the activities of the Vietnamese Association and explains the number of Vietnamese living in Chemnitz. In the sequence just prior to the excerpt, Hong and the interviewer speak about the question of whether there are Germans who are actively involved in the Vietnamese Association.[5]

Transcript 1

Eine konTAKT zu diesen vietnamesen und deutsche sin auch schon DA. ist nicht dass wir nur ABseits sin nur isoLIERT sin is NICHT ne sonnern (--) wir haben zum BEIspiel (1.5) bei trung thu FEST (---) ich kann au (---) au diese (.) ANdere (-) AUSschländische (.) MITbürger oder ANdere (-) migrantn (.) AUCH (-) JA. EINgeladen (--) äh EINgeladen und (--) ja (.) und mit un MITzufeiern (.) oder weil (.) ja (-) (wir) (--) bei integration in die gesellschaft ham wir auch (.) EINgeladen (--).

Contact between these Vietnamese and Germans is also already there. it is not like we are only apart only isolated is not like that but we have for example at the Trung Thu holiday, I can also these other foreign residents or other immigrants also yes invited um invited and yes and to celebrate with us or because yes (we) at the integration into the society we've also invited.

Through both his vocal style and his repetition of a statement with very similar content, Hong strongly emphasises that there is *contact* between Germans and Vietnamese, and that the Vietnamese are not merely *apart* and *isolated.* His statement has a very markedly defensive tenor. This is shown particularly in his hedge when claiming that there is *also already* contact, and in the double direct negation about the Vietnamese being *apart* and *isolated.* He explicitly contradicts the unspoken, implicit criticism that the Vietnamese are separating themselves from the rest of society by means of their association. This criticism is an aspect of the latent impression on the part of the German population that Vietnamese immigrants show little readiness for integration. In the public debate, immigrant organisations are always in the position of having to justify their existence as ethnically homogeneous organisations within the context of the integration discourse. Presenting integration as an organisational goal is one of their most important strategies to assure the receipt of public financial support. Since the interviewer is not known to Hong and is both a member of the majority society and a representative of a German institution, Hong probably assumes that his interlocutor knows and potentially shares German prejudices concerning immigrant organisations in general and the Vietnamese in Chemnitz in particular. He thus takes a clear stand against these prejudices during the interview and cites examples to illustrate how deeply committed he is to *integration*.

5.2.1.2 Integration as event?

In what follows, we will analyse how the word *integration* is actually used. The context of the phrase 'at the integration into the society we've also invited' is initially unclear. Are we dealing with a grammatically wrong use of the preposition *at* (German *bei*), which can be seen simply as an error of a non-native speaker, or might this instead represent a significant semantic shift? We argue that this is a semantic shift with a change in the predicate class (Polenz 2008: 159). Paired with the German preposition *bei*, the concept of *integration* as used here by Hong can no longer refer to a process as it is intended in the official definition. Instead it seems to refer to an event or a function, just like the previously cited Trung Thu Festival. Thus, while the official linguistic formula *integration into society* has been completely adopted, its meaning has been fundamentally transformed. Integration turns into an event that one may celebrate along with other 'fellow foreign nationals' while cultivating one's own traditions.

This seems a bit odd at first, but when considered from the perspective of his day-to-day activities, the meaning Hong gives to the term *integration* in this excerpt is not as unusual as it initially appears. For example, events lasting from one to three days are supported by funds 'for the promotion of integrating immigrants'. The concept of integration is thus prescribed by policy, and government publicity campaigns have increasingly imparted the term with an official meaning.[6] In daily practice, however, the concept is not just passively assimilated, but rather critiqued, modified, varied and strategically appropriated against the backdrop of one's own experiences. For example, Hong strategically links the two goals of the association: preserving traditions and integration into society. The traditional Trung Thu Festival, a festival carried out for children with performances in Vietnamese and an audience consisting primarily of Vietnamese, is transformed into an integration event through appropriate labelling and the invitation of other immigrants.

In addition, implicit in this event is a reversal of the unidirectional concept of integration. Whereas in the official interpretation, x (the immigrant) is to be integrated into y (German society), here the concept is thought of in terms of others (Germans or other immigrants) becoming integrated into the immigrant culture of x. Thus, in addition to a predicate class change (process to event), a reversal in the sense of a semantic conversion also occurs (Polenz 2008: 181).

This example demonstrates how elastic the integration concept has become in the current debate. It is a typical umbrella term that holds together highly divergent strands of discourse. It is remarkable that Hong uses *integration* to refer to an event, not a process. On a very temporary and local level, projects and events may certainly promote good neighbourly coexistence, but the promotion of integration as a cross-sectional task requires a great deal more. This entails reappraising institutions, structures and systems with respect to their potential for inclusion and exclusion and with regard to their impact upon the course of individual lives and upon processes, which shape coexistence. Otherwise a social concept such as *integration* may only be understood as an event, despite any political rhetoric. In the following case study, we will focus on the potential for institutions to include and exclude as we look closely at the experience of history teaching in schools.

5.2.2 Post-Holocaust identity construction in school and public discourse

A key role in the integration process has been assigned to the education system since school performance is closely tied to opportunities for training and successful entry into a career, thereby influencing social acceptance (Beauftragte der Bundesregierung für Migration, Flüchtlinge und Integration 2007: 13, 25). It is particularly in school that young people learn how to position themselves in society as they define their own identity and sense of belonging within the context of society as a whole. Because school is a social institution that one generally cannot avoid, it exercises a large measure of influence. It is primarily in school that children and adolescents learn which social categories exist and which stereotypes and prejudices confront them. Those belonging to minority groups in particular must learn how to deal with these processes of social categorisation and to assert themselves in relation to them.

In the following section, we will present a case study addressing this topic. We discuss an interview with Ariella, a young Jewish woman who emigrated from Ukraine, and analyse how she frames the subject of identity formation in the context of her school experience. She reports on her years at school retrospectively, as by the time of the interview, she was already a medical student at the University of Jena. It is apparent that Ariella has great difficulties in positioning her own sense of belonging in Germany and in becoming accepted even though she appears to be well integrated: having arrived at the age of 12, she learned German very well, successfully completed her baccalaureate degree, and is currently studying without any academic difficulties. However, according to what she says in the interview, she appears to be rather isolated personally and socially.

5.2.2.1 Stigmatisation in the school setting

In the course of the interview, it becomes apparent that Ariella feels connected to two potentially stigmatising affiliations, her Ukrainian and her Jewish identities. She deals with each of these quite differently. Her Eastern European origin is generally known and, moreover, is unmistakeably present in her accent. She often uses the designation *Ausländer*, or 'foreigner', when referring to herself, thus positioning herself as a social outsider. At the same time she conceals her Jewish identity from both her fellow students and teachers. In dealing with this situation, she faces a task which Goffman (2007: 56) refers to as information management. The following excerpt serves as a point of departure for interpretation; it follows a sequence in which Ariella reports about a fellow immigrant Jewish student who presents himself as a German.

Transcript 2

A: und der war AU:CH (.) so: (.) kontingentflüchtling; das das DARF man nicht erzählen; du ka' du ka' KANNST doch nicht ner klasse erzählen (.) warum du nach deutschland gekommen bist; weil das DARFST du nicht.
I: wieso NICHT?
A: na (weil) du KANNST doch nicht sagen ich bin JUde, HALlo- (-)
I:kannst du [nicht?]
A:[da ich] hab das noch kein MENSCH gesagt, also (.) vielleicht DIR; du bist die EINzige deutsche (die das weiß) o:kay; na, naJA; ( ) aber SO hab, (-) kannst du NICHT sagen; (wenn du sagst) und (.) wenn dich jemand FRAGT, ja warum bist du nach DEUTSCHland gekommen dann sagst du naJA::? also ich wollte immer irgendwie (emiGRIE:ren)? (-) Aber so richtigen grund hab ich AUCH nicht? weil (-) wenn i' wenn ich plötzlich in der schule sage dass ich also (.) gesagt HÄTte dass ich (ne) JÜdin bin, man muss WIRKlich die schule wechseln; (-) (GEHT nicht)-das KANN nicht sein;

A: and he was also like a contingent refugee; that that must not be spoken about; you ca' you ca' cannot speak about this in your class (.) why you came to germany; because you must not speak about it
I: why not?
A: well (because) you cannot really say I am jewish, hello-
I: you can't?
A: cause I haven't told a single person about it, now maybe you; you are the only german (who knows it) okay; well, well yes; ( ) but well, you cannot say it; (if you say it) and if someone asks you, well why did you come to germany then you say, well? well, I always wanted to (emigrate) somewhere? But then I really don't have a proper reason? cause if I suddenly say in school that if I like had said that I am a jew, you really would have to change schools; (it's impossible) no way.

Ariella starts out with an indirect reference to her being Jewish by describing the student she had previously focused on as *also* being a contingent refugee. She thereby admits that she belongs to this group too. Strictly speaking, the expression *contingent refugee* refers primarily to a legal status that denotes a very specific, planned, controlled and institutionalised form of admitting immigrants into Germany (Körber 2005: 53). Since 1991, Jews from the successor states of the former Soviet Union who can prove their ethnic affiliation may apply for admission to Germany under certain circumstances (ibid.: 55). The term *contingent refugee* thus connotes a person's origin in the former USSR and their Jewish descent.

Thus, at this moment Ariella is already referring – implicitly, and yet unmistakeably – to her Jewishness while at the same time attesting to what she considers its taboo nature. When the interviewer persistently inquires about the necessity for such secrecy, Ariella is astonished. She simply repeats her assertion about the taboo. Her use of the generic, historically stigmatised term *Jude* is striking in the way that it reveals this hallmark of her identity in an especially direct fashion. In strongly emphasising a common word from youth-slang, *hello*, she expresses her astonishment at the naivety, if not ignorance, shown by the interviewer in this matter. For a total of four instances, she characterises revealing her Jewish identity as impossible. She then describes an avoidance strategy and sums up by remarking that the alternative would be to change schools. The forceful intonation, the repetitions, and the rapid, sometimes harried manner of speaking suggest that Ariella struggles emotionally with assuming her Jewish identity and finds it very difficult to talk about it in the interview.

After the interviewer's persistent inquiries, Ariella explains why it is so difficult to reveal her Jewish identity in a school setting. Her answers are primarily related to German history and the discursive engagement with it. After two rhetorical questions in which she makes reference to the interviewer's familiarity with the history of the persecution of the Jews ('how were Jews always treated?'), she arrives at a detailed explanation of her situation in Germany:

Transcript 3

A: ZWEItens-äh:- (.) das ist IMmer so; weil (--) ist jetz immer (.) verhasstes THEma das (.) << acc >wenn man jetzt den zweiten weltkrieg behandelt=sagt man immer> jA:: ihr seid die DEUtschen und=die juden sind die gu:ten und=die deutschen sind die schlechten und << all >das geht immer aufn keks>. weil (.) es is schon SECHzich jahre her - ja das weiß jetz JEder <<all> un=da sagen sie> << h > ja gucken sie doch mal> ähm; (.) << h > indianer hatten auch (.) Irgendwie einen krieg ähm (.) mit amerikanern;> (-) keiner sagt jetz doch dass ameriKAner schlechte menschen sind; weißt du

A: second of all um it's always like that; because this is always a hated topic now << acc >when they talk about the second world war now=they always say> yeah you are the germans and the jews are the good guys the germans are the bad guys << all >that always gets on your nerves>. because it's already been sixty years gone by yeah, everyone knows it <<all> and so they say> << h > yea, just look> um << h > the indians also had some kind of war um with americans;> and today nobody says that the americans are bad people; you know.

She reports that the Second World War is *always* a hated topic. By stressing the word *always* three times in the course of the passage, she highlights the excessively frequent attention to German Nazism in the curriculum and the constant public and media debate about this issue. Later in the interview she comments on her school experience,

[I]t's always there, 'cause we do it in just about every year, in the eighth, in the ninth, in the tenth and in the twelfth it was extensive.

Not only is the Second World War 'always' treated, but Jews and Germans are also constantly contrasted as 'good' versus 'bad'. In another excerpt, she further substantiates this and reports that, 'the teacher always says we are guilty, [...] that always, yes, always causes stress', or as she puts it, 'it always gets on your nerves'. Both formulations are ambiguous. It is not quite clear who is being stressed or whose nerves are affected: is she referring to herself or to her fellow students? Both are plausible according to the interpretation that follows.

In the excerpt above, the perspectives become blurred, and at first, the basis of Ariella's reaction to the treatment of the National Socialist past in school is not clear: is she expressing her own views, the views of her fellow students or what she takes to be a general perception? Ariella points out the passing of time ('sixty years gone by') as an argument for a different pedagogical approach to the National Socialist period. She thus effectively rejects the idea of a strong emotional and personal engagement with a past that she considers quite distant. Ariella disguises her voice as she quotes what appears to be her fellow students as they address their teacher during a heated debate ('<<all> and so they say> <<h> yea, just look here >') and then point out the case of the Americans and the Indians. For Ariella, this debate and the everyday practice of teaching history are highly relevant, and at the same time stressful and threatening. In what follows, we will attempt to uncover the reasons for this.

The teacher, Mr Hansen, frames the group of 'the Jews' as the *good guys*. The high standard associated with this label – to always be 'good' – can never really be fully met, and Ariella rejects such an idealised characterisation of Jews. In the image of the 'good victim' as constructed by the teacher, there is no room for real-life Jews as complex human beings (Georgi 2003: 178). Ariella portrays the reaction of her fellow students to the teacher's attempt to instil a consciousness of collective guilt or 'badness' in them as a vehement rejection of a *hated subject*. Ariella expects neither grief nor the acceptance of moral responsibility from non-Jewish students. For her, it is only important to deal less, or less emotionally, with the National Socialist period.

For Ariella, a topic like Nazism poses the risk of forcing her to take a stand and reveal her Jewishness, which renders the topic even more unpleasant for her. In the interview, she reports on a number of situations in her history class which she perceived as deeply unpleasant because her own emotional reaction nearly led her to disclose her Jewish identity. Her determination not to reveal her Jewish origins might not only cause her constant unease in history classes at school, but also in the course of ordinary social interaction. Being uncertain about her ability to completely control stigma-relevant information (Tröster 2008: 144) turns even routine situations into complex management tasks (Goffman 2007: 112).

The discussions that Ariella quotes from the history classroom bear strong resemblances to German public discourses about coming to terms with the Nazi past. In the 1980s the so-called 'historicisation' of National Socialism was debated (Fischer 2007: 235–8).[7] Furthermore, the moral uniqueness of the Holocaust was discussed in the context of the so-called Historians' Debate (Knäpple 2007: 238).[8] In the late 1990s, the well-known writer Martin Walser triggered a public debate with his Peace Prize speech, in which he argued for a stronger individualisation of memory and less collective and media emphasis on the Nazi past (Lorenz 2007: 297–8).

The interview vividly suggests that for Jewish immigrants more widely, the way in which National Socialist history is dealt with – both in public debates and in history classrooms – is extremely significant. German guilt has also informed the political and symbolic order of the immigration system, as a separate category of immigrants only came into being because of a sense of moral responsibility for the crimes of National Socialism (Körber 2005: 53). The decision to admit Jewish immigrants from the former Soviet Union, like the strengthening of Jewish communities in Germany which this measure is intended to support (Haug 2005: 5–6), generally occurs within an internal, self-referential, discursive framework whose origins lie in concepts of historical responsibility and reparation. According to Körber, the presence of a Jewish community is important primarily for its representative function in documenting and legitimising the democratic transformation of German society after the Holocaust (2005: 62). This has the consequence that individual immigrants must also contend with a nexus of meanings that embed their own situation into a very specific moral framework. As the discourse regarding Jewish immigrants and Ariella's example more specifically shows, the issue at stake is not primarily the needs, aims and feelings of the immigrants but the historical sensitivities and moral anxieties of the German majority society.

5.2.2.2 Historical memory in a multicultural society: Implications for teaching History

At a more general level, this example illustrates that majority Germans are not 'among themselves' when they address the question of collective guilt and debate the ethics of a responsible relationship towards the past. In multicultural schools, different perspectives on the German past may become relevant. When students in history lessons are addressed uniformly as 'Germans', a community of shared fate and guilt is postulated, which excludes those students who may not be able to share this particular relationship with the past. Engaging with the German past in terms of a vehement self-attribution of collective guilt and 'badness' intensifies the division of humans into bounded collectives, into an 'us' and a 'them', thus reinforcing the perception of Germans as a naturally given homogeneous people. Such a concept of national identity excludes both Jewish Germans and their experience of persecution (Lorenz 2007: 298), as well as Germans of different ethnic or national origins (Georgi 203: 152–6). Because children in today's German schools represent such diverse backgrounds, teaching history and confronting the difficult German past presents many challenges and opportunities.

If schools are to perform an integrative function without excluding any of their pupils on the basis of what is taught and how it is taught, they will have to offer curricula that take this into account. Georgi and Ohliger (2009), for instance, have assembled a collection of new insights and reflections for teaching history that point in this direction. Indeed every consideration of history and form of engagement with the past is part of the cultural processes that lead to the formation of historical self-awareness for a particular collective, regardless of how this collective is actually constituted (Rüsen 2007: 212). According to Rüsen (2007: 213), the consideration of history is based on an ethnocentric construction of meaning, and should be critically challenged through the ongoing development of methods of historical research and teaching. Reflection about these kinds of issues in schools and as a part of teacher training is one aspect of the institutional changes that have become necessary as Germany recognises itself as a country of immigration.

5.2.3 'No-go areas'? An Afro-German family responds to discrimination in Chemnitz

In this final case study we examine an Afro-German family's perceptions of risk and security in Chemnitz and compare these to the public discourse. Unsafe places, or 'places where you don't go', as the interviewer puts it, are called *no-go areas* by the interviewees. As a whole, the interviewees refer strongly to the public and media discourse on this subject. We thus begin with a brief overview of the origins of this term.

5.2.3.1 The history of the term and its discursive use

There are different terms and expressions for places that could be risky or dangerous for certain groups at certain times (Münnich 2008). The concept of no-go areas originated in a military context, referring to areas where military control could not be ensured. Used in a civilian context, this term is associated with areas in which government bodies and law enforcement mechanisms have lost control. In its broadest sense, the term denotes dangerous locations or areas where individuals or groups from certain segments of the population fear becoming the victims of crimes directed against them for specific reasons (gender, age, skin colour, sexual orientation, etc.). From the perspective of the victims, such areas have been described as a space of fear (Döring 2008: 98; Paul 2008).

In German public discourse, the expression no-go area surfaced with particular frequency in the months leading up to the 2006 Football World Cup. The Berlin/Brandenburg Africa Council apparently planned to publish a map of Germany to identify specific areas, which they deemed unsafe for non-white visitors attending the matches (Schultze 2006). This plan took on a particular relevance after an Afro-German scientist in Potsdam was attacked and critically injured. The Africa Council later denied that they had planned to publish such a map, but would instead issue a guide recommending rules of conduct for non-white World Cup visitors (Afrika Start 2006). During the course of this debate, many political representatives, journalists and inhabitants of the regions – particularly in eastern Germany – which were suspected to be possible candidates for the label no-go areas, protested against this 'defamation of entire regions'[9] (Greven 2006).

5.2.3.2 Experiencing discrimination and threatening places

How do potentially targeted people who live in eastern Germany and do not stand in the public spotlight deal with the question of no-go areas? To answer this question, we will present an individual case analysis based on an interview with several members of an Afro-German family. The interview partners are the white German mother, Karin (K) and two daughters, Annina (A) and Ilona (I), aged 16 and 17. The African[10] father was not present, as he works for a large corporation in western Germany and only comes home at weekends. As the following interpretations will demonstrate, for members of the F. family, the subject of no-go areas does not merely represent a theoretical or political issue. As potential victims of racism, they have to find their own personal, practical strategy for dealing with this problem in their everyday life and compare the public discourse with the reality of their own life on the ground. An excerpt from the early segment of the interview will serve as a point of departure for our analysis. Confronted with the interviewer's question about 'places where one does not go, or that one wants to avoid', Annina, who generally takes up the largest share of the conversation, begins with an answer.

Transcript 4

A: also ich (-) möchte das eigentlich nich dass ich irgendwas meide wegen irgend wegen meiner hautfarbe oder so. deswegen also ich geh einfach überall hin, och wenns da vielleicht (.) gewisse gefAHrengebiete gibt oder so was das is mir eigentlich relativ egal. also weil ich das (-) nich tolerieren möchte und dann (-) mich da auch gerne drüber hinwegsetze sozusagen.

A: well I actually don't want that i avoid things because of some because of my skin colour or something like that. that's why well I simply go everywhere, even if there are maybe certain dangerous places or things like that for me it's actually pretty much all the same. well because I don't want to tolerate it and then I prefer to ignore it, so to speak.

5.2.3.3 'No-go areas' and the need for personal freedom

In forming the question about specific places where one does not go, the interviewer engages in a kind of self-correction as he uses the expression 'that one wants to avoid'. In this phrase, the modal verb *wants to* suggests free will and intentionality. Annina's reply makes it clear that she understood the question in these terms because she answers directly in the negative, repeating the word *want* from the question ('well I actually don't want that'). In addition, Annina immediately connects the question about places that she avoids with her skin colour. The preceding exchange thus shows how the relevance of skin colour has already been established at this point in the interview.

However, this first statement from Annina also contains the restrictive particle, *actually*, and Annina reaffirms her assertion by saying, 'well I simply go everywhere'. She also repeats this again later as she develops the topic further, 'yes as I said, so I just don't avoid anything'. In her words, 'even if there are maybe certain dangerous places' which she nonetheless deliberately ignores; for her, 'it's actually pretty much all the same'. However, by expressing lack of attention and defiance she implies that there are problematic circumstances. These dangerous places are not *all the same* to her in the sense of indifference because they represent a problematic phenomenon, which she 'does not want to tolerate'. Hence if there are symbolic limits for dark-skinned individuals, she 'prefers to ignore' them, emphasising her own self-determined strategies. Annina appears to be driven by a quest for unrestrained freedom of movement and for individual freedom of action. Rather than complying with socially constructed boundaries she makes a point of crossing them. These intentions are emphasised in the way she frames her statements: she begins by stating that there are no places she wants to avoid and ends with a sequence in which she indicates that even though she has already had some bad experiences, she chooses to ignore them, 'because I really want to have the freedom to go wherever I want'.

In her talk Annina presents herself as independent and strong. There is no point in concealing who she is (as Ariella does, for instance) since her skin colour is readily visible to everyone. In addition, she describes herself as a *punk*, and points towards the 'style markers' (Kallmeyer 1994: 31) she likes to wear such as colourful clothes and combat boots. Thus, she identifies with a group that has chosen its own symbols of stigmatisation. Through her punk appearance, Annina thus intensifies her distance from people who would reject her on account of her skin colour, and shows them that she does not shy away from a confrontation with them. After the end of Annina's turn in Transcript 4, the interview continues as follows:

Transcript 5

U: ja. (-) also es gibt offensichtlich gebiete die in der stadt,
A: das is halt nich so direkt. das des is halt mehr so (1.0) .hh na doch schon also im heckert gebiet un so da is manchmal ganz schön komisch, also da sind halt v::iele die dann n bisschen (--) komisch reagieren wenn man da rumläuft und so aber. (-) also (-) ich hab da ooch nich so viel zu tun dort aber trotzdem also manchmal (--) is man halt da wegen der schule und so was (-) un aber ich (--) mach mir da jetzt nich son kopf und ich mach mir auch keen kopf wenn mir jetzt jemand irgend(-) was sagt oder so, also

U: yes. so there are, apparently areas in the city,
A: it's not that straightforward really, it is just more like this .hh but even so in the heckert area and such it's sometimes really quite strange, well there are lots of people who like react a little bit strangely if you hang out there and so on, but. well I don't really have much to do there, but still, despite that, well sometimes you just happen to be there 'cause of school and so on and but me I don't really think about it, and I don't think much about it if somebody says something to me or something like that, well.

At the beginning of the passage above, the interviewer alludes to Annina's implicit acknowledgement of the existence of dangerous areas when he interrupts her and states, 'yes. so there are apparently areas in the city'. He is unable to complete this statement, for Annina quickly takes back the right to speak and paraphrases the *areas in the city* more clearly. While there are no clearly defined places where one doesn't go, in certain places, as she puts it, it is sometimes 'really strange'. Rhetorically, many interruptions, hedge words and paraphrases reveal an insecurity and ambivalence in dealing with this subject. In contrast to the concrete, clearly demarcated spaces suggested by the term no-go areas in the media discourse, Annina's description is vague. She only once mentions a relatively large area, *the Heckert area*, triggering a *strange* feeling, a diffuse feeling of fear and intimidation. She uses the expression *strange* where one might have expected her to say *threatening* or *hostile*. However, Annina does not use these terms, just as she demonstrates throughout the interview that she does not let herself be easily intimidated by potentially threatening behaviour by others. *No-go areas* is simply not the appropriate designation for what Annina calls *certain dangerous places*, because entry into such areas is a necessity for people who live or go to school there. The practical problem for the F. family is not how to avoid certain areas, but rather how to deal with a diffuse feeling of threat as they pursue their daily activities in public space.

5.2.3.4 Racism and discrimination: Special challenges in provincial areas

Racism and discrimination are of paramount importance for integration processes (Sassenberg et al. 2007) because people tend to retreat into their separate groups if they do not feel accepted. There are, however, a number of different strategies employed by people faced with experiences of discrimination. Members of the F. family initially try to keep their experiences with discrimination in public at a distance and thus portray them as unimportant or not overly bothersome. In this way, they acknowledge unpleasant experiences but, by emphasising their own strength, they portray these experiences as manageable and not overly threatening. This presentation of the self as strong and independent may also be reflective of a conversational situation in which an unfamiliar white German researcher who is not personally affected by racism poses questions about this subject. Such an interview situation may not provide a 'safe space' for speaking about discrimination. In these interview narratives, members of the F. family resort to their own individual strategies for managing danger. Interestingly, references to other Afro-Germans cannot be found in their stories. This may suggest that much needed emancipatory networks or 'safe spaces' are still difficult to create in provincial places such as Chemnitz (see also Chapter 9).

5.3 Conclusion

All three case studies described above demonstrate that the people interviewed for this study grapple with elements of the public discourse, albeit in different ways than one might have anticipated. The key concept of integration is strategically reinterpreted. Attempts to provide moral reparations to Jews lead to added identity conflicts. No-go areas are disclaimed, even while their existence is confirmed, albeit in a distinct perception as places where one is made to feel 'really strange'. This might actually be a plausible description, since one cannot choose to avoid such places, and because the threat is often latent and thus remains all the more incalculable. Based on our research, we would like to highlight the following three points.

First, in an immigration society like Germany, there is a need for a reflective process to determine which institutional practices (for example, the teaching of history) have an exclusionary and divisive effect, and how these practices can be changed to become more inclusive. This also means that integration should not become an 'event', a tendency fuelled by the strong focus on providing financial support for 'projects'. Instead, a political process for restructuring social institutions needs to be instituted.

Second, in eastern German provincial areas, the challenge of communicating the 'normality' of an immigration society is much greater than in large cities that have traditionally been characterised by immigration. The kind of ordinary, everyday intercultural contact which Yildiz (1999) and Bukow (2007) describe in their research on large western German cities is rare in eastern German towns and cities. It is thus crucial that these areas should not be passed over in the current debate on immigration.

Third, the discrepancy between formal integration (both in the case of Ariella and the F. family) and the problems of exclusion and stigmatisation actually experienced draws attention to the limited validity of global integration indicators (such as, for example, in Woellert et al. 2009) and emphasises the need to determine the specific relevance of crucial issues for immigrants as well as their individual perspectives on the basis of a direct and open exchange.

Table 5.1 Transcription conventions (cf. Selting et al. 1998)

KEEne	accented syllable
kann=ich	rapid, instant connection of new subjects or entities
a::, a:::	elongation, stretching, according to length
(.)	micropause
(-),(--),(---)	short, medium and longer pauses 0.25–0.75 sec, max 1 sec
(6.5)	timed pauses, length in seconds
[ ]	overlapping and simultaneous speech
((lacht))	non-verbal behaviour
( )	incomprehensible sequence
(etwas)	not completely clearly comprehensible sequence
,	pitch slightly rising
?	pitch rising high
;	pitch slightly falling
.	pitch falling strongly
-	pitch remaining the same
<<h> >	high pitch register
<<t> >	deep pitch register
<<p> >	soft speech
<<f> >	loud speech
<<all> >	rapid speech
<<len> >	slow speech
<<acc> >	becoming faster
<<rall> >	becoming slower

Notes

1. German original: 'Angesichts des demografischen Wandels und des wachsenden weltweiten Wettbewerbs um die besten Köpfe müssen wir auch zukünftig Zuwanderung gezielt für die wirtschaftlichen und gesellschaftlichen Interessen Deutschlands nutzen. Auch dafür ist eine nachhaltige Integrationspolitik dringend erforderlich' (Beauftragte 2007: 12).
2. We are grateful to Gerd Ulrich Bauer who conducted approximately half of the interviews. He also compiled most of the historical survey and the survey on immigrants in Chemnitz. The other interviews were conducted by Inken Carstensen-Egwuom.
3. German original: 'In der bundesdeutschen Debatte um Zuwanderung und Migration, so scheint es, existieren die ostdeutschen Bundesländer nicht. Mit dem Hinweis auf die geringe Quantität der Zuwanderung wird dabei die besondere Qualität der Zuwanderung übersehen' (Weiss 2007: 119).
4. All personal names are pseudonyms.
5. The transcriptions used in the English translations are greatly simplified because the placement of, for example, pauses and stressed syllables cannot be adequately translated. For the transcription of the German originals see conventions shown in Table 5.1.
6. See e.g. [http://www.bundesregierung.de/Content/DE/Publikation/IB/nationaler-integrationsplan-plakate.html].

7. German original: 'Historisierung' (Fischer 2007: 235–8).
8. German original: 'Historikerstreit' (Knäpple 2007: 238).
9. German original: 'Verunglimpfung ganzer Regionen' (Greven 2006).
10. We chose the expression 'African' here in order to protect the anonymity of the participants. Their precise country of origin is known to the authors and the generalisation that is connected with not designating African countries of origin by name is only adopted here in the interest of anonymity.

References

Afrika Start (2006). 'Afrika-Rat: Fokus auf Überwindung von Rassismus'.http://web.archive.org/web/20070819230521/http://www.afrika-start.de/artikel-176.htm, accessed 2 December 2008.

Beauftragte der Bundesregierung für Migration, Flüchtlinge und Integration (2007). *Der Nationale Integrationsplan: Neue Wege – Neue Chancen* (Berlin: Presse und Informationsamt der Bundesregierung).

Bukow, W. D. (2007). 'Die Rede von Parallelgesellschaften: Zusammenleben im Zeitalter einer metropolitanen Differenzgesellschaft', in W. D. Bukow, C. Nikodem, E. Schulze and E. Yildiz (eds). *Was heißt hier Parallelgesellschaft? Zum Umgang mit Differenzen* (Wiesbaden: VS Verlag für Sozialwissenschaften), pp. 29–51.

Döring, U. (2008). *Angstzonen: Rechtsdominierte Orte aus medialer und lokaler Perspektive* (Wiesbaden: VS Verlag für Sozialwissenschaften).

Fischer, T. (2007). 'Historisierung der NS-Zeit', in T. Fischer and M. N. Lorenz *Lexikon der 'Vergangenheitsbewältigung' in Deutschland: Debatten- und Diskursgeschichte des Nationalsozialismus nach 1945* (Bielefeld: transcript), pp. 235–8.

Georgi, V. B. (2003). *Entliehene Erinnerungen: Geschichtsbilder junger Migranten in Deutschland* (Hamburg: Hamburger Edition).

Georgi, V. B. and R. Ohliger (eds) (2009). *Crossover Geschichte: Historisches Bewusstsein Jugendlicher in der Einwanderungsgesellschaft* (Hamburg: Ed Körber-Stiftung).

Goffman, E. (2007 [1963]). *Stigma: Über Techniken der Bewältigung beschädigter Identität* (Frankfurt am Main: Suhrkamp).

Glaser, M. (2006). 'Interkulturelles Lernen in Ostdeutschland: Voraussetzungen, Entwicklungslinien und Perspektiven', in L. Reiberg (ed.) *Berufliche Integration in der multikulturellen Gesellschaft: Beiträge aus Theorie, Schule und Jugendhilfe zu einer interkulturell sensiblen Berufsorientierung* (Bonn: Bundeszentrale für politische Bildung), pp. 55–63.

Greven, L. (2006). 'No-Go-Areas: Brandenburg meiden', *Zeit Online*. http://www.zeit.de/online/2006/20/Nogoareas-Heye, accessed 25 June 2009.

Haug, S. (2005). 'Jüdische Zuwanderer in Deutschland: Ein Überblick über den Stand der Forschung', *Working Papers der Forschungsgruppe des Bundesamtes* (Nürnberg: Bundesamt für Migration und Flüchtlinge), No. 3/2005.

Holly, W., U. Püschel and J. Bergmann (eds) (2001). *Der sprechende Zuschauer: Wie wir uns Fernsehen kommunikativ aneignen* (Wiesbaden: Westdeutscher Verlag).

Jung, M. (1997). 'Die Sprache des Migrationsdiskurses: Ein Überblick', in M. Jung, M. Wengeler and K. Böke (eds). *Die Sprache des Migrationsdiskurses: Das Reden über 'Ausländer' in Medien, Politik und Alltag* (Opladen: Westdeutscher Verlag), pp. 9–16.

Jäger, S. (1996). *BrandSätze: Rassismus im Alltag* (Duisburg: DISS).

Kallmeyer, W. (1994). 'Das Projekt Kommunikation in der Stadt', in W. Kallmeyer (ed.) *Exemplarische Analysen des Sprachverhaltens in Mannheim. Kommunikation in der Stadt, Teil 1* (Berlin: de Gruyter), pp. 1–38.

Keppler, A. (1993). 'Fernsehunterhaltung aus Zuschauersicht', in W. Holly and U. Püschel (eds). *Medienrezeption als Aneignung: Methoden und Perspektiven qualitativer Medienforschung* (Opladen: Westdeutscher Verlag), pp. 101–13.

Klein, J. (1995). 'Asyl-Diskurs: Konflikte und Blockaden in Politik, Medien und Alltagswelt', in R. Reiher (ed.) *Sprache im Konflikt: Zur Rolle der Sprache in sozialen, politischen und militärischen Auseinandersetzungen* (Berlin/New York: de Gruyter), pp. 15–71.

Knäpple, L., 'Historikerstreit' in T. Fischer and M. N. Lorenz (eds). *Lexikon der 'Vergangenheitsbewältigung' in Deutschland: Debatten – und Diskursgeschichte des Nationalsozialismus nach 1945* (Bielefeld: transcript), pp. 238–40.

Körber, K. (2005). *Juden, Russen, Emigranten: Identitätskonflikte jüdischer Einwanderer in einer ostdeutschen Stadt* (Frankfurt am Main: Campus-Verlag).

Lorenz, M. N. (2007). 'Walser-Bubis-Debatte', in T. Fischer and M. N. Lorenz (eds). *Lexikon der 'Vergangenheitsbewältigung' in Deutschland: Debatten – und Diskursgeschichte des Nationalsozialismus nach 1945* (Bielefeld: transcript), pp. 297–9.

Meißner, B. and G. Ruhrmann (2000). *Das Ausländerbild in den Thüringer Tageszeitungen 1995–1999: Eine quantitative und qualitative Inhaltsanalyse* (Erfurt: Der Ausländerbeauftragte der Thüringer Landesregierung).

Münnich, N. (2008). 'No-Go-Areas in Deutschland', http://www.nogoarea.de, accessed 25 June 2009.

Niehr, T. and K. Böke (eds) (2000). *Einwanderungsdiskurse: Vergleichende diskurslinguistische Studien* (Wiesbaden: Westdeutscher Verlag).

Paul, M. (2008). '"National befreite Zone", "Angstraum", "No-Go-Area": Herkunft und Bedeutung verräumlichter Begriffe', Lecture *at a STHK Workshop* (Oberwiesenthal: STHK).

Polenz, P. (2008). *Deutsche Satzsemantik: Grundbegriffe des Zwischen-den-Zeilen-Lesens* (Berlin, New York: de Gruyter).

Ruhrmann, G. and J. Kollmer (1987). *Ausländerberichterstattung in der Kommune: Inhaltsanalyse Bielefelder Tageszeitungen unter Berücksichtigung 'ausländerfeindlicher' Alltagstheorien* (Opladen: Westdeutscher Verlag).

Rüsen, J. (2007). 'Interkulturelle Geschichtswissenschaft', in J. Straub, A. Weidemann and D. Weidemann (eds). *Handbuch Interkulturelle Kommunikation und Kompetenz. Grundbegriffe – Theorien – Anwendungsfelder* (Stuttgart: Metzler), pp. 211–15.

Sächsischer Landtag, Die Sächsische Ausländerbeauftragte (2008). *Jahresbericht 2007* (Dresden: Sächsischer Landtag).

Sassenberg, K., J. Fehr, N. Hansen, C. Matschke and K. A. Woltin (2007). 'Eine sozialpsychologische Analyse zur Reduzierung sozialer Diskriminierung von Menschen mit Migrationshintergrund', *Zeitschrift für Sozialpsychologie*, vol. 38, no. 4: pp. 239–49.

Schultze, C. (2006). 'Gefahrenatlas Deutschland: No-Go-Areas für Schwarze', *Spiegel Online*, http://www.spiegel.de/politik/deutschland/0,1518,412226,00.html, accessed 25 June 2009.

Selting, M., P. Auer, B. Barden, B. Jörg, C.-K. Elizabeth, G. Susanne, M. Christoph, Q. Uta, S. Peter, U. Susanne (1998). 'Gesprächsanalytisches Transkriptionssystem (GAT) ', *Linguistische Berichte*, no. 173: pp. 91–122.

Stadt Chemnitz (2002). *Sozialreport der Stadt Chemnitz 2000–2002* (Chemnitz).

Stadt Chemnitz (2008a). *Sozialreport der Stadt Chemnitz 2003–2007* (Chemnitz).

Stadt Chemnitz (2008b) *Chronik der Stadt Chemnitz*, http://www.chemnitz.de/chemnitz/de/stadt_chemnitz/geschichte/chronik/chronik_index.asp, accessed 10 November 2008.

Thomas, T. (2003). *Deutsch-Stunden. Zur Konstruktion nationaler Identität im Fernsehtalk* (Frankfurt a.M.: Campus).

Tröster, H. (2008). 'Stigma', in K. E. Petersen and B. Six (eds). *Stereotype, Vorurteile und soziale Diskriminierung. Theorien, Befunde und Interventionen* (Weinheim: Beltz PVU), pp. 140–8.

Wengeler, M. (2003). *Topos und Diskurs. Begründung einer argumentationsanalytischen Methode und ihre Anwendung auf den Migrationsdiskurs (1960–1985)* (Tübingen: Niemeyer).

Weiss, K. (2007). 'Zuwanderung in die neuen Bundesländer', in W. Woyke and D. Halm (eds). *Integration und Einwanderung: Eine Einführung* (Schwalbach/Ts.: Wochenschau-Verlag), pp. 119–40.

Woellert, F., S. Krönert, L. Sippel et al. (2009). *Ungenutzte Potenziale: Zur Lage der Integration in Deutschland* (Berlin: Berlin-Institut für Bevölkerung und Entwicklung).

Yildiz, E. (1999). *Fremdheit und Integration: Ausführungen zum besseren Verständnis, Anregungen zum Nachdenken* (Bergisch Gladbach: BLT).

6

Integration into What? The Intercultural Week, Mental Borders and Multiple Identities in the German Town of Bayreuth

Hauke Dorsch

> However, I wonder whether this is not asking too much, to somehow jump over walls on such an evening. Well, walls is maybe too strong a word, but to suddenly jump over borders that are so present in everyday life, whether this is not way too ambitioned.[1]

This was the disillusioned résumé of Reverend H. after the 'Festival Evening of Cultures' (*Festabend der Kulturen*) which was planned to be the highlight of the *Intercultural Week* 2008 in Bayreuth, Germany. Reverend H. uses both terms 'walls' and 'borders' to define what he considers a strong separation between 'natives' and 'foreigners'.[2] For a number of years he was the main person responsible for the Intercultural Week, but had resigned from this position at the time of the interview. The Intercultural Week (*Interkulturelle Woche*, or IKW) is the largest single event celebrating Bayreuth's cultural diversity. I participated in the meetings preparing the Week for 2008, during which the organisers also evaluated the IKW of 2007. The atmosphere of these meetings was friendly. But emotions were stirred when participants discussed an incident during the IKW of 2007: a dance troupe of ethnic Germans from the former Soviet Union had overstayed their allotted time on stage. Once they had finally finished, the audience – mainly other Germans from the former Soviet Union – left the venue, leaving the remaining artists behind, who had to perform in a nearly empty hall. After heated discussions about this issue, from which the organisers of the dance troupe remained absent, it was decided that this troupe should not participate in the Intercultural Week of 2008. The following year, the Week's programme was reduced.

This chapter will be about absences: the absent audiences at events of the IKW, the Russian-Germans' (*Spätaussiedler*) lack of interest in other migrants' activities, and the absence of the 'native' German population in Bayreuth, which reduced the event to a meeting of what could be called the 'integration scene'. I will ask why other groups were absent from the IKW in 2008, and why encounters between those groups who did participate did not take place. I will try to explain these findings by focusing on performances, and on how these reveal existing mental borders not only between 'natives' and 'foreigners' but also between different groups of 'natives'.[3]

6.1 The research setting in the town of Bayreuth

Bayreuth is the regional capital of Upper Franconia, the most north-eastern region in the German federal state of Bavaria. It borders on Thuringia and Saxony, both of which were part of the German Democratic

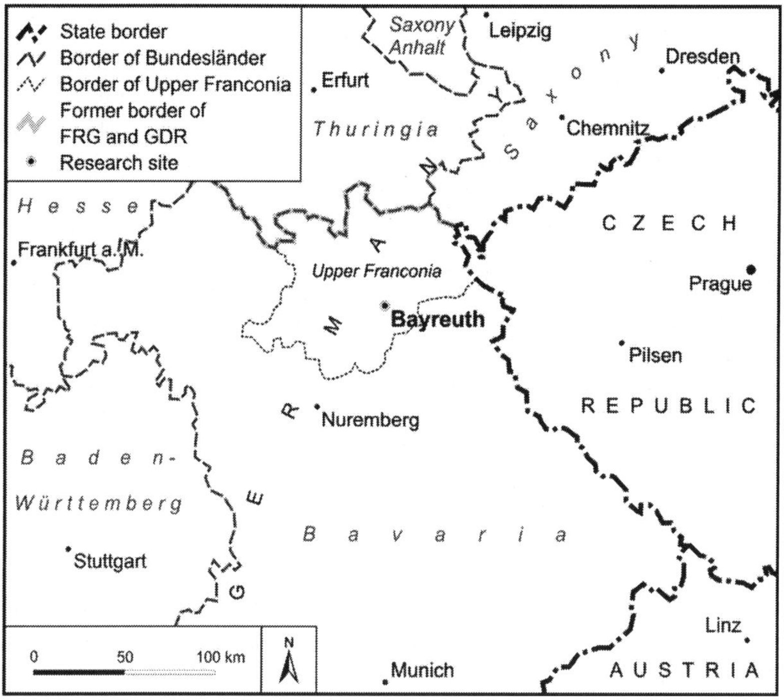

Map 6.1 Bayreuth in the German region of Franconia

Republic (GDR) until 1990, and on the most western tip of the Czech Republic (see map 6.1). German unification as well as EU enlargement have transformed the political geography of Upper Franconia from a remote border region in West Germany to a mid-central region within Germany as well as within the new Europe. The constitution as a peripheral borderland that was located at the front lines between 'East' and 'West' deeply shaped – and in many ways disadvantaged – the economic and demographic fabric of Upper Franconia. The region is both, a political and a symbolic reality: its territorial boundaries mark a *Regierungsbezirk* (administrative district) in Bavaria and form part of people's collective identity.

Bayreuth is the regional centre and largest town in Upper Franconia. It has long served as an urban pull-centre for the entire region, and has absorbed migrants who left structurally weaker areas of Franconia, as well as neighbouring areas of East Germany after 1989. The foundation of the university in 1975 has consolidated the town's pull-effect, attracting a large contingent of national and international students. Bayreuth and Upper Franconia have a long history of local, international and even intercontinental migration and trade exchanges due to the region's long-standing industrial tradition.

Bayreuth has about 73,000 inhabitants, roughly 5500 of whom are foreign nationals.[4] The largest group of recent immigrants are the so-called *Spätaussiedler*, ethnic Germans from the former Soviet Union, who do not count as foreigners in immigration statistics because they received German citizenship on entering the country. Roughly 6,500 of them live in Bayreuth. Apart from being an important cultural location thanks to the annual Richard Wagner Festival, Bayreuth is also an administrative centre. Thus, it is wealthy compared to its neighbouring regions. However, this characteristic creates a difficult situation for migrants, because many jobs in the public sector are reserved for nationals. Bayreuthers describe themselves as reserved towards foreigners and often explain this as an expression of their *Beamtenmentalität*, or public servants' mentality.

Research took place from October 2007 to October 2008, and again in March, June and September 2009. I focused on institutions, individuals, spaces and activities facilitating or aiming at integration and 'good neighbourhood' in Bayreuth. Participant observation took place at meetings or events organised by different institutions, associations and groups. These included religious groups, the municipality, migrant associations, political groups, professional and administrative bodies. Some participant observation and interviewing was also conducted at sports and youth clubs, restaurants and snack bars that offer 'ethnic' food, and in a school which was known for its high percentage of immigrants. Furthermore I visited festivals, concerts, theatre performances and other cultural activities. Media analysis and the observation of the City Council election campaigns helped determine whether and in which way integration was a debated issue. Looking at these spaces of encounter and at institutions which implemented targeted integration policies helped to avoid the 'methodological nationalism' (Glick Schiller et al. 2006) that would follow ethnicity or nationality-based groupings only. Thus it is important not only to think beyond the national or ethnic constructions of immigrants, but also to understand the heterogeneity of the respective host societies. Focusing on the heterogeneous identifications of members of the 'host society' helps one to avoid the unhistorical and homogenising perspectives of society that are increasingly successful in today's Europe, especially, but not exclusively, among right-wing populist parties (see Geschiere 2009: 166).

6.2 Bayreuth's intercultural scene and the 'Week'

The IKW brought some of Bayreuth's major 'intercultural scene' players into the limelight. First, there was the established body of welfare organisations, solidarity groups, anti-Nazi-groups and liberal church activists, many of whom were linked to the Lutheran Church. The IKW in general showed that Bayreuth's major intercultural activities take place in the framework of the Lutheran Church. Four of the 16 institutions organising the event were linked to the Lutheran Church, the former IKW organiser, Reverend H., is a Lutheran cleric, and most meetings and events took place in venues owned by it. Other organising groups included three Roman Catholic groups, 'Third World' solidarity groups, the municipality, the university, the local cinema and three migrant associations (all of which represented people from Eastern Europe, especially Germans from the former Soviet Union). Other activists and associations important in this field were notable through their absence, the reasons for which I will explain below.

Recently, the municipality joined the group of IKW organisers. For many years, Bayreuth's mayors have been merely 'patrons' of it, but starting in 2008, the newly inaugurated Commissioner for Integration joined the organisational committee and used the municipality's infrastructure to support this event. This new role of the municipality reflected changing local and national policies. Chancellor Merkel's new National Integration Plan in 2007 included the acceptance that Germany was shaped by immigration and invoked the need to integrate migrants (see Carstensen-Egwuom and Holly, this volume). When Bayreuth's new

Conservative mayor was elected in 2006 he declared, that integration policies would be a major concern of his term in office. Consequently, he established a new administrative position, the Commissioner for Integration.[5] The person chosen for this position was a 'native' German civil servant, whose experience in the field was limited. Apart from the new Commissioner the so-called Advisor for Foreigners[6] and her vice-commissioner, both of whom are immigrants, continued to work from the municipality on a voluntary basis. They operated from not more than a desk and a telephone in a municipal office.

6.3 Absences

The Jewish community has never participated in the IKW. In fact, it is hardly visible in town. Its leaders are consciously avoiding too much presence,[7] despite the community's growth with the arrival of Jewish refugees from Eastern Europe. They had left a growing anti-Semitic climate in the former Soviet Union and emigrated to Germany where they were admitted as so-called Kontingentflüchtlinge (see also Carstensen-Egwuom and Holly in this volume). In the 1980s the few remaining Jewish citizens of Bayreuth feared for the future of the community, as they could hardly find enough participants for the service in the synagogue. According to the Chair of the Jewish community (conversation, 17.12.2007, cf. Aas 2007), today roughly 200 of Bayreuth's c.500 Jewish citizens are regular visitors to the synagogue. There are inter-religious working groups with Christians and other forms of encounter, e.g. visits of Christian groups in the synagogue. However, their concept of 'integration' focuses on internal concerns, such as on teaching Judaism to Jews from the former Soviet Union, most of whom have little knowledge about religion. In this case, the comparison with the findings of our colleagues in Chemnitz is striking. There, the Jewish community is a major player in organising the IKW. Among other reasons, existing bourgeois anti-Semitism in Bayreuth may be a reason for the Jewish community's choice to keep a low profile. The spirit of Wagnerian circles is still felt in town, and the head of the Jewish community (and others) told me about incidents that revealed anti-Semitism in Bayreuth. Recently, however, there have been signs of change and more active efforts towards overcoming the mental borders between Christians and Jews. The Lutheran Church, local historians and politicians organised a number of events focusing on National Socialism in Bayreuth, thereby tackling the ongoing local silence about the Third Reich.[8] The Jewish community opens the synagogue for visitors or on special occasions like Hanukkah.

It supported an exhibition on Jewish history in a local museum in Bayreuth in autumn 2010.[9] In the near future, the community plans to open a community centre, which will be open to the public and include a museum on the centuries of Jewish presence in Bayreuth.

The mosques did not participate in 2008's IKW. One interviewee told me this was because they missed the deadline for having their activities published in the programme; another said it was because they were not aware of the event (Interviews with A., 10.09.08; E. 30.09.08). The mosques participated in earlier IKWs, however, and did so again in 2010.

Apart from some refugees, there were hardly any African or Asian migrants present at the IKW. Again the comparison with Chemnitz is interesting, where Angolan, Mozambican, Nigerian and Vietnamese associations are active in intercultural events. In Bayreuth, Africans – mostly students and academics – organise in the AASAB (Association of Africans Students and Academics in Bayreuth). They use the yearly Afro-Caribbean Festival as their forum of exchange, rather than the IKW. Furthermore, none of the many restaurants, takeaways, pubs and tea houses, which are run by immigrants, participated in the IKW.

An important player in the field of Bayreuth's integration and immigration policies did not participate in the IKW. This is the Immigration Authority, called Ausländeramt which translates best as Foreigners' Office. This institution often heavily informs the lives of non-EU immigrants in Bayreuth. In contrast to other German towns and *Länder*, none of its officers has a 'migration background', although intercultural competence in similar institutions reportedly reduced misunderstandings and conflicts. Furthermore, the head of the Immigration Authority told me (Interview with Mrs D., 15.09.2008) that they had not received any intercultural training so far, although, again, other immigration authorities had seemingly good experiences with such training.[10] The Bayreuth Office has the image of harbouring hardliners who cling to Germany's elites' earlier denial of Germany being a country of immigration. Its employees are seen as gatekeepers who try to prevent the 'floods of refugees' from entering the country. This image prevails among the activists of the 'Round Table', whose main labour is devoted to preventing deportations of asylum seekers, and in the local Bavarian and national German press, which reported on deportations from Bayreuth, suggesting that the local authority is particularly strict.[11] Often being the first authority any non-EU immigrant coming to town is confronted with, it is understandable that many immigrants are not eager to participate in events that they perceive to represent 'officialdom'. As a result, few immigrants participated in the official reception in the town hall at the end of the IKW in 2008.

6.4 The diversity of local identities

Current research on migration and multiculturalism largely ignores the existing complexity and interplay of religious, ethnic and local identities within 'native' populations in the respective host countries. I will therefore apply an 'integration' perspective to the town's majority society, in order to scrutinise some of its historical and contemporary fissures.

Multicultural influences in Bayreuth and Upper Franconia can be traced back to the multi-religiosity established in the eleventh century, with Jews settling in the region, followed by the changing dominance of Prussian Lutherans and Bavarian Catholics, and the immigration of French Huguenots. More recently, the region's multicultural reality was shaped first by migrations of ethnic Germans who were expelled or fled from Eastern Central and Eastern Europe after the Second World War, second by labour migrants recruited mainly in Southern and South-Eastern Europe, and third by East Germans and Eastern Europeans who immigrated after the fall of the 'Iron Curtain' (Maier 1997; Maier and Dittmeier 1996; Mayer 2010; Reinhardt 1994; Roth 1990; Schiener 2008).

Today, Bayreuth's international migrants stem from more than 100 different nations. The largest groups originate from Turkey, followed by Eastern Europeans, former Yugoslavians, Italians, and other EU nationals. This mirrors the migration structure in Bavaria and West Germany at large, with the former *Gastarbeiter* (Turkish, Italian, Greek) having the longest duration of residence, the number of citizens from ex-Yugoslavia rising in the 1990s, and Russians, Poles and Ukrainians among the more recent arrivals. Thus, Bayreuth hosts a diversity of neighbours: 'native' residents anchored in a regionally defined urbanity; residents who have moved 'west' after the Second World War and those who did so with German unification; residents who have lived the guest-worker experience of the old Federal Republic of Germany; residents who have origins in the 'old' and 'new' Europe; and residents who have roots outside Europe.

Historically the town of Bayreuth gained national and international fame through the nineteenth-century composer Richard Wagner, who built an opera house which still hosts the Wagner Festival that draws a yearly crowd of opera lovers. The Wagner family clan, his admirers and the town of Bayreuth have never lost the stigma of being too close to Nazism. Hitler's Wagner-adoration and his close friendship with Winifred Wagner – the composer's British-born daughter-in-law and director of the Bayreuth Festival in the 1930s and 1940s – turned the provincial city into a cultural centre of Nazi Germany. At the same time, Bayreuth turned itself into the capital of the new Nazi creation Bayerische Ostmark: a fusion of the Bavarian regions Upper Franconia, Upper Palatinate and Lower Bavaria. This Ostmark was to serve as a borderland against the propagated threat of a Slavic invasion, a spectre created by *völkisch* circles in the late Weimar Republic. After the Second World War the 'denazification' of the Bayreuth Festival (dubbed as *Neubayreuth*) allowed for its continuation as an important representational event for Germany's political, economic and cultural elites. Today the Festival visitors bring a kind of seasonal international flair to the town (cf. Friedländer and Rüsen 2000; Gebhardt and Ziegerle 1998; Haller 2000; Hamann 2002).

This paradoxical symbolism of the Wagner Festival – a history steeped in German nationalism and anti-Semitism on the one hand, and its cosmopolitan outreach on the other – is also reflected in the town's self-image. It has continuously aimed at presenting itself as an important location in the global world of opera while, at the same time, sending contradictory messages about its links to Nazi history. This has meant both downplaying its role during the Nazi period and expressing outright sympathies with Nazi ideology. Thus, the fact that a Wagner bust by Arno Breker, Hitler's favourite artist, was erected in the 1950s, or that a street named after the racist and anti-Semitic author Houston Stewart Chamberlain, who was married to Wagner's daughter and inspired Hitler's worldview, was only removed in the 1990s, speaks to this ([www.stadtbayreuth.de/pressearchiv/5284/details_576.htm], accessed 26.09.2010; Leupold 2001). During our research, the town's Green politicians and the Jewish community campaigned to rename a street that bears the name of Hans Meiser, a Lutheran pastor whose anti-Semitic statements even after the Second World War made him a doubtful candidate for such honours. Thus, while Munich and Nuremberg, for example, had already renamed their Hans Meiser Streets, in Bayreuth there was an uproar against these plans in letters to the Editor of the local newspaper, stressing Meiser's importance as the founder of the School for Church Music in Bayreuth, and, more importantly, as a symbol of Franconian identity and Franconian Protestantism.[12] These issues were not only brought up in media debates, but also in encounters of the Jewish community with Christians (e.g. during the visit of a Catholic group to the synagogue on 09.04.08) and in many of my conversations with the head of the Jewish community.

My research suggests that native Bayreuthian perspectives on identity are, at base, nourished by a symbolic dichotomy of Franconian and Protestant versus Bavarian and Catholic. Politically this tendency would be represented by the Social Democratic Party (SPD) and the Christian Social Union (CSU). When looking more closely, though, this dichotomy does not stand an empirical test as there are many combinations of political, local and religious identifications. However, there are ongoing debates on how much Franconia is actually part of Bavaria or should become an independent *Bundesland* (federal state), and whether the region is discriminated against by the Bavarian government in Munich. An example for this was the election of a Franconian protestant as Bavaria's Prime Minister. It created media headlines about whether Franconians were too powerful in Bavarian politics, and after he was ousted, the Franconian media hinted at a Bavarian intrigue against him.[13] There is not enough space to discuss the complexities of these local identities and mental borders within the 'native' Germans of Bayreuth. A few examples will suffice to illustrate the complex interplay of local, regional, religious and political identities: in a guided tour at an exhibition focusing on 'Bayreuth during the Third Reich', the presenting historian stressed the election success that the Nazi Party had especially in Lutheran areas of Germany; the head of the Jewish community often pointed at anti-Semitic statements of Bayreuth's Social Democrats, as he was convinced that most of the local former Nazis found (untypically for the rest of Germany) their postwar political home in the SPD which was dominated by Protestants. While examining historical evidence for these politico-religious identities cannot be pursued within this chapter, it is important to understand how these claims are used to negotiate the relations of different religious and political groups in today's Bayreuth, Franconia, Bavaria and Germany.

Local identities are best described as segmented, in the way that Upper Franconians stress their difference from neighbouring regional groups like the inhabitants of Upper Palatinate or Central and Lower Franconia. However, they identify as Franconians vis-à-vis Bavarians, but as Bavarians vis-à-vis other Germans, especially the so-called Prussians, i.e. Germans living to the north of Bavaria. The construction of the Prussian as the 'other' of the Bavarian is rooted in the Prussian dominance in the German Empire (1871–1918) and has religious overtones, as the governing Prussian elite was Protestant and challenged the power of the Catholic Church in Germany (Erichsen and Brockhoff 1999; Kirmeier 2006). After the Second World War and the dissolution of the Prussian state, whose militaristic tradition was widely regarded as a root of Nazi aggression, it was common in some parts of Germany to associate the Third Reich with the Prussian (and thus the Protestant) tradition in order to downplay local responsibilities. For Bayreuth there was no such exit option, as the town was not only steeped in Nazi cultural politics, but furthermore marked by the historical presence of the Prussian margraves, who resided in Bayreuth in the eighteenth century. In addition, Franconia's higher percentage of Protestants made it Bavaria's 'other', or Bavaria's Prussia within the gates. It is thus not surprising that a local historian would describe Franconians as being 'colonised' by Bavarians (interview A. 11.01.08); or, similarly, that a famous Franconian singer ironically referred to the Bavarians as a 'master people' (*Herrenvolk*) who were not interested in the culture of their subjugated Franconians – and that 'Old Bavaria' (that is, Bavaria without the Franconian provinces) was the only place in the whole of Germany where he was not invited to perform (Conversation with Wolfgang Buck, 09.08.08). Clearly these opinions were brought forward *cum grano salis* or with outright irony. Nevertheless, a specific 'Franconian' identity was an issue for informants. Interestingly, it also came to the fore in an interview with a founding member of Bayreuth's German–French Association. In an attempt to give the Franconians an historical identity outside Bavaria, he linked them to the Empire of the Franks (which existed long before Prussians or Bavarians had even thought of establishing states), and thus to French history and its cosmopolitan republican mission (Interview with W.W., 05.09.2008).

Public discourse in Bavaria reveals a keen awareness of this potentially disintegrative tribalism. Originally it included 'three tribes' living in Bavaria (Bavarians, Franconians, and Suebes). Recently it has been widened to include a fourth, the ethnic German refugees who immigrated after the Second World War (see Endres 1998, and Endres 1985 on Franconian–Bavarian relations), and a fifth tribe of Jewish Bavarians as Beckstein, the former Prime Minister of Bavaria claimed (see Kraus 2008: 1).

Interestingly, though, the tribal trope has not been extended to include other groups of immigrants. The recent heated debate, sparked by the publication of an Islamophobic book by the former Berlin Minister of Finance (Deutschlandstiftung Integration 2010; Sarrazin 2010), about whether Muslims in particular, should be seen as part of the imagined community of Bavaria or Germany clearly suggests this. When the federal German President Wulff announced in a speech commemorating German unification that, alongside Christianity and Judaism, Islam had to be considered part of Germany, one of the first protests came from the Bavarian Prime Minister Seehofer who stated that Germany was not in need of further immigration from Muslim countries. The claim to the 'Christian–Jewish tradition' as part of German history was used by some politicians as a means to deny Muslims' belonging to German society.[14]

The comments above indicate that local and regional history feeds into the negotiation of sometimes diverging local political and religious identities. Even in a small town like Bayreuth, identities form in response to grown and emergent, local, social and historical processes, only one of which is immigration. This is not meant to suggest that belonging to any of these groups would expose a person to discrimination or racism in a way comparable to what many immigrants go through. I have not heard of discrimination on the job market for either Catholics or Protestants, and intermarriages are not uncommon; but in conversations I gained the impression that the memories of serious discrimination (e.g. against Catholics in Bayreuth, and against Franconians in Bavaria) were very vivid, and a sense of difference was clearly felt. I suggest that it is precisely the presence of immigrants that allows the different groups of Germans living in Bayreuth to develop an in-group feeling and to construct themselves as 'natives', as I will show below.

6.5 The Bayreuth Intercultural Weeks in 2007 and 2008

The IKW in Germany was established in 1975, taking place in different West German cities and towns. Its original name was Woche der ausländischen Mitbürger, or 'Week of Foreign Co-citizens',[15] highlighting the label 'co-citizen' that became particularly established in the language of politicians, signifying that immigrants were more than 'guest-workers' even if not quite real 'citizens'. Nationally, the Weeks were initiated by the Roman Catholic, Lutheran and Greek Orthodox Churches, supported by unions, welfare organisations and migrant organisations. The organisers of IKW state the following aims on their website:

> Until now the aim of the 'Week' has been to provide advocacy for improving the political and legal conditions that guide the shared lives of Germans and immigrants. In addition the initiative aims to increase mutual understanding and fight prejudice through personal contact and exchange.
>
> ([http://www.ekd.de/interkulturellewoche/343.html], accessed 13.112010, translated by H.D.)

The Week's motto of 2008 in Bayreuth was *Teilhaben – Teil werden*, roughly translatable as 'participate – become part of' (German society). The programme included an opening service in a Lutheran church with many references to this year's motto, and an opening speech by the Catholic Mayor of Bayreuth. Information evenings about different countries were organised, surprisingly, though, not about those countries where most immigrants in Bayreuth originate from. Associations representing migrants from Eastern Europe and ethnic Germans from the former Soviet Union staged a Volga-German wedding ceremony, organised an evening on Russian-German and Bavarian traditions and customs, and other events. Furthermore, the Week included an open-day at the centre for asylum seekers, readings by a Senegalese and a Turkish author, and the 'Festival Evening of Cultures' Reverend H. referred to. This featured music, dance and theatre performances mainly from Russian-speaking artists, food prepared by women living in the centre for asylum seekers, speeches by the 'Advisor for Foreigners' and a representative of the Catholic welfare organisation, and a quiz show mocking the newly introduced 'German citizenship test'. The IKW was officially closed with a service at the Catholic church, where no reference whatsoever was made to the IKW or the issue of integration. Shortly after the IKW, but still as part of its programme, the Mayor invited Bayreuth's new citizens 'with migration background' into the town hall for an official welcoming ceremony. The following day, the municipality organised a guided tour through the town for its new citizens.

Differently to 2007, in 2008 the performers at the 'Festival Evening of Cultures' adhered to the schedule but the problem in 2008 was generally a very low attendance. The welcome ceremony in the town hall brought together mainly professionals and activists of the 'intercultural scene' but hardly any migrants. Some events had as few as four persons attending. And even at well-attended events like the Festival Evening the audience remained clearly divided in groups, that is the asylum-seekers stayed among themselves, and so did the ethnic Germans from Russia.

With regards to the stated aims, the IKW was not a success. An obvious reason for this was the fact that publicity for it had been poor. Other reasons for the failure are to be found in the dynamics of integration policy and intercultural activities in Bayreuth and the players involved.

6.6 Analysis of the Week's problems

A glance back at the 2007 Week and the problems with the Russian-German dance troupe will help one to analyse the situation. Discussions about their overly long stage performance and demonstrated lack of interest in other groups' performances came up at every organisational meeting of the IKW in 2008. What angered the organisers even more than the group's 'disrespect' for the schedule was what they saw as the rationale behind it. I was told that this was a professional group who had used their time on stage to showcase their skills and turned the event into an advertisement for their dance school. This may well have been the case. However, when asking members of the group I was told that, due to a misunderstanding, they were not aware of the strict schedule, and that they had announced beforehand which dances they would perform.

None of these two explanations can help us understand, however, why the Russian-Germans had left the venue after their performance, or why Russian-Germans and refugees from other (mainly Middle Eastern) countries had kept apart during the following year. Mostly, ethnic Germans do not identify with other immigrants due to their essentialist concepts of German identity – and indeed some of my interviewees resented being 'lumped together' with immigrants from Southern Europe or Turkey as 'persons with migration background'. This was simply not 'their' stage.

However, while the Russian-Germans refuted being put into the immigrant category, this was precisely what most 'native' Bayreuthers were doing. 'Russians' is the shorthand reference that is generally used by the locals. I even heard people blaming them for only 'pretending' to be Germans. In heated debates in a gas station on a night after a football match that Russia won, where hundreds of Russians and presumably Russian-Germans celebrated in the streets, 'native' Germans fantasised about sending them to Russia, even about killing them (Conversation overheard on 21.06.08). Although this may have been a single and extreme case, it was however indicative of a general unease among 'native' Germans with ethnic Germans from the former Soviet Union, that I encountered during my research. Interviewees talked about 'ghettos', referring to quarters where many Russian-Germans lived, and stories about them were routinely linked to crime, fear and violence.

This observation is supported by statements of many of my interviewees. When talking about racism in German society, I heard fewer complaints from interviewees of Turkish and/or Muslim background than from those of Russia-German origin. Clearly, some interviewees of Turkish origin talked about experiences of racism and about the feeling of being treated like second-class citizens. However, it was remarkable that when I discussed this in a mosque, people often referred to events that they heard or read about in the media[16] rather than to problems in Bayreuth itself. Some interviewees explained this by the spatial and cultural integration of Muslims in Bayreuth society. This is not say that anti-Turkish racism or Islamophobia does not exist or that Bayreuth's Muslims do not face problems with schooling or language, but to my surprise these were less obvious and less explicitly stated than both national media discourses and scientific studies would have one believe.[17]

The ethnic Germans from the former Soviet Union, in contrast, often referred to racist experiences in Bayreuth. Furthermore, during the meetings of working groups on integration in the town hall, the only person explicitly referring to issues of racism was a representative of Russian-German origin (Field notes, 03.06.08). Many interviewees of Russian-German origin complained that their Germanness was constantly questioned, that 'native' Germans as well as the media often referred to them as 'Russians', thereby ignoring their history of suffering in Russia. Interviewees were very serious about how they wanted to be called: *Russlanddeutsche* or *Deutsche aus Russland* (Russian-Germans or Germans from Russia) but not simply *Russen* or *Deutsch-Russen* (Russians or German-Russians), as both terms denied their German identity.

Given this focus on Germanness, it is not surprising, that Russian-Germans joined the umbrella organisation of ethnic Germans from Poland, Czechoslovakia, Romania or elsewhere (Bund der Vertriebenen), who came to Germany immediately after the Second World War. It is often forgotten that these immigrants, too, suffered from severe racism and discrimination after arriving in Germany. Their Germanness was questioned, and – in the tradition of Nazi racism and essentialism – they were seen as characterised by a supposed 'Slavonisation', that would not make them fit into West German society (Kossert 2008; for the region of Upper Franconia see: Bernreuther 2005: 156,180). This experience did not necessarily translate into solidarity with migrants arriving later in Germany.[18] After having to defend their 'Germanness', many former Aussiedler believed that other groups of immigrants, who were not of ethnic German origin, did not belong to the country in the same way they did. Thus, as refugees they reproduced ideas of Germanness based on *jus sanguinis* rather than the republican *jus soli*.

Although there are signs of a development towards a more hybrid identification among some Russia-Germans, who acknowledge the Russian experience as part of their collective identity, the following quotation of Mrs D., a representative of the Russia-German *Landsmannschaft* in Bayreuth, illustrates the unwillingness of Russia-Germans to fit into the multicultural idea of diversity as expressed in the IKW:

> Well, you see, Intercultural Week. I organised these events here, the movies etc., within the framework of this Week. But, Intercultural Week, this doesn't really concern us, because it's about the foreigners, and somehow we slipped into this (laughs). And now we participate,

> although, actually, we're Germans, even if we come from another culture. We have another mentality. [...] You see, we don't belong there [to the Week, H.D.], someone from Ecuador, yes, but why should *I* be part of it. [...] I don't think a German from Russia would want to learn from an Iranian or Iraqi or whatever.
>
> (Interview with Mrs D., 29.04.08, translation by H.D.)

The absence of 'native' audiences partly serves to explain the reaction of the Russian-German dance troupe. They addressed their performances specifically at 'native' Germans, because they are the ones who need to understand about their Germanness and 'natural' belonging in Germany. Consequently, they were not interested in performances of people of other ('non-German') background. Preserving their Germanness and being discriminated for it has been instrumental in opening the way to Germany. This message was not addressed at others who in their eyes belonged less than they did. The remarkable absence of persons with migration background among the organisers helps to explain some of the Week's problems. It is important to note that most of the persons involved in organising the Week were 'native' Germans who saw their contribution as aid for migrants on whose behalf they took a stand in opposition to the policies of the municipality, the immigration authorities or hostile popular views. Although politically well-meaning, these activists also displayed substantial paternalism. It seemed not only that no-one had seriously invited migrants to become involved. No-one seemed to have asked them whether they felt represented by these types of events, whether they felt the need to be 'integrated' and, more importantly, what 'integration' would mean to them beyond staging such cultural events. It might very well be that not only the Russian-Germans but everybody else felt that their right to 'Germanness' was in denial.

A brief look at the ritualistic aspect of the Intercultural Week itself might serve to give a further answer. The 2008 event was framed by church services, with the Lutheran Church opening and the Catholic Church closing the event. Thus, two dominant institutions representing the 'native' Bayreuthers performed their authority as organisers of the Week by staging the crucial moments of framing, or to use anthropological language, by marking the beginning and the end of this ritual, and assuming the symbolic position of gatekeepers. Many of the Week's events did not reflect the possible perspectives and interests of those who were performing 'cultural difference'. Instead they reflected the interests of 'native' Germans who talked about their experiences in other countries, or about their visions of integration. Those who 'are to be integrated' were supposed to present the cultural capital they would add to German society. These events were thus staging the multiculturalism of the 1980s for an imagined audience of those who wanted an ethnically homogenous Germany. Thus it was an argument among German political camps over the question of immigration. With the changing discourse and practices following the acceptance of the realities of immigration and the global competition for well-educated human capital, this multicultural argument is now supported by national integration policies. It became thus an argument of German elites directed at the general public. Consequently, the Week seemed like an event that served as a space for local elites and activists to talk to each other or to immigrants, rather than as a platform where all these groups would have the chance to enter into dialogue.

Interpreting the Week as a ritual reveals not only the dominant churches' performance of power, but also local power inequalities and the mental borders between different groups of 'native' Bayreuthers. The Catholic Mayor joined the opening service for the Intercultural Week that took place in the Lutheran church, and gave a speech with reference to the Week and integration policies. Many activists of the 'intercultural scene' were present. However, the Mayor and the other two Catholics present sat totally isolated from the Lutheran community. Although representing the political power in town, they were not seen as part of the community in this church. In a marked display of the reverse, none of the Lutherans active in the 'intercultural scene' joined the closing service at the Catholic church.

6.7 Conclusion

It is obviously not easy to answer the question in this chapter's title. What is the society into which immigrants are supposed to integrate: Germany, Bavaria, Franconia or Bayreuth? The diverse, partly mutually exclusive identifications that exist in a small town like Bayreuth – be they religious, political, ethnic or even 'tribal' – make it impossible to define a typical 'Bayreuther'. However, they may also be seen as an opportunity to extend the existing cultural diversity to include more recent groups of Bayreuthers.

The absences and problems at the IKW help to focus on local issues that are not sufficiently referred to in national discourse. One is the understanding that festivals and cultural events do not suffice to address the issues at stake. Exchange does not take place, and although the lack of knowledge of different actors' culture may be still a problem, educational and professional inequalities will not be changed by such events. Furthermore, events like the IKW are not successful in overcoming the dichotomist constructions of 'natives' and 'immigrants'. Through focusing mainly on the others' 'culture' these events reproduce boundaries between us and them, fall back behind the debate on 'old' and 'new Germans', and reproduce the mental borders they aim to overcome.

In Bayreuth integration policies led to new local coalitions. The activists who support refugees and organise events such as the Intercultural Week are dominated by church activists, mostly Lutherans, and have a supposedly Leftist leaning. They found themselves cooperating with a municipality dominated by conservatives and Catholics. However, this new cooperation aiming at integration did not change the patronising character vis-à-vis those who are seen as being in need of integration, i.e. specific groups of immigrants and ethnic Germans from the Soviet Union. Conflicts arise, as we saw in our introductory example, when some challenge the rules. Rather than assuming the role of performers of a friendly multiculturalism, as the organisers had intended them to do, some decided to interpret the event differently or stayed away altogether. African migrants avoided this conflict by concentrating on the Afro-Caribbean festival, Muslims by staying away. Germans from the former Soviet Union hijacked the stage in order to present their culture to themselves. This may be interpreted as the outcome of an absent dialogue between the different groups involved about what these events should be used for, on how the different groups want to see themselves represented. The performing Germans from the Soviet Union, it seems, had the self-awareness that MacAloon (1984) describes as being characteristic of performers.

When referring to the problems of the Week in 2007, Reverend H. interpreted the events as being too demanding. In his view, the immigrants present were unable to handle the cultural diversity they encountered. He suggested that future events should be restricted to encounters between people from the white German majority on one side and people from the respective immigrant groups on the other. This, he hoped, would allow both sides to get to know each other, and would not confuse them with too many different cultural expressions. I think this strategy would be a problematic reaction to the given problems because it would normalise the perspective of white 'majority' Germans. It would put these 'native' Germans again in a position of control and reproduce the dichotomist mental border of 'natives' and 'immigrants'.

In closing, I would like, once more, to stress, that intercultural exchange does take place in very specific localities and that national discourses and policies are only one part of the whole picture. Local practices and understandings of group identities, of guarding group borders or boundaries, come into play. And these are not only the borders between 'new' and 'old' Bayreuthers. I referred to a number of surprising absences in the introduction to this chapter. With reference to performances during this Week a striking absence is marked by the lack of an ecumenical or interreligious service as opening or closing event for the Week, something one would expect of a 'Week' that is largely organised by church groups. Instead, the church services reproduced existing rifts between Lutherans and Catholics. After some hundred years of living together in the same region, the mental border separating these denominational groups is still being reproduced. So, there are even older borders than the ones Reverend H. referred to. If we take seriously the Bayreuthers' self-definition as public servants who open up very slowly, and if we take into account the local obsession with in- and out-grouping, we may end up less surprised about the local Russia-Germans' interest in performing their identity to themselves. Engaging all important actors in the field in dialogue and acknowledging the existing diverse identifications rather than aiming at 'integration' into a seemingly homogenous society may be fruitful starting points for overcoming the many mental 'borders' and 'walls'.

Notes

1. Interview with Reverend H., 17.03.2009, translation by the author.
2. These are quite awkward terms, but they come closest to a literal translation of the German *Einheimisch* and *Ausländer*, which are the emic concepts most commonly used in everyday discourse. Media and academic discourses tend to prefer *Migranten, Einwanderer* and *Zuwanderer* which are best translated as migrants and immigrants, with slightly different political connotations. *Person mit Migrationshintergrund/Migrationserfahrung*' (person with a migration background/migration experience) were widely used terms, but are now often ridiculed. Conservatives reject them because of their 'political correctness', and those labelled 'migrants' often refute them because they eternalise their connection to migration. In official statistics, 'persons with migration background' include all persons who immigrated to Germany or those who have at least one parent who immigrated. Recently, the more inclusive terminology of 'old' and 'new' Germans or citizens (*Altdeutsche* and *Neudeutsche* or *Bürger* and *Neubürger*) has been proposed (cf. Laschet 2009) but so far these are hardly used. Although they have slightly different connotations, *Einheimische* and *Ausländer* as emic terms draw our attention to naturalising and territorialising discourses of inclusion and exclusion, which are comparable to the concept of autochthony, discussed by Geschiere

(2009). (*Einheimische* is based on the word *Heim*, or home, thus claiming for 'natives' that they live at their 'home', whereas *Ausländer* are associated with coming from 'outside'.)

3. Due to spatial constraints I will not be able to discuss other absences, which would deserve a closer analysis. These include the absence of recognition of the role of the former German–German and German–Czech borders in Bayreuth by both the researcher and his interviewees, to whom it did not seem to be an issue, although the changing status of these borders influenced the region economically (cf. Dittmeier et al. 1998; Fleischer et al. 1999; Maier 1997; Maier and Dittmeier 1996). A different, methodological issue that cannot be discussed here is my absence from the event that was crucial in showing the factions of the activists involved in organising the IKW.

   This chapter focuses on events and performances as these may offer highly condensed representations of social issues. Following Richard Bauman (1992), I define performance as an aesthetically intensified form of communication that both presupposes and creates a heightened awareness of the given situation as well as of society at large. Whereas earlier functionalist theories of performance in anthropology – following theories of ritual – stressed its ability to represent, integrate and stabilise society, more recently studies looked at the emerging quality of rituals and performances, i.e. their ability to change society. This transformative power of rituals and of performances in general gives the performer a position of power in performance. MacAloon (1984) discusses the self-reflexivity in rituals and performances – performers are, like their audiences, reflecting and evaluating their art and the quality of their performance. Furthermore rather than looking at unified societies, recent studies tend to look more at how rituals represent societies' heterogeneities, e.g. how different groups within societies – migrants for example – use rituals to represent their perspective on society (e.g. Baumann 1992).
4. These and the following numbers are based on the town's official statistics, see: [http://www.bayreuth.de/rathaus/statistisches_jahrbuch_26.html, last accessed 21.06.2011]).
5. Note the self-representations of the Mayor and the Officer of Integration at their respective homepages: http://www.bayreuth.de/integration/integrationsbeauftragter_1087.htm, last accessed 21.06.2011].
6. Bayreuth's 'Advisors for Foreigners' (*Ausländerbeauftragte*) are in charge of supporting and advising the town's residents with foreign nationality regarding their legal status, orientation in their new surroundings, or whatever problems they may encounter. However, this being an honorary post, the two advisors were able to open their office for visitors only once a week for two hours.
7. The decision – that although Bayreuth's Jewish community supported a concert celebrating the 60th anniversary of Israel, it would not announce this support – was explained by its head as aiming not to expose the community too much (Conversation, 28.4.2008).
8. This may seem quite late compared to elsewhere in Germany (cf. Fischer and Lorenz 2007). However, in many other small towns and rural areas, public debates of the Nazi past started only recently.
9. [http://bayreuth.de/pressearchiv/6595/details_576.htm], accessed 14.11.2010.

10. This information is based on discussions I had with representatives of Immigration Authorities in other Federal *Länder*, namely North-Rhine-Westphalia and Berlin at the Symposium 'Governmental Institutions and Integration: Anthropological Perspectives' held at the Haus der Kulturen der Welt, Berlin, organised by the German Anthropological Association (DGV) on 30.06.2009.
11. See the articles in the local newspaper *Nordbayerischer Kurier* ([http://www.nordbayerischer-kurier.de/nachrichten/1283121/details_8.htm, last accessed 21.06.2011]) and the statements from activists ([http://www.fluechtlingsrat-bayern.de/lagerinventour-news/items/id-4-tag-oberfranken-bayreuth---brunch-hinter-martialen-zaeunen.html], accessed 14.11.2010).
12. [http://www.frankenpost.de/nachrichten/regional/ofrbay/art2389,1251108], accessed 14.11.2010.
13. See e.g. *Nordbayerischer Kurier*, 10.10.07, p. 1; an interview with Beckstein on his election and Bavarian–Franconian issues: [http://www.frankenpost.de/nachrichten/serien/interview/art3294,724432], accessed 14.11.2010.
14. Thilo Sarrazin, the former Berlin Minister of Finance, now dismissed member of the executive board of the German Federal Bank and (currently still) member of the Social Democratic Party, instigated a debate on whether 'Germany abolished itself' (Sarrazin 2010), using a crude mixture of Islamophobia, racism, classism, simplistic statements on the inheritance of intelligence, and eugenics. Although most comments by politicians and journalists criticised the book, it seemed to have struck a chord, as it turned out to become the most best-selling book in Germany since the Second World War. The disrespectful tone of the book informed the debate, and politicians such as Germany's Federal President Wulff – who tried to cool it down – were only partly successful. See the *Irish Times* on President Wulff's speech: [http://www.irishtimes.com/newspaper/world/2010/1006/1224280471804.html, last accessed 21.06.2011]. Several commentators have criticised the instrumentalisation of the newly claimed 'Jewish–Christian German tradition' as a means to out-group Muslims. Most prominently, Jürgen Habermas in the *New York Times* and Heribert Prantl in the *Süddeutsche Zeitung*: Habermas, 'Jürgen: Leadership and Leitkultur' in [http://www.nytimes.com/2010/10/29/opinion/29Habermas.html?_r=1andemc=eta1, last accessed 21.06.2011]; Prantl, Heribert: Der Missbrauch der Juden durch die Politik [http://www.sueddeutsche.de/politik/gedenktag-november-der-missbrauch-der-juden-durch-die-politik-1.1021220], accessed 14.11.10.
15. For more information, see: [http://www.interkulturellewoche.de/, last accessed 21.06.2011].
16. At the time of our research, the fire in a house in Ludwigshafen was debated strongly. While it turned out later that it had been caused by an accident, at the time it was discussed as a possible arson attack by racists. See articles: 'Fire Sets German–Turkish Race Relations on Edge' ([http://www.dw-world.de/dw/article/0,,3112847,00.html]), or 'Baby saved after being dropped from third-storey inferno' ([http://www.guardian.co.uk/world/2008/feb/05/germany]), or 'German ambassador says Turkish community is a part of German society' ([http://www.hurriyet.com.tr/english/8272472.asp?gid=74andsz=92097]); 'Opinion: A Turkish–German Tragedy' ([http://www.spiegel.de/international/germany/0,1518,533713,00.html]); all sources accessed 24.09.2010.

17. See e.g. the weekly *Der Spiegel* special on Muslims in Europe: [http://www.spiegel.de/international/europe/0,1518,k-6817,00.html], accessed 08.10.2010. The interviews I refer to include: H., 17.10.07 and 18.12.07, Y.; and discussion at the DITIB-Mosque, 11.01.08, T. 14.01.08, R. 16.01.08, B. 12.02.08.
18. Although I noticed that many of those Germans supporting intercultural activities in Bayreuth were descendants of ethnic German refugees from Central or Eastern Europe.

References

Aas, N. (2007). *Juden in Bayreuth 1933–2003 – Verfolgung, Vertreibung und das Danach* (Bayreuth: Bumerang Verlag).

Bauman, R. (1992). *Folklore, Cultural Performances, and Popular Entertainments – A Communications-Centered Handbook* (New York and Oxford: Oxford University Press).

Baumann, G. (1992). 'Ritual Implicates "Others" – Rereading Durkheim in a Plural Society', in D. de Coppet (ed.). *Understanding Ritual* (London, New York: Routledge), pp. 97–116.

Bernreuther, A. (2005). Soziokultur als Einflußfaktor der Regionalentwicklung – Die Beispiele des historischen Sechsämterlandes in Oberfranken und des Stiftlandes in der Oberpfalz Bayreuth', *Arbeitsmaterialien zur Raumordnung und Raumplanung Heft 242*, Universität Bayreuth.

Deutschlandstiftung Integration (ed.) (2010). *Sarrazin – Eine deutsche Debatte* (München: Piper).

Endres, R. (1985). *Franken und Bayern im 19. und 20: Jahrhundert* (Erlangen, Erlanger Geographische Arbeiten), no. 45.

Endres, R. (1998). *Bayerns Vierter Stamm: die Integration der Flüchtlinge und Heimatvertriebenen nach 1945* (Bayreuther Historisches Kolloquium 12), http://stabikat.sbb.spk-berlin.de/DB=1/SET=6/TTL=1/MAT=/NOMAT=T/CLK?IKT=1008&TRM=%3C&cvtourl%3 (EKöln: Böhlau).

Erichsen, J. and E. Brockhoff (eds) (1999). *Bayern and Preußen and Bayerns Preußen: Schlaglichter auf eine historische Beziehung* (Augsburg: Veröffentlichungen zur Bayerischen Geschichte und Kultur), no. 41.

Fischer, T. and M. Lorenz (eds) (2007). *Lexikon der 'Vergangenheitsbewältigung' in Deutschland – Debatten – und Diskursgeschichte des Nationalsozialismus nach 1945* (Bielefeld: Transcript).

Fleischer, A. et al. (eds) (1999). *Nachbarn im Haus Europa – Perspektiven der EU-Erweiterung für die Region* (Tutzing: Evangelische Akademie).

Friedländer, S. and J. Rüsen (eds) (2000). *Richard Wagner im Dritten Reich* (München: Beck).

Gebhardt, W. and A. Ziegerle (1998). *Pilgerfahrt ins Ich – Die Bayreuther Richard Wagner-Festspiele und ihr Publikum. Eine kultursoziologische Studie* (Konstanz: Universitätsverlag Konstanz).

Geschiere, P. (2009). *The Perils of Belonging – Autochtony, Citizenship, and Exclusion in Africa and Europe* (Chicago and London: Chicago University Press).

Glick Schiller, N., A. Caglar and T. C. Guldbrandsen. (2006). 'Beyond the Ethnic Lens – Locality, Globality, and Born-again Incorporation', *American Ethnologist*, vol. 33, no. 4: pp. 612–33.

Haller, J. (2000). '"Die Heilige Ostmark" – Ostbayern als völkische Kulturregion "Bayerische Ostmark"', in *Bayerisches Jahrbuch für Volkskunde*, pp. 63–73.

Hamann, B. (2002). *Winifred Wagner oder Hitlers Bayreuth* (München: Piper).

Kossert, A. (2008). *Kalte Heimat – Die Geschichte der deutschen Vertriebenen nach 1945* (München: Siedler).

Kraus, U. (2008). 'Der fünfte Stamm Bayerns – Charlotte Knobloch wurde mit der Moses Mendelssohn Medaille ausgezeichnet', in *Dialog*, vol. 1, no. 38: p. 1.

Laschet, A. (2009). *Die Aufsteiger-Republik – Zuwanderung als Chance* (Köln: Kiepenheuer and Witsch).

Lengle, P., Kirmeier, J. and J. Schumann (eds) (2006). *200 Jahre Franken in Bayern 1806 bis 2006* (Augsburg: Veröffentlichungen zur Bayerischen Geschichte und Kultur), no. 51.

Leupold, B. (2001). '"Ehre wem Ehre gebührt?" Straßennamen als Spiegel des Zeitgeistes, Bayreuth und Bamberg im Vergleich' in H. J. Hiery (ed.). *Der Zeitgeist und die Historie*, Bayreuther Historische Kolloquien 15, (Dettelbach: J. H. Röll), pp. 53–78.

MacAloon, J. John (ed.) (1984). *Rite, Drama, Festival, Spectacle – Rehearsals toward a Theory of Cultural Performance* (Philadelphia: Institute for the Study of Human Issues).

Maier, J. and V. Dittmeier (1996). *Der Landkreis Bayreuth: Ein sozioökonomisches Strukturbild der Gemeinden* (Bayreuth, Materialien zur Raumordnung und Raumplanung), no. 151.

Maier, J. (ed.) (1997). *Oberfranken im Strukturwandel – ein Grenz- und Anpassungsraum* (Bayreuth, Materialien zur Raumordnung und Raumplanung), No. 160.

Maier, J., V. Dittmeier and D. Sehič (1998). *EU-Osterweiterung und Auswirkungen auf Oberfranken* (Bayreuth, Materialien zur Raumordnung und Raumplanung), no. 181.

Mayer, B. (2010). *Kleine Bayreuther Stadtgeschichte* (Regensburg: Friedrich Pustet).

Reinhardt, M. (1994). *Die Entwicklung Bayerns durch die Integration der Heimatvertriebenen und Flüchtlinge* (Bayreuth: Abschlußbericht der Dokumentationsstelle Bayreuth).

Roth, E. (ed.) (1990). *Oberfranken im 19 und 20 Jahrhundert* (Bayreuth: Oberfrankenstiftung).

Sarrazin, T. (2010). *Deutschland schafft sich ab* (München: Deutsche Verlagsanstalt).

Schiener, A. (2008). *Kleine Geschichte Frankens* (Regensburg: Friedrich Pustet).

7
Immigrants and Natives: Ways of Constructing New Neighbourhoods in Catania, Sicily

Orazio Licciardello and Daniela Damigella

Within the framework of the *SeFoNe* project, the research carried out by Sicily's Catania team concerns mental border experiences in multi-cultural EU regions. It suggests a coming together of people who coexist within the same geographical space but who are nevertheless separated by a myriad of internal borderlines which isolate, segregate and exclude people without any obvious institutionalisation of boundaries. These people are strongly marked and visibly 'other' as a result of their different ethnicity, the colour of their skin or their cultural practices.

According to Allport's Contact Hypothesis Theory (1954), still valid today and confirmed by research projects on inter-group relations carried out in Catania (Licciardello et al. 1997a, 1999, 2003, 2004a, 2004b, 2007a, 2007b), simple contact is not sufficient to create a sense of good neighbourliness between people of different cultures; on the contrary, it could increase mental barriers. To realise positive contact, some further conditions are necessary, such as equality of status, cooperation, long and intimate/friendly contact, common aims as well as some level of institutional support. These would provide ideal contact conditions that are difficult to find in everyday life contexts. Allport also notes that simply sharing a physical space is not sufficient in itself to establish harmonious relationships, but may even have the opposite effect. This would seem all the more true if social identity is defined in terms of in-group identification, leading to the phenomenon known as inter-group bias, that is the tendency to regard one's in-group in a more positive light than the out-group, so as to share in the positive reflection which being a member of a valued entity bestows (Tajfel 1981).

In multicultural contexts it seems therefore desirable to help create genuine integration processes, based on the enhancement of mutual belonging (Brown and Hewstone 2005), while preventing assimilation, in-group closing or self-denial (see also the example of Ariella discussed by Carstensen-Egwuom and Holly in this volume).

Our chapter is based on a research project conducted in Catania, one of the main cities in the island of Sicily (see map 7.1). Catania hosts a growing number of migrants who live scattered across the city. We used qualitative methods within a social psychological framework in order to investigate the perceptions of Catania's multicultural reality by migrants themselves. We have paid particular attention to the way in which neighbourhood and possible mental barriers are experienced by immigrants. To gauge the opinions of the majority population we have also analysed prevalent media discourses about migration and policy proposals designed to improve migrants' quality of life and the relationships between people of different cultural backgrounds. Our bottom-up perspective – which gives a voice to the migrants themselves – aims to achieve a better understanding of intercultural neighbouring, while the combination of analysis with action research hopes to bring about positive changes in migrants' quality of life and improve the relationships between all local people.

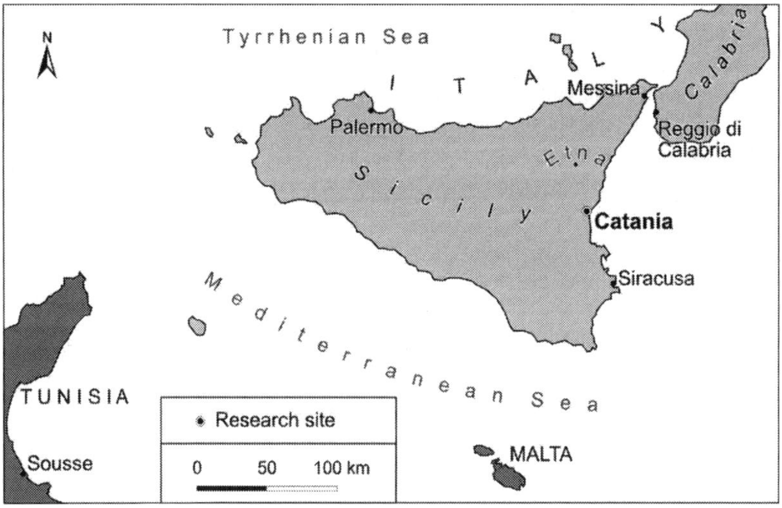

Map 7.1 Catania in Sicily

7.1 The Italian framework of immigration

In the period of post-colonial and economic migration into Europe after 1945, Italy was a late-comer, for immigration only started in the mid-1970s. Today, however, immigration is as much a reality in Italy as in other countries in Europe. The first migrants, mainly students and political dissidents, came from Africa, the Middle East, Latin America and Asia. These emigration processes were usually caused by push factors, such as the wish to escape from oppressive regimes and persecution. Pull factors became significant in the early 1980s (Zincone and Caponio 2004: 2), when three main types of immigrants can be identified: men from North and Sub-Saharan Africa working illegally in Southern Italy as fishermen, carpenters, street-vendors or farm labourers; women from Eritrea, Somalia and the Philippines, mainly working as domestics; and Chinese entrepreneurs running restaurants or cottage industries and employing fellow-nationals of both sexes (Ambrosini 2001).

Since the 1990s, immigration has risen almost tenfold, reaching the Figure of 4.3 million, or more than 5 million if we consider non-regular migrants (Caritas 2009: 8). Regarding migrant flows, institutional actions at national level seem to swing between respect for fundamental human rights on the one hand and, on the other, the need for national security, seemingly under threat by migrants. This is a view that is greatly fostered by the national and local media.

At both national and local levels, politicians tend to deal with this phenomenon using short-term emergency measures. Intercultural and interethnic networking is rare and very limited in scope. Moreover, migration is a highly politicised issue and often a direct link can be observed between the negative bias of Italian public opinion towards migration and the restrictive measures undertaken by politicians worried about the next election.

7.2 Sicily: Not only an entry port to Europe

The island of Sicily, the largest and southernmost region of Italy, is marked by centuries of multicultural history, which have had a profound impact on Sicilian culture. The wealth of historical sites, the great variety of food traditions and the existence of deep-rooted long-established minorities testify to this reality. Sicily was historically a region of strong out-migration. Today it is a cross-roads of different people who use it as an often illicit point of entry to Europe but also as a final destination to settle in. In the 1960s and 1970s, migrants first came from the Maghreb, especially Tunisia, to the west of Sicily. They settled in places such as Mazara del Vallo, Trapani, Santa Croce, Camerina and Ragusa where they were employed in fishing and farming.

Subsequently and still continuing today, many migrants from Africa have been arriving in Sicily illegally, via the sea in overcrowded vessels. The arrival of migrants across the Mediterranean Sea is often seen as an 'invasion'. However, we should point out that it is only the minority of migrants who enter Italy via the sea. According to the Italian Home Office (2009), 63 per cent are so-called overstayers, that is migrants who stayed on after the expiry of their residence permits. Some 24 per cent came by road from France, Austria and Slovenia; and only 13 per cent entered Italy illegally via the Mediterranean Sea.

Today, Sicily is home to 114,632 regular immigrants who represent 2.3 per cent of the total population (Caritas 2009: 444). Migrants in Sicily come from 103 different nationalities and they live dispersed across the nine Sicilian provinces. Moreover, since the entrance of Romania to the European Union, the opening of borders has resulted in a significant increase of Romanian migrants. According to the Caritas Dossier (2009: 445), Romanians are nowadays the largest immigrant community in Sicily. This multiplicity of nations raises the question of the relationship between social groups who are often characterised by very different cultural identities.

Because of its location in the middle of the Mediterranean Sea and its EU membership as an Italian region, Sicily is part of the Euro-Mediterranean partnership development (PEM), in which it plays an important role as a 'fluid' border region. This Partnership started with the Barcelona Declaration in 1995, whose purpose it was to create in this area a zone of peace, political stability, safety and free trade and also to empower human resources and support mutual respect and cultural recognition. In relation to the latter aim, many projects realised at national and international level could have an important role in improving the understanding of the Mediterranean migrants' culture. This could further good neighbourhood relations between EU and Mediterranean regions and promote a feeling of super-ordinate membership, an identity dimension that recognises the specific social group affiliations as well the larger one (Gaertner et al. 2000; 2007).

Because of Sicily's geographical position as entry point for illegal immigrants, expectations towards the EU concern a better management of migrant flows coming from the Mediterranean, including those of asylum seekers. Hence the EU is considered as an entity that can act as a guarantee for all parties involved. However, those who fear for national security and the risk of 'invasion' expect policies that would prevent entry and increase the militarisation of borders; others, especially the migrants themselves expect policies of cooperation and recognition of human rights so as to avoid the risk of further closing the 'European fortress'.

An important fact that contributes to the reinforcement of negative views on migrants is their representation (Moscovici 1989) by the media. In this respect the national literature testifies to the negative role that the media has in the process of constructing the image of migrants and in fuelling stereotypes and prejudices against them (Cospe 2003; Mazzara 2008; Sibhatu 2004). The data we obtained through content analysis of relevant media texts from regional newspapers and local news also confirms this. More specifically, most news reporting is related to crimes such as drug smuggling and drug dealing, theft, bag-snatching on the streets, prostitution, exploitation, violence, and the associated arrests and trials, as well as to illegal immigration. In the latter case, there is a focus on criminals who organise these illegal immigrations and none on illegal immigrants themselves, their motivations for coming to Italy, or the conditions prevalent in their own countries. The only immigrants *not* seen in a negative light are those who become victims of violence themselves, children or pregnant women. In these cases, media reports express pity for them. There are very few in-depth articles about immigrants' personal experiences where one might find interviews in which migrants could express their point of view, including their grievances. Little attention is given to integration measures such as civil actions, changes in the law, or proposals. On the whole, the media do not pay much attention to the politics of integration and the problems faced by migrants, their cultures and their needs. According to the literature, these results support the stereotypical correlation between immigration and deviance, with the risk of creating suspicion, fear, and distrust among the public, based on the prevalent image of the migrant as a social threat. Given this situation, a better understanding of migrants' way of life within and with majority society is of enormous significance.

We attempted to approach this understanding by asking how 'neighbourhood' was experienced in different parts of Catania and what expectations people had of it. As already described in Chapter 1 of this volume, the concept of a 'neighbour' comprises different meanings – from close relationships, to isolation from and rejection of others. In order to promote positive changes, it is useful to know mutual social representations.

7.3 Catania's neighbourhood contexts

From the 1980s onwards, Catania has become one of the Sicilian cities with the largest number of migrants. According to Caritas (2009: 446), legal migrants in the province amount to 20,550 and in the city alone there are 7,825 migrants, broadly balanced by gender. In Catania itself, the majority come from the Indian Ocean island of Mauritius and from Sri Lanka. Despite their medium to high educational levels, they are overwhelmingly employed as maids, porters, gardeners, and workers in bars, restaurants or pubs. Other groups come from the Maghreb and Sub-Saharan Africa, especially Tunisia, Morocco and Senegal. They work as street vendors or, in rural areas, as farm labourers. Moreover, there is a significant number of immigrants from China and Romania.

In relation to Catania's growing and permanent presence of migrants, one of the major problems is that politicians have frequently dealt with this reality using emergency policies that do not consider the complexity of the phenomenon, and ignore the needs of migrants and the importance of intercultural relationships and activities at different levels. Moreover, it is important to highlight the fact that offices and associations that deal with immigrants have not yet formed a network to pursue their aims in spite of these being at times very similar. This gives the impression of a multiplicity of isolated cases that do not relate to one another, with little or no communication between the different agents. A possible explanation for this fact is the lack of a coordinating institution which would be able to rationalise resources and link different groups. Recently, this situation has changed somewhat with the promotion of integration processes that focus more on the complex situation of immigrants, and thus approach migration not as a temporary but as a stable phenomenon, and as a resource which should be addressed in a more systematic way.

In order to reach a better understanding of neighbourhood and networking contexts, we have conducted an ethnographic observation in some relevant contexts of the city. According to Lewin (1935 [1965]: 77) we consider the environment as a psychological environment, i.e. made up of many objects and events of a quasi-physical and quasi-social nature. All these things are defined partly by their appearance but above all by their functional possibilities, in the sense that objects are not neutral but have an immediate psychological effect on behaviour. In other words, the environment is more than physical aspects of the reality; it comprises people, objects, and present, past and future situations that could be real, possible or imagined, and that could have positive or negative meaning for each person.

With these considerations in mind we conducted an ethnographic observation in the open-air 'Carlo Alberto Square Market', situated in the centre of Catania, where native Italians and immigrants share the same space to sell their goods. The market dates back to the ninth-century Saracen rule of the island, which explains its striking similarity to Arab souks. It is perhaps the best-preserved reminder of Sicily's Arab tradition, as it presents the visitor with a cacophony of sights and sounds and a colourful assortment of fruit, vegetables, fish and meats. The ambience is enhanced by colourful tarpaulins erected to protect the stalls.

Observation in this place has highlighted a physical segregation of people expressed by a concentration of vendors from specific ethnic groups in certain market areas. To give some examples of this spatial and social distribution: the majority of Chinese vendors with their stands and shops are located in specific streets such as Giordano Bruno, Teocrito, Giacomo Puccini and S. Gaetano alla Grotta. The Chinese marketeers tend to be seen as hard-working yet temporary stayers who do not learn the language and display strong in-group behaviour. This becomes a barrier to social interaction with the Italians, suggests a problem for integration, and lends support to negative stereotyping towards them. For example, Chinese newcomers are suspected of belonging to the 'Chinese mafia'. There is even talk of customers disappearing in changing rooms in Chinese shops. Moreover, their growing presence and the very low cost of their goods are considered to cause unfair competition, leading to conflictual relations between the Chinese and other migrant and non-migrant vendors. A considerable, but changing number of vendors from the Maghreb run moveable stalls and locate them at the fringes of the market with a specific concentration in Cosentino and Castiglione Streets. Frequently, they do not have residence permits and often sell counterfeit goods. For these reasons, they are often subject to police controls, which reinforces the common local stereotype that 'a black skin always implies an illegal worker'. In general, neighbourhood relationships are not good in this market context because of the competitive nature of the vendors' activities and the subtle or manifest prejudice on the part of natives towards them. Nevertheless, everyone – regardless of ethnic affiliation – buys from any stall.

Other neighbourhood contexts of our ethnographic observation are Service Centres, the *Casa dei Popoli* (literally: the House of the People) and the CGIL Immigrant Office, and schools.

The *Casa dei Popoli* is an Intercultural Municipal office, active in Catania since 1995. It offers many services to migrants, such as assistance with employment or residence permits, job search, Italian language courses, and legal and political support more widely. It also promotes initiatives such as intercultural projects, workshops and events carried out with schools or local associations to develop closer and more positive relationships among people with different cultural backgrounds. For many migrants, even if their relationships with advisors are asymmetrical or top-down, this is an example of good neighbourhood and a place where they can obtain assistance and support. Moreover, it is an important place that should be strengthened in some aspects and that could become a coordinating institution able to create a network between different organisations that promote the same aims. Furthermore, the *Casa dei Popoli* is linked with schools in order to support students, offers afternoon Italian courses, and provides books or journals on immigration and intercultural issues for teachers. However, their facilities are restricted and also not sufficiently known by the relevant target group.

This leads us to consider the school context. Schools are important institutions where contact among people of different cultural backgrounds could produce progressive effects. The results of this physical contact are related to a number of variables such as mental barriers, the social climate in the schools, the level of institutional support and teachers' attitudes. For these reasons, schools could act as important mediators between different groups of people and challenge segregation and marginalisation processes.

In our context this is a crucial aspect because, in spite of the considerable presence of first- or second-generation migrants and migrant students, schools seem unprepared for educational innovations based on multicultural integration. Among teachers there is some confusion about the meaning and the processes that lie at the heart of integration: even if some of them recognise the importance of mutual respect and cultural exchange, others put it on a par with assimilation. In many cases, teachers, even if driven by goodwill and by a form of 'sentimental multiculturalism', often recognise their own incompetence, and that of the school system, and have difficulties in dealing with this 'new' reality and the tendency of segregation among students. For example, in some schools, projects that promote learning Italian reveal 'one-way' strategies that address only migrant students. The cultural mediator in these instances is merely considered as a learning-support teacher. There are very few projects oriented to intercultural negotiation or to preserving some aspects of the second generation migrant parents' culture, such as mother-tongue retention. These results seem to reveal a complex reality in which teachers first need to be supported and trained in order to obtain new cultural and relational competences, starting from their own experiences, difficulties and stereotypes.

Our ethnographic observation also involved the CGIL Immigrant Office. This is a non-denominational trade-union office that helps immigrants with employment formalities, and supports them in legal and political battles for the acknowledgment or execution of rights, especially in the employment sector. However, according to one of our migrant informants, trade-union interest is often lukewarm:

> Even if CGIL defend us, there is no strong interest towards migrants' rights and needs.
>
> (A.M., Tunisian male, Catania, 25.01.2008).

Furthermore, it seems that the effects of the economic crisis are being felt. Trade unions tend to prioritise the rights of native workers while the dominant culture uses minorities as scapegoats. Using an intergroup perspective, we could understand this phenomenon as fraternal or group-specific deprivation. As Runciman puts it, 'the magnitude of a relative deprivation is the extent of the difference between the desired situation and that of the person desiring it' (Runciman 1966: 10). In other words, the group perspective includes a perception that one's reference group as a whole is deprived in comparison to the other group. This process produces a lateral solidarity, a sense of kinship with the members of the perceived in-group that becomes the basis of subtle or manifest prejudice against vulnerable targets like members of minorities groups.

7.4 Immigrants' points of view

The foundations of our fieldwork are a bottom-up approach coupled with methods of action research, because they provide both a tool to discover the rules that govern everyday life and a potential strategy for effecting social change. Hence, what our informants stated is important not only for understanding their quality of life and inter-group relationships, but also for laying the groundwork for improving their situation. The data from our in-depth interviews can be used as an argument in favour of interventions aimed at a fruitful coexistence that is respectful of different cultural backgrounds. It means socio-educational and political actions that avoid non-recognition phenomena which represent a real distortion of reality and result in a form of oppression that imprisons people in a false, distorted and impoverished way of life (Taylor 1992). Thus, it is possible to avoid the risk of a reaction that leads to in-group closing. On the contrary, the issue should be the recognition of the out-group, no longer seen as 'the other' and 'the enemy' but as a partner with whom it is possible to achieve peaceful coexistence.

7.5 Barriers to good neighbourhood

The data from interviews reveal an ambivalent representation of neighbourhood. Contact with local people is superficial and suffers from prejudice, distrust, ignorance and fear. For example, a Mauritian Brahman stated that in the early stages of Mauritian migration to Catania in the 1980s, local citizens feared the Mauritian community. They ascribe such behaviour to lack of knowledge and fear of the 'other', even if with the passing of time things have changed for the better (Interview with R.R., 10.12.2007). Moreover, one female Senegalese informant recounted a story in which a local who was not a person in authority exerted power over her, demanding to see her papers and calling the police because the woman's child was riding a bicycle too fast in the playground (Interview with M.C., Catania 03.12.2007). Eritrean and Mauritian migrants highlighted the marginalisation of immigrants because they are not involved in cultural activities (or only very sporadically), and some Palestinian and Maghrebi women stated that many veiled women prefer to remain in their homes in order to avoid the uncomfortable stares of locals. Only a small proportion of respondents reported that relationships were good or based on similarities. Below are three examples from our interviews that give a more positive account:

> Here people are very warm and they treat foreigners very well [...] I have a lot of local friends.
>
> (Interview with A.H., Philippino male, 03.02.2008, Giarre)

> Catania is like Eritrea [...] there are a lot of similar things [...] you don't feel like a foreigner [...] then the weather, when it is sunny and then rainy, you feel as if you are in Eritrea.
>
> (Interview with C. A., Eritrean female, 10.02.2008 Catania)

> Arabic and local culture are very similar, the same way of thinking, behaviour, even physical appearance, the weather [...] but we care more than you about religion and traditions.
>
> (Interview with C.S., Palestinian female, 11.02.2008, Catania).

Immigrants reported a number of boundaries they face regarding accommodation, work, and recognition of their qualifications:

> It's difficult to find a house to rent: costs are high and they don't rent to blacks.
>
> (M.L., Mauritian female, 03.12.2007, Catania)

> We have to rent a house [...] that was abandoned, damp and then the children get ill.
>
> (A.T., Sri Lankan male, 17.12.2007, Catania)

> The problem is that a lot of immigrants work illegally!
>
> (Interview with B.A., Eritrean male, 30.11.2007, Catania)

> I found myself in a precarious situation because I was unable to find a job related to my qualifications and expectations.
>
> (N.M., Brazilian female, 21.12.2007, Catania)

> I am forced to declare I am less qualified than I am, because my qualifications are not recognized.
>
> (B.A., Tunisian male, 14.01.2008, Catania).

The social boundaries of the everyday include relationships with public institutions and especially with the police, or with immigration bureaucracy:

> Documents are a problem, every year it gets worse [...] After 30 years each time is as if I had just arrived [...] they make you feel a foreigner every day! [...] It's getting worse at the police station.
>
> (B.A., Eritrean male, 30.11.2007, Catania)

> We live in anxiety [...] There aren't laws to protect you.
>
> (B.A., Eritrean male, 30.11.2007, Catania)

> There aren't any initiatives and policies because so far there have been only emergency policies.
>
> (G.B., Senegalese male cultural mediator, 10.01.2008, Catania)

Language, too, can act as a boundary mechanism:

> The first difficulty I had was the language because I prefer to have a stomach-ache rather than not be able to communicate. In my opinion it's terrible not to be able to communicate.
>
> (P.R., Philippino priest, 12.12.2007, Giarre).

The media discourse itself represents a barrier these migrants are faced with. Italian media reporting on countries of origin tends to be one-sided and to follow a limited range of stereotypes. Africa, for example, is usually shown as a suffering continent at war, Muslims are seen as terrorists. Migrants have the feeling that the media do not listen to them and are not really interested in them.

These obstacles to good neighbourhood combined with data about the way in which migrants spend their free time reveal the risk of in-group closing. Migrants are often completely absorbed in their work and spend what little free time they have with family or compatriots, especially when there are formal or informal homeland or cultural associations that provide a sense of familiarity and safety.

7.6 Proposals for good neighbourliness

It is important to note that our respondents did not limit themselves to evaluating problematic aspects of their experience in Catania, but also made some proposals for positive change. Many would like to see the creation of intercultural neighbourhood centres where different groups (including native Italians) could meet to get to know each other and develop shared activities.

> because there is a world [...] there is a curtain and nobody knows the other, both are afraid.
>
> (A.F., Algerian male, 10-12-2007, Catania)

With the same aim, immigrants propose the realisation of periodic intercultural events in public spaces using, for example, music and dance not in a folklorist way but as tools for cultural mediation. These proposals seem to highlight the need for mutual social identity and cultural recognition (Brown and Hewstone 2005). This can be seen from proposals regarding the building of a new mosque to replace the derelict building that is currently used, a Muslim cemetery and a 'Mediterranean library' that could also be used as a cultural centre. By the same token, many parents missed the opportunity to develop bicultural practices of integration that would allow their children to acquire both knowledge in Italian and the homeland culture. In this respect, respondents suggested introducing the language of origin as a subject in school and the inclusion of intercultural activities into the curriculum of secondary schools, thereby working against prejudice and stereotypes at educational institutions more effectively.

7.7 The school project

Following these suggestions in the framework of the *SeFoNe* project, a project was carried out in schools, entitled 'The Mediterranean as a key of integration in a school of common belonging'. It was based on an institutional partnership between the University of Catania's Department of Educational Processes, the primary school Campanella Sturzo, the hotel management secondary school Karol Wojtyla, and the municipality represented by the office of the Casa dei Popoli. Two chefs with immigrant backgrounds coordinated the project. Using Mediterranean cuisine as an expression of multicultural identity and as a tool of cultural mediation, it aimed at a better understanding and respect of cultural differences. It represented a good example of cooperation between institutions and an occasion at which immigrants had a recognised and valued status. Moreover, it provided conditions of contact characterised by cooperation, institutional support, long-lasting relationships and face-to-face settings. The students involved felt initially uncertain but became quite enthusiastic as the project carried on.

7.8 The second generation

It is difficult to give a comprehensive definition of second-generation migrants. The group comprises migrant children who were born in Italy or in their country of origin, some of whom began their education here, while others did not; and minors who came to Italy without parents or relatives as refugees or adopted children. In all these cases, observers have often spoken about a double affiliation and related problems. In Italy, one-sixth of the newborns can be defined as second-generation migrants (Caritas 2009: 8). The presence of a second generation in a specific context testifies to a stable and active migration process and to a cultural change that involves the whole society at different levels. It should lead to a process of biculturalism (Hong et al. 2000), a complex psychological and social phenomenon which enables the combination of elements of the cultural systems of origin and of destination, and stimulates the creation of a multiethnic society that values diversity and encourages the development of new and more advanced forms of culture. On the basis of second-generation interviewees' responses, biculturalism seems to be at the basis of their identity development. In fact, they are satisfied to acquire some aspects of the local culture while also preserving elements of their parents' culture and traditions, even though the latter is a difficult issue, because the school does little to support it:

> The children of other immigrants arrived, new friends. With them I have found another culture. There was a new change! Then little

> by little I have balanced things. In fact, there are aspects that I like in Italian culture and others in the Philippine one.
>
> (N.J., Philippine male, 20.01.2008, Giarre)

> We are Palestinian, but Italian too, half and half. This is good because we can see two points of view.
>
> (C.S., Palestinian female, 11.02.2008, Catania)

> There are a lot of stories about Romania and I'd like to listen to them at school [...] to listen to the name of Romania, my Romania, where I was born.
>
> (A.H., Romanian female, 08.02.2008, Catania)

Especially dark-skinned respondents of Mauritian, Eritrean or Singhalese descent stated that native Italians racialised them as 'foreign' and did not consider the possibility of their having a double identity. Parents, by contrast, seemed to be worried about the possibility that their children could lose their parents' culture and traditions:

> I hope that my child won't have any problems [...] like loss of identity [...] the most important thing is to create something for our children.
>
> (B.A., Eritrean male, 30.11.2007, Catania)

> Children who were born here don't have the sense of Philippine affiliation. People without a history, it's not a good thing, they can't discern white from black.
>
> (P.R., Philippine priest, 12.12.2007, Giarre)

Many parents also feared that their children would be excluded from upward mobility on account of their ethnic origins:

> Our children must get more respect and a job different from ours, a better life than what we have had.
>
> (R.R., Mauritian male, 10.12.2007, Catania)

In many cases, parents put a lot of effort into making sure that their children learned their own language and religion, a role which cultural associations in particular were designated to fulfil:

> We are teaching our language to all Mauritian children [...] It's a glory for us that our children learn Italian but also our language.
>
> (R.R., Mauritian male, 10.12.2007, Catania)

> They read and write Arabic, but they have to apply themselves more to studying this language because the future will be international all over Europe.
>
> (A.M., Tunisian male, 25.01.2008 Catania)

In very few cases did parents consider integration equal to assimilation:

> I encourage my child to be like Italians.
>
> (P.M., Philippine female, 08.02.2008, Giarre)

> He doesn't know my culture, he was born here, he has local tastes, he lives and eats like local people [...] as all other children do.
>
> (P.S., Mauritian female, 26.11.2007 Catania)

As has emerged in the interviews with first-generation migrants, they see the future for their children in Catania and Italy. Children were also claimed to be the strongest reason for why parents wanted to stay in Catania:

> Every time we think about going back, we always stay because our children are growing up here and it's difficult to uproot them.
>
> (C.R., Mauritian male, 15.02.2008, Catania)

Statements such as these confirm that children represent an important influence on the plans of their parents while, at the same, the children are very aware that they are expected to advance socially and economically:

> I'd like to became a paediatrician [...] my mother is a house maid and my father is a cook.
>
> (F.A., Mauritian female, 25.01.2008, Catania)

Even if the risk of job discrimination is real, it seems that the second generation does not accept a 'subordinate integration', but aspires to upward social mobility (Tajfel 1981 [1985]).

7.9 Conclusion

Regarding our research results, the concept of neighbourhood has been a good theoretical framework for analysing relationships and practices that define the processes lying at the bottom of positive or conflicting neighbourhood building. Its usefulness is based on the fact that neighbourhood is a more 'neutral' term, less characterised by ethical connotations and open to different levels and typologies of neighbourhood that emerge from the reality of our research context. For instance, in some cases physical and territorial neighbourhood can be one of the conditions that favour positive relationships between people of different cultural and religious backgrounds. For example, Mauritians and Salesian priests, immigrants of the 'Borgo-Consolazione' quarter and a neighbouring institute of nuns are all harmoniously sharing one neighbourhood of Catania. In other cases, the same situation could lead to conflictual relationships, such as for example seems to be the case between the vendors at the 'Carlo Alberto Square Market'. In a third-case scenario one could observe total indifference among people who share the same space in the city. In this respect, our results reveal different types of neighbouring dynamics.

School is an example of potentially positive or negative neighbourhood where physical contact could generate segregation or integration. In other words, it is a context where chances of in-depth contact, risks of discrimination and of assimilation are equally possible. These effects of contact are related to all those processes, realised at different levels – educational, institutional, mediatised – that contribute to openness and to respect for the 'other' or do the opposite.

In order to contribute to realising good neighbourhood relationships, in schools or elsewhere, our research suggests that they do not necessarily develop 'naturally' but need to be helped along by socio-political or civil society interventions that, following a bottom-up approach, put into action the real needs and proposals of immigrants and locals. In this respect, second-generation migrants seem to have an important role to play. First-generation migrants expressed desire for a future in Italy to guarantee a better life for their children than they themselves had experienced. Moreover, in a relatively new multicultural region like Sicily, the presence of a second generation could represent a unique opportunity to realise practices of integration, understood as respect of diversity and openness to the 'other'. It is a complex task that needs competences and the participation of civil society.

References

Allport, G. W. (1954). *The Nature of Prejudice* (Cambridge: Addison-Presley Publishing Company).

Ambrosini, M. (2001). *La fatica di integrarsi: Immigrati e lavoro in Italia* (Bologna: Il Mulino).

Brown, R. and M. Hewstone (2005). 'An Integrative Theory of Intergroup Contact', *Advances in Experimental Social Psychology*, no. 37: pp. 255–343.
Caritas (2009). *Immigrazione: Dossier Statistico 2009: XIX Rapporto* (Roma: IDOS).
Cospe (2003). *Media e Immigrazione: Rapporto sulla settimana europea dei media in Italia* (Firenze: Cospe).
Gaertner, S. L. and J. F. Dovidio (2000). 'The Common Ingroup Identity Model for Reducing Intergroup Bias: Progress and Challenges', in D. Capozza and R. Brown (eds). *Social Identity Processes: Trends in Theory and Research* (London: Sage Publications), pp. 133–48.
Gaertner, S. L., B. M. RiekE. W. Mania and J. F. Dovidio (2007). 'Quando l'identità duplice riduce la differenziazione intergruppi?', in R. Brown, D. Capozza and O. Licciardello (eds). *Immigrazione, acculturazione, modalità di contatto* (Milano: Franco Angeli), pp. 19–31.
Hong, Y., M. W. Morris, C. Chiu and V. Benet-Martinez (2000). 'Multicultural Minds: A Dynamic Constructivist Approach to Culture and Cognition', *American Psychologist*, vol. 55, no. 7: pp. 709–20.
Italian Home Office (2009). http://www.interno.it.
Lewin, K. (1935). *A Dynamic Theory of Personality* (New York: McGraw-Hill Book Company), Trad. (1965) *Teoria dinamica della personalità* (Firenze: Giunti e Barbera).
Lewin, K. (1951). *Field Theory in Social Science* (New York: Harper and Row) translated (1972) *Teoria e sperimentazione in psicologia sociale* (Bologna: Il Mulino).
Licciardello, O., D. Damigella and G. Di Marco (2007b). 'Relazioni con il territorio e qualità della vita degli extracomunitari a Catania: contributo di ricerca sul campo', in G. J. Kaczynski (ed.). *Stranieri come immigrati. Fra integrazione ed emarginazione* (Roma: Bonanno), pp. 65–82.
Licciardello, O., D. Damigella G. Di Marco and M. Mauceri (2004b). 'Immigrazione e lavoro: La rappresentazione che ne hanno gli extracomunitari che vivono a Catania', *Iniziativa comunitaria Equal*, Progetto IT-G-SIC-096 AZIMUT – Azione per lo sviluppo del sistema di integrazione sociale degli immigrati-Dipartimento di Processi Formativi, Università di Catania, Report N. 3, Catania.
Licciardello, O., M. E. De Caroli, L. Calì, G. Lombardo, M. Mauceri and T. Ramaci (1999). 'La similarità/distanza nei confronti degli stranieri di colore: rilevanza del contatto, livelli di scolarizzazione, dimensioni dell'identità: Una ricerca con i liceali di due diverse città siciliane', in S. Di Nuovo (ed.). *Da stranieri a cittadini* (Troina: OASI), pp. 105–31.
Licciardello, O., M. E. De Caroli, C. Castiglione, D. Damigella, G. Di Marco, M. Mauceri and E. Sagone (2007a). 'Il contatto e le condizioni della sua possibile funzionalità: Contribuiti di ricerca nella realtà siciliana', in R. Brown, D. Capozza and O. Licciardello (eds). *Immigrazione, acculturazione, modalità di contatto* (Milano: Franco Angeli), pp. 99–112.
Licciardello, O., M. E. De Caroli, C. Castiglione D. Damigella M. Mauceriand E. Sagone (2003). 'Identità Sociale, ipotesi di contatto e contesti formativi: confronto sugli effetti di diverse politiche culturali', in *Riassunto delle comunicazioni, V Congresso Nazionale A.I.P. – Sezione di Psicologia Sociale*, Bari, 26/27 settembre 2003, pp. 21–3.
Licciardello, O., M. E. De Caroli, G. Ficili and M. Nucifora (1997a). 'Vissuti di distanza sociale degli studenti stranieri dell'Università di Catania e livelli di

accettazione espressi dai colleghi', in O. Licciardello (ed.) *Relazioni fra gruppi e identità sociale* (Catania: C.U.E.C.M.), pp. 131–50.

Licciardello, O., G. Di Marco and E. Scuderi (2004a). 'Gli extracomunitari a Catania: Una ricerca sulla qualità della loro esperienza di immigrati', *Iniziativa Comunitari Equal*, Progetto IT-G-SIC-096 AZIMUT-Azione per lo sviluppo del sistema di integrazione degli immigrati-Dipartimento di Processi Formativi, Università di Catania, Report N.2.

Mazzara, B. (ed.) (2008). *I discorsi dei media e la psicologia sociale* (Roma: Carocci).

Moscovici, S. (1989). 'Il fenomeno delle rappresentazioni sociali', in R. M. Farr and S. Moscovici (eds). *Rappresentazioni sociali*, (Bologna: Il Mulino), pp. 23–94.

Runciman, W. G. (1966). *Relative Deprivation and Social Justice* (London: Routledge and Kegan Paul).

Sibhatu, R. (2004). *Il cittadino che non c'è: L'immigrazione nei media italiani* (Roma: Edup).

Tajfel, H. (1981). *Human Groups and Social Categories: Studies in Social Psychology* (Cambridge: Cambridge University Press), Trad. (1985) *Gruppi umani e categorie sociali* (Bologna: Il Mulino).

Taylor, C. (1992). *Multiculturalism and 'the Politics of Recognition'* (Princeton: University Press).

Zincone, G. and T. Caponio (2004). *Immigrant and Immigration Policy-Making: The Case of Italy*, Country Report Prepared for the First IMISCOE General Conference, Coimbra 3rd–4th December 2004.

8

Networks and 'Safe Spaces' of Black European Women in Germany and Austria

Cassandra Ellerbe-Dueck

Research indicates that the current situation of people of the African/Black[1] Diaspora living in European societies is inextricably linked with racism and discrimination.[2] African/Black people face disproportionate exposure to hate violence and racial profiling.[3] Of major importance is the fact that racism(s) is a gender-oriented phenomenon. African/Black women living in Europe endure not only sexism from the dominant white society, but also, in certain situations, from within their own communities. Thus, Black women in Europe experience and grapple with these realities on two distinct fronts. The issue of visibility vs invisibility of Black women in the current sociopolitical landscape makes this a subject for in-depth discussion.

This chapter focuses specifically on the German-speaking countries. In that context we can observe that the participation of Black women and men is virtually absent in the political arena. I will address primarily the grass-roots activism of Black women in Germany and Austria, especially the formation of the Black European Women's Council (BEWC) in Vienna. I explore these women's activities in light of how they utilise the European Commission's infrastructure in order to obtain greater representation and participation of Black women in policy making on a European level. I argue that the BEWC functions not solely as a type of cross-border 'neighbouring', which fosters links between these groups in Germany and Austria, but that this network also provides Black women with a self-defined 'safe space'. Employing a mix of discourse analysis, anthropological and intersectional theory, I broadly sketch the current sociopolitical situation of Black female subjects and their political participation in Germany and Austria; examine the issue of black feminism; and look at the term Black European as used by the BEWC. Black women's voices in Switzerland will be cited, but this essay concerns primarily Germany and Austria.

8.1 Fieldwork and self-reflexivity

From September 2007 till October 2008, I travelled throughout Germany and Austria to conduct research with members of seven different networks. The core of my research data is based on participant-observation, a large number of conversations and 40 recorded ethnographic interviews. The interviews and conversations were distributed equally between the sexes. And as conventional fieldwork dictates, female and male respondents were interviewed separately with one exception. As a Black female ethnographer, who moves about freely in the German language and society, I was easily and quickly 'in-corpo-rated'[4] into the various activities of these networks. While in the process of mapping out the nodes, making contact with key informants, and conducting the first interviews, I became strongly aware of Black male informants and their dominance in the organisations. At that point, I consciously decided to focus on and document Black female voices within these organisations. I was particularly interested in the views of Black females about grassroots organising, and the development of strategies for tackling the major challenges facing African/Black people in the German-speaking world.

I used participant observation and qualitative interviewing as main ethnographic methods. Intersectionality (Crenshaw 1991; Patricia Hill-Collins 2000) is an additional methodological tool that assists in the understanding of the axes of differentiation (gender, 'race', class, legal status, physical ability/disability etc.) and social location, and how they crisscross in systems of oppression. These methodological approaches allowed me to gain insights into the lives and concerns of the members of the BEWC, but also to analyse Black women's experiences and coping mechanisms with the intersections of race, gender, social class and nation. Mobilisation and collective activism are the means through which the women I interviewed are attempting to become visible, empowered, and to gain political agency within local and national political structures in Europe. Based on my personal connection to these women, it is my sincere hope to contribute to the development of activist ethnography regarding the sociopolitical activism of Black women in German-speaking countries. I envisage activist ethnography as not simply the 'writing-up' of my fieldwork, but believe that it is also a product of significant value in that it looks at the activism of one particular Black European population. Research, documentation and the production of knowledge that examines political activism as part of the Black experience in the German-speaking world is an under-researched area.

While the research project originally sought to examine the networks of African immigrants in Germany, the inextricable connectedness of the African and Black German[5]/Black Austrian[6] communities surfaced during fieldwork, and was not to be ignored. While many Blacks who self-identify as German, Austrian and Swiss do not view themselves as immigrants, it is the common experience of racial positioning and exclusion that prompts these groups to form strategic alliances with individuals of the African Diaspora with a migrant status. Thus, it became clear to me that the networks of African or Black individuals could not be seen as disparate webs, separate from those of the Black German/Black Austrian community. Instead one could view these networks as inextricable webs of associational ties rooted in sociocultural interests and political concerns.

8.2 The Black Diaspora and German-speaking landscapes

Before examining the significance of networks and 'safe spaces' in relation to Black women in the German-speaking world in particular, it is helpful to understand the sociohistorical trajectory of Black citizens in Europe. The presence of African/Black diasporic peoples across the European space is not a new phenomenon. There are essentially four significant eras involving African/Black diasporic peoples in European history: the colonial period, the First World War, National Socialism and its occupation of Europe, and post-Second World War. While an in-depth discussion of these periods is beyond the scope of this chapter, I will briefly mention that the demonisation of African/Black diasporic soldiers (First World War), hypersexualisation of Black bodies, infantilisation, sterilisation, and fears of miscegenation ('race'-mixing) were a few of the dominant discourses that influenced the lives and positioning of Blacks in Germany[7] during these periods. Due to the constraints of this chapter, I will focus mainly on the current situation of Black people in Germany, but will make references to the Austrian and Swiss contexts.

Only recently have the hidden histories of the Black Diaspora in German-speaking countries been unearthed.[8] The transatlantic slave trade and colonialism in general are historic events not immediately associated with sociohistorical trajectories of the German-speaking countries. However, the fact is that Africans did endure slavery in Germany and Austria.[9] In the seventeenth and eighteenth centuries, African children and young adults were often given as personal gifts (in the form of servants) to members of the German and Austrian aristocracy. The acquisition of an African (*Mohr*) adult or child servant was a highly prized exotic accoutrement for aristocratic households (Johnston-Arthur 2007: 425). The objectification of black bodies as luxury items to be acquired, utilised and dispensed with points to a form of oppression often overlooked in mainstream German and Austrian historical accounts. Enslaved Africans during this period were not able to return to their countries of origin, nor did they possess any agency or negotiating power to determine their fate. The current African/Black diasporic population in Germany and Austria mainly consists of people with a 'dual heritage'[10] or a migrant experience. Voluntary migration or a refugee experience is the main characteristic of Switzerland's Black Diaspora. Blacks in Switzerland assess their situation as linked to the issues of 'race'-racism,[11] such as discrimination, exclusion and feelings of rejection by the white Swiss population (Froehlicher-Stiness and Mennel 2004: 7–8).

8.3 Space and issues of belonging

In looking at the dispersal of Blacks around the globe, the issue of space and belonging is extremely significant. Black individuals who live in the German-speaking world often find themselves in the position of having to answer a barrage of questions from white Germans and Austrians about their personal life stories. These questions serve to explain and 'make sense' of the presence of Black bodies within an 'imagined' white space. This mindset regarding the presence of Blacks in Germany can be traced to the concept and existence of *Blinde Flecken* (blind spots) in German historiography. These *Blinde Flecken* are a kind of collective amnesia regarding German direct and indirect links to the transatlantic slave trade, and participation in the division and colonisation of the African continent. Not until recently has scholarly work critically examined Germany's role and participation in the colonial system. This work is significant because it has shown how the colonial *Weltanschauung* informed racialised views of the German 'self-imaginary', identity and images of 'others'. These deeply engrained perceptions still thrive in contemporary German and Austrian society (Gummich 1994; Johnston-Arthur 2007: 423–5). To be Black while claiming 'German-ness', 'Austrian-ness' or 'Swiss-ness' is viewed as anomalous or a 'mismatched identity formation' (El-Tayeb 2003: 462; Unterweger 2005: 7–9).

African students began arriving in Europe during the late 1960s and early 1970s. However, it was from the 1980s onwards, that a vast increase in African outward migration (often as political refugees) to Western European took place. This was due to the ravages of civil war, failing economies, and the chaos of striving to create Western style democratic institutions in their home countries. These migratory movements significantly added to the Black population in Germany and Austria. Precise statistical data related to this population is non-existent. Demographic data in Germany and Austria indicate nationality, but do not include factors such as skin colour or 'race'.

An increased flow of migrants during the late 1980s to Germany and Austria from Eastern Europe, South and Central Asia, Latin America, Africa and the Caribbean has been an issue of major concern for these two nations. Migrants coming from the US, EU countries, or Japan are not considered as problematic as the 'less desirable' nationals from the global South. Unrelenting in their political credos, West German and Austrian governments for decades refuted being immigration countries. They refused to acknowledge that many of the so-called guest-workers and other migrants in Germany (El-Tayeb 2003: 463–4) and Austria[12] had no intention of returning to their impoverished or repressive home countries. It follows that both nations have been grappling with the growing ethnic, racial and cultural diversity. Since the sociopolitical upheavals of the 1980s and 1990s, 'racialised' ethnic minorities and migrant citizens in Europe have come increasingly under fire from political parties advocating anti-immigration legislation and racist positions. In particular, individuals socially constructed as Black have increasingly become the targets of hate crimes and racial profiling. Racial profiling takes on a gendered dimension in that Black males are commonly associated with the dealing and consuming of illegal drugs. Characterised as lazy, uneducated and aggressive, Black women often struggle to find appropriate employment that corresponds to their levels of education. In many cases, Black women are forced to accept low-wage menial labour despite their qualifications. There is also the perception that Blacks are hypersexual beings, and in particular that Black women gravitate towards working in the sex trade. In addition, negative depictions and distortions from the general media have helped to propagate and fixate the notion of Germany and Austria being inundated by duplicitous migrants who cause havoc and endanger economic prosperity.

8.4 Why the need for 'safe spaces'?

Unlike in the urban centres of many former European colonial powers (e.g., France, Belgium and the United Kingdom), larger and predominantly Black neighbourhoods in Germany and Austria are virtually nonexistent. Faced with marginalisation, exclusion and the threat of racist attacks in Germany and Austria, Black individuals have been prompted to seek spaces of 'safety' that provide not only retreat and refuge from an environment often experienced as hostile, but also an activity space for alliance building. In addition, it is important to keep in mind the multilayered-ness of the issue of violence. While it is not possible within the scope of this article to fully explore this topic, I will point to the fact that physical violence is not the sole threat to the wellbeing of Black people(s) in these countries. Verbal and visual violence are also contributing factors to the psychological distress experienced by Black people in Germany, Austria and Switzerland. The prevalence of graffiti-like racist epithets (*'N'-raus*)[13] daubed upon walls in public spaces, particularly in Vienna (this I have witnessed myself) is only one such example of non-physical forms of violence. In the Swiss case, we need only mention the 2007 anti-immigrant, black-sheep campaign poster of the Swiss People's Party (SPP). The campaign poster depicts three white sheep positioned upon a Swiss flag. One of them kicks a black sheep off it. Below this depiction one reads the slogan *Sicherheit schaffen* (creating security). The poster underpins the SPP initiative to rid Switzerland of foreign criminals who, in its view, are non-white and male. Further, the violent deaths of Marcus Omufuma[14] (died 1999) in Austria, Alberto Adriano[15] (died 2000) in Eastern Germany, and N'deye Mareame Sarr[16] (died 2001) in Western Germany, have also been significant indicators to the Blacks that the geographical spaces in which they reside can be life-threatening.

8.5 Theorisation of 'safe space'

In underscoring my argument that the networks of Black women in Germany and Austria have come to function as 'safe spaces', I align myself with the theoretical framework proposed by social-movement theorist Francesca Polletta (1999: 1–38) and Black feminist theorist Patricia Hill Collins (2000). While Polletta offers us a theorisation of the term 'free spaces', I have chosen to use the term 'safe spaces' in my research because the issue of safety in relation to space was prevalent in the ethnographic data. Polletta describes 'free spaces' as 'small scale settings within a community or movement that are removed from the direct control of dominant groups, are voluntarily participated in, and generate the cultural challenge that precedes or accompanies political mobilisation' (Polletta 1999: 1).

Patricia Hill Collins (2000: 110) also offers an analysis of the importance of 'safe spaces'. She asserts the following:

> Historically, safe spaces were 'safe' because they represented places where Black women could freely examine issues that concerned us.

> By definition, such spaces became less 'safe' if shared with those who were not Black and female. Black women's safe spaces were never meant to be a way of life. Instead they constitute one mechanism among many designed to foster Black women's empowerment and enhance our ability to participate in social justice projects.
>
> (Hill Collins 2000: 110)

I have meshed these two theoretical considerations. I found both to be useful in examining Black female subjectivity in relation to the issue of space and political participation in Germany and Austria, in whose local and national political arenas Blacks and particularly Black women are virtually invisible. Moreover, the Black women who shared their experiences and knowledge with me did not consider themselves wholly represented or included in the decision-making processes within these spheres. Social stratification and marginalisation constitute processes that are intertwined with 'race'-racism, class, postcoloniality, sexism, homophobia and legal status. Moreover, these socially constructed forces contribute not only to the specific location allotted to Black women, but also co-form[17] their social locations and the perceptions frequently ascribed to this group by whites. The analysis and theorisation of space is a significant factor in examining the conditions of social stratification and marginalisation as experienced by Blacks, particularly in the German-speaking world. Theoretical considerations from human geography (Delany 2002; Duncan 1996) and queer theory (Ahmed 2007) have expanded forms of analysis to closely examine how space(s) intersect with 'race', gender and sexuality. In addition, new work is emerging that looks at how space(s) is/are infused with power, and how people of colour and their communities negotiate and transform the arduous situation in which they are located while living in white-dominated spaces.

Rendered invisible, and relegated to spheres of subalternity within their respective European societies, many of the Black women I interviewed expressed a desire to acquire a political voice, engage with the major players within this area, and exercise political leverage. Further, many of the informants believed that the creation of a strong cross-border network of Black women in Europe is one of many crucial steps necessary for tackling the numerous societal issues that impact the lives of Black communities.

8.6 The Black European Women's Council

The past decades have witnessed the creation of several transnational and cross-border networks and organisations striving towards the advancement and political mobilisation of women in Europe (Rolandsen and Roth forthcoming 2011). Valentine Moghadam (2000: 57–85) asserts that networks appear to be the best means for doing this type of mobilisation work. The Black Russian scholar Lily Golden states: 'There is much to be done to join forces among diverse Black communities in Europe to find a common ground'.[18] Golden also points to the necessity of establishing networks and adds that Black People in Europe must 'think themselves into the New Europe' (ibid.). The formation of the Black European Women's Council is a current example of just how this might happen. Initiated by AFRA[19] (Vienna) and Tiye International (Utrecht), 120 Black female delegates from 16 European countries gathered together from 27–9 September 2007 for the Black European Women's Conference in Vienna. The BEWC Congress participants represented various Black women's organisations, non-governmental organisations (NGOs), initiatives and projects from across Europe. The congress participation list indicated the diversity of Black women in Europe and their organisations. Many of the participants were either acquaintances already or had shared histories of activist collaboration. These collaborative efforts cut across various societal sectors, e.g. education, politics, healthcare, culture and the economy. According to Beatrice Achaleke (AFRA) and Helen Felter (Tiye International), many more women answered the call that went out over the Internet and by word of mouth to attend the conference. Due to limited funding (travel was at one's own expense) and staff, over 40 women were placed on a waiting list for lack of sufficient accommodation. Those who managed to attend represented the diversity and complexity of the Black Diaspora in Europe in terms of language, ethnicity, religious background, socio-economic level, legal status, sexual orientation, political involvement and experience. English was the working language and multilingual participants were asked to interpret for non-English speakers. Written translations were also organised, and the BEWC Vienna Declaration appears online in English, German, Portuguese, Swedish and French.

The European Commission declared 2007 as the 'European Year for Equal Opportunities for All.' This campaign urged all 27 member states along with Iceland, Liechtenstein and Norway to participate by hosting initiatives and events that would promote awareness about rights to equal treatment and anti-discrimination legislation. In recent years the topic of diversity has gained attention from the European Union (EU). Diversity has come to be seen as a positive aspect of European societies, and was also propagated as a key issue of the yearlong campaign. Ferree (2008) has discussed the significance of the EU in putting political norms and frames into place for the creation of the 'new Europe'. Campaigns such as the 'Equal Opportunity for All' (2007) and 'Intercultural Dialogue' (2008) are indicative of this attempt. While the EU has come to be equated with the notion of 'Europe', it is nonetheless important to remember that this notion and its institutions are not one and the same. One should note that the EU has served not only as an arena for the development of equal opportunity and diversity 'norms', but also for the implementation of stringent immigration regulation (see also chapter 9 this volume).

The concept of promoting diversity within the EU led one initiative in Austria to post the following statement on its website: 'The European Union can be proud of its anti-discrimination laws, which belong to the most modern laws in the world'.[20] While the EU appeared to be proud of its advancement in the pursuit of social justice and inclusion, the women at the BEWC conference did not appear to be totally convinced. According to Béatrice Achaleke, many Black women in Europe continue to live isolated lives, and do not always have access to or information about networks or Black women's organisations (Personal communication, 28.9.2009). Thus, such EU campaigns may have little or no impact on the lives of Black women, who are not 'linked in' or connected to networks. Achaleke also mentioned her frustration with the fact that the BEWC received no funding from the EU for the Vienna conference. In her view, the efforts of the BEWC to implement and mainstream Black women's empowerment were a concrete 'invitation' to the EU to not merely come up with sweeping visions and promises, but to actually offer 'real, hands-on' support.

The conference participants were keen on a critical evaluation of the methods and strategies used by the European Commission to promote equal opportunities and ensure inclusion. The development of a strong Europe-wide network and collective strategies to confront common challenges literally became the 'mantra' throughout the entire conference. Moreover, the women of the BEWC believed it necessary to examine the EU's progress and future plans from a Black female perspective. Brainstorming and critical evaluation took place in the form of working groups where BEWC participants discussed issues to do with 'identity and self-empowerment', 'challenges faced by the younger generation of Black children and youth', 'psychosocial conflicts affecting black communities', 'qualification and access to the labour market', or 'political participation'.

After two days of lively and at times heated discussions, the conference culminated in the formation of the Black European Women's

Network (later renamed Council). Within this exclusively Black female space, the organisation's Vienna Declaration was drafted; a definitive name for the organisation was voted upon; and the groundwork laid for the creation of a European-wide umbrella organisation of Black women. The BEWC conference was hosted for and by Black women with the main goal of strengthening Black women's communities across Europe for the purpose of increased political mobilisation and participation at various levels. While membership criteria were and remain determined along lines of gender and self-definition as a member of the African/Black Diaspora in Europe, the BEWC also strives to build EU partnerships, lobby for funding at national and EU levels, promote the participation of Black women in European politics at various levels, utilise the Lisbon Strategy[21] as a platform for socioeconomic and political advancement of Black Europeans, and fortify transatlantic alliances such as the Helsinki Commission[22] in Washington, DC. Regarding the political advancement of Blacks in Europe, the women of the BEWC believed that if the EU truly seeks to reach its ultimate potential via the implementation of the Lisbon Strategy, it must tap into and make better use of the already existent human-resource potential, and not draw solely from a limited sector within European society/ies.

Laying emphasis on the goals and strategies (more on this in a later section) of the BEWC is not meant to discount prior endeavours at mobilisation among Black women in Europe.[23] However, the official launch of the BEWC in Brussels on 9 September 2008 does point to an important step in the articulation of a politicised Black and gendered voice within the EU arena which was also noted by Vladimir Spidla (Commissioner for Employment, Social Affairs and Equal Opportunity of the European Commission), who stated: 'I would like to congratulate you for having made yourself heard on an international level [...] The Black European Women's Council is a new voice to represent an important part of European society'.

8.7 Creating the framework

In April 2009, representatives from 31 Black women's organisations from 12 EU member states gathered in Utrecht-Soesterberg, Netherlands to elect the BEWC's first Management Board members, and to focus on capacity building strategies. The four BEWC current Executive Board Members are from Austria, Greece, the Netherlands and France. The women elected to the board represent the diversity of the *Western* European experience as well as different ethnic origins, socioeconomic backgrounds, languages, migration/non-migration trajectories, and experiences in political mobilisation. However, English has become the working language for BEWC activities and written correspondence.

It was also within the space of the third European-wide meeting that the BEWC developed a public-relations motto. The BEWC defines itself as 'a vehicle for the recognition and visibility of Black women in Europe, through which they can reach their optimum potential'.[24] The meeting in Utrecht–Soesterberg ended with a clear plan of action and definition of BEWC's future priorities. BEWC Board Members and participants agreed upon the following priorities:

- Establishment of an equipped BEWC office and staff in Brussels
- Drafting of annual reports and statistical data on the situation of Black women and their communities in Europe
- Capacity building
- Mentor, leadership and empowerment strategies for African/Black diasporic youth
- Black female empowerment and increased political participation
- Black women's health issues.

8.8 Top-down versus bottom-up

The formation of the BEWC drew attention to the specific strategies employed by this group of Black women in pursuit of social justice, political participation and inclusion. Besides, it is important to gain an understanding as to exactly why some of the members of the BEWC believe in the 'European' value of the organisation and in a certain supranationally driven top-down approach. As the sociopolitical upheavals of the 1990s (including the tightening of Europe's outer borders) began to transform Europe, people of colour became increasingly the targets of racism, and the EU responded immediately. It adopted anti-discrimination legislation,[25] and the EU Parliament declared 1997 as the 'European Year against Racism'. This endeavour was the beginning of awareness campaigns sponsored by the EU with the intent of reaching out to all its citizens. In addition, the EU Parliament also considered this campaign to be a clear signal of disapproval and non-tolerance towards far-right political parties such as France's Front National and Austria's Freedom Party, both of which had captured the European political spotlight by spouting neo-racist[26] and exclusionist rhetoric. One of the significant outcomes of the 'European Year Against Racism' was the establishment of the European Network

Against Racism (ENAR). ENAR is a monitoring body composed of nearly 600 European-wide NGOs working to combat racism and discrimination in all the EU member states.

Representatives from ENAR have collaborated with members of the BEWC prior to the Council's establishment and were also in attendance at the BEWC 2008 launch in Brussels. The 1997 campaign also opened the door for the establishment of the European Monitoring Centre on Racism and Xenophobia, and in 1998 the European Commission adopted the 'Action Plan Against Racism'. The goal here was to mainstream anti-racism initiatives into the EU member states' actions and policies at all levels. In June 2000, the European Union drafted the Council Directive 2000/43/EC (Race Equality Directive). This implemented the principle of equal treatment between all persons irrespective of their 'racial' or ethnic origin in the areas of employment, education, housing, access to goods and services, and social protection ([www.europarl.europa.eu/sides/], accessed 10 July 2010). The Directive became law in July 2000, and all EU member states were expected to implement this new legislation by 2003. Some member states, such as Germany, only reluctantly followed this directive. The issue provoked heated debates in Germany and was met with great opposition. In certain political circles the EU directives were viewed as an infringement upon Germany's rights as a sovereign state. Arguments against the directives claimed that upon implementation they would increase bureaucratisation and result in a surge of anti-discrimination litigation. It was feared that this would inflict damage upon the German economy, thus curtailing job-growth (Howe and Wilpert 2008: 175). The Christian Democratic Union (CDU), Germany's centre Right party, contended that the directive would unnecessarily restrict an employer's 'freedom of contract'. The ongoing debates and critique surrounding the directives appeared to be never-ending. While in 2005 the German Parliament did pass a corresponding bill, the directives were not actually adopted until 18 April 2006, and the General Act on Equal Treatment[27] was finally implemented in August 2006.

In my many conversations with members of the BEWC, the impact and usefulness of the 'top-down strategy' came to light. They believed that countries such as Germany or Austria would not have implemented such legislation unless placed under intense pressure from the European Union. BEWC President Béatrice Achaleke put it this way:

> We need punishment. We need sanctions and these sanctions have to be made public. If the sanctions are there and the public doesn't

know that people are being sanctioned for certain crimes of course many people will continue to perpetuate them.[28]

While in the first half of this excerpt Achaleke employs the term people, a later discussion of this topic indicated and confirmed that she was indeed making reference not only to *individual* 'people' but also to nation-states. Sanctions can only be imposed upon a European member state by the European Union. For example, in 2000, sanctions were imposed upon Austria in reaction to the entrance of the extremist right-wing Freiheitliche Partei Österreichs (FPÖ) into the Austrian Parliament. While the sanctions against the Austrian government were of a more symbolic nature, they were indicative of the EU's attempt to clearly distance itself from anti-foreigner rhetoric and racist mottos. BEWC President Béatrice Achaleke expressed an adamant belief that the 'top-down' approach may be the only method to ensure the enforcement of anti-discrimination legislation. Although Austria does have Equal Treatment Laws (*Gleichbehandlungsgesetze*), this legislation in its current form is lacking in measures that would successfully fight racism and other mechanisms of exclusion (Achaleke 2007: 26). Referring back to Germany, the trajectory of the General Act of Equal Treatment (AGG) Directive illustrates an example of a member state's resistance to EU legislation. Germany's resistance to the legislation from 'above' also prompted the German members of the BEWC to believe that there was something to be gained from addressing local and national issues by appealing directly to the EU. At this time, there exists no documentation or case study/studies where minority groups in Germany have actually appealed to the EU for intervention on their behalf. However, various independent anti-discrimination offices, reports and press releases[29] have indicated that the feared wave of discrimination-based litigation cases in Germany never took place.

8.9 Starting the journey and the importance of networks

During the roundtable discussions at the BEWC conferences in Vienna and Brussels, Brenda King, President of the EU Commission on Employment and Citizenship, pointed to the significance of the EU's legislation, and to the power of its jurisdiction. She stressed that it was extremely important for Black women in Europe to become better informed about their rights, and to exercise them. EU member states must comply with legislation and guidelines passed by the Parliament. According to juridical protocol, citizens can first exercise their right to appeal to the European Union court after local and national judicial avenues have been exhausted. Brenda King also encouraged BEWC members to overcome their fears of inadequacy in terms of legal know-how and experience, and to become unyielding in the pursuit of justice and equality. King also insisted upon the collection of statistical data about Black women. She stated: 'There is no data about Black women who are citizens of the EU, nor is there data on how many Black women are involved in politics etc. Without statistics we are invisible' (BEWC 2007 Congress Report: 15).

Another important issue that dominated the roundtable discussions was the necessity of creating new networks and fortifying those which existed already. The women envisiaged utilising various social websites and blogs such as Facebook, BEWC, Black Women in Europe Blog, Afro European Sisters Network websites, word of mouth, or organised cultural, educational and kitchen-table activities to reach out to Black women throughout Europe. The BEWC is intended to function as a meso-mobilisation[30] actor, and to exercise a mentoring function for micro-mobilisation actors (i.e. smaller Black women's groups and initiatives). Information from and the concerns of these smaller groups/ initiatives would be gathered, consolidated and presented to EU governance bodies. Based on the activities and future goals of the BEWC, one could define this network as a transnational advocacy network, working on behalf of Black women and their communities at EU level. The significance of transnational networks (TANs) cannot be overlooked. TANs in Europe have gained continuous influence in various policy arenas (Lang 2007: 3). Since the 1980s women's TANs have become the most active of such network formations (Silliman 1999; Moghadam 2000, 2005; Desai 2005). Women's TANs have become targets as well as carriers of gender-mainstreaming. The increase in Black women's organisations across the globe is associated with Black consciousness movements of the 1960s and 1970s (McLaughlin 1995). The 1995 Beijing Conference and process prompted new efforts to tackle gender inequality (Verloo 1999). Various conversations with several BEWC members uncovered not only that some of these women attended the 1995 Beijing Women's Conference in China, but that many also had a long history of feminist activism and networking in Africa, USA, Latin America and the Caribbean. For example, Béatrice Achaleke often spoke of her deceased Cameroonian grandmother who committed her life to helping defend the rights of the women in her village and improving their situation. The grandmother also sparked Achaleke's interest in pursuing political activism. BEWC members such as Achaleke (Austria), Hellen Felter, Rita Naloop (Netherlands), Virginia

Wangare Greiner (Germany), Angela Shaw (France), and Yvette Jarvis (Greece) have been involved in trans-European networking and activities for many years. Clearly, gender intersects with 'race'. Many of the BEWC women felt that the topics of gender equality and gender-mainstreaming as dealt with by organisations such as the European Women's Lobby were far too often seen as being 'race'-neutral. Many of the women expressed to me that gender equality must be preceded by racial equality (Personal communication, 09.04.2009, Utrecht).

While I have described activities and views of the interview partners that can be categorised as feminist/Black feminist, none of the interview partners ever explicitly mentioned feminism or Black feminism. In the BEWC Congress Report (2007: 54), the transcription of Hellen Felter's keynote address does refer to the work of Black feminist theorist Patricia Hill Collins, but feminism or Black feminism did not constitute part of the discussion and workshop topics at the conference. However, what Black feminist theorist Barbara Smith (1983) describes as 'an innate feminist potential' (which she sees arising from Black women's long-standing experience of resistance to various forms of oppression) was undeniably present in these women's debates and activities.

8.10 Action, partners and coalitions

As mentioned earlier, the initiators of the 2007 Black European Women's Conference (AFRA and Tiye International) decided to make strategic use of the 'European Year for Equal Opportunity for All'. In 2008, the BEWC made use of another EU theme. The 'European Year of Intercultural Dialogue' served as an opportunity to launch the newly established council as an official representative body at the European Union level. And while the BEWC limits its membership to Black women in Europe, the Black European Women's Council does seek to liaise with the organisations of predominantly White European women or African/Black diasporic organisations of mixed gender, e.g. European Women's Lobby and Virtcom Consulting.[31] However, the words of Black Swiss activist Zeedah Meierhofer Mangali – 'We must not barter our space for temporary collaboration, which in the long term may disempower Black women' (Black European Women's Conference Congress Report (2007: 61)) – are reflected in the BEWC Board Members' adamant stance on maintaining and protecting Black women's organisations and political autonomy.

The creation of the BEWC was inspired by the prior participation of several of its current members in other European women's organisations. Several members of the BEWC have been and are still currently active in organisations such as the European Migrant Women's Forum and the European Women's Lobby. However, many of these women felt that the specific needs and concerns of Black women and children had often been neglected by these large umbrella organisations. In addition, several BEWC members expressed frustration with the fact that no Black women held positions of power within the aforementioned EU-based organisations. BEWC President Béatrice Achaleke addressed these sentiments by stating in an interview I conducted with her: 'Schwarze Frauen wollen handeln und nicht behandelt werden'. ('Black women want to take action and not be acted upon'), thus rejecting the stereotypical role ascribed to Black women as passive objects. She alluded to the infantilisation of Black women during the BEWC's April 2009 Management Board elections in Utrecht/Soesterberg. While discussing issues related to capacity building and lobby strategies at the EU level with BEWC participants, she stated: '[W]e are a group of Black women who have had enough of being mothered'.[32] This statement was in reaction to Achaleke's previous experience while collaborating with established White-dominated NGOs and migrant women's groups. In her opinion, the relationships between these two groups had been akin to that of the parent–child dyad. According to Achaleke, these relationships unfolded such that the more established NGOs (often predominantly White) commonly saw their role as that of the 'protector' of migrant women and their organisations. When migrant women's groups decided to assert their views and forge self-determined paths that differed from the guidance of the NGOs, their actions were met with resistance, and strife often erupted within these alliances. During the preparation for the 2008 BEWC launch in Brussels, Achaleke stated:

> Just to be a bit provocative, I have the impression, that these majority organisations are not really interested in migrant women becoming emancipated. When suddenly we want to do more than just get their help. From the moment we want to realise our full potential and position ourselves, a power struggle emerges, and sometimes there is even intrigue.

BEWC members invest hope and ambition in this newly formed self-defined 'safe space' in which self-empowerment can be achieved and political agency exercised. The above quotation underscores why it is so important for this group of politically active Black women to negotiate the conditions in which they find themselves. These aspirations carry political significance for Black women residing in Europe, who wish to enter political arenas at local, national and EU levels. These are spheres that have been elusive not only for Black women, but also leave much to be achieved and desired in regard to gender equality between White women and White men.

Clearly not all BEWC members were convinced of the sovereignty and fairness of the EU as a partner for Black people in Europe. Belgian BEWC member, lawyer and journalist Joyce van Genderen-Naar expressed staunch criticism of the EU in regard to its decisions and policies towards African Caribbean Pacific (ACP) banana-producing countries. She agreed with the Chairman of the ACP's Working Group on Bananas that 'The EU is not a real partner'[33] in that is has chosen trade over development. She found certain EU decisions reflective of its disregard for those less powerful. Without a strong and powerful lobby, such countries have a lesser chance of challenging the EU. She sees a correlation here with the situation of Black people in Europe and in particular with Black women. In order to implement real changes, a powerful lobby, vocal constituency and a 'real partner' is needed (personal communication, 10.04.2009).

8.11 The politics of a name

The self-ascription of a name carries much importance in both social and political life (Fischer 2002: 145). This appears to be the case with the BEWC. While in the midst of organising the Black European Women's conference and seeking sponsorship, Béatrice Achaleke mentioned to me that several donor organisations questioned her about the term Black European and wondered why she refused to employ the term 'African' women in Europe. In the following interview excerpt, she recounts the thoughts and strategies linked to the term Black European:

> This term, Black European women, is a strategic working definition, which I think is very important. When they speak about us, then we will be one step in the direction of being recognised as a European population, and not be seen as *these* [emphasis mine] second and third generation migrants. The name Black European came out of the reflection that I don't want my children to forever be considered migrants [...] And that my children can at some time define themselves as part of the European population. They were socialised here. They should be at home here.

The process of determining self-ascribed names, embracing ideas concerning 'racial' selfhood, and the creation of a sense of a collective identity

(Hanchard: 1999:245), have been integral to nearly all transnational Black movements of the past two centuries. In Germany, the self-ascribed term Afro/Black German was certainly a crucial ingredient of the Afro/Black German movement, and has also been implemented among Black Austrians. Prior to 1986, Afro/Black Germans were subjected to a myriad of blatantly derogatory insults, i.e. *Neger* (negro/nigger), *Mulatto, Soldatenkind*.[34] These were descriptions that were definitely not of their own choosing. And just as Afro/Black Germans found it necessary to call attention to their German identity along with their 'imagined'[35] African/Black diasporic identity, so the participants of the 2007 BEWC Congress also found it crucial to the cohesiveness of the Council to agree upon a self-designated term. During the drafting of the BEWC Vienna Declaration, the term Black European Women was selected and the women decided that it would be utilised to encompass all Black women living in Europe regardless of their migrant or non-migrant trajectory.

While yet to be conclusively defined, this term has gained political and academic accreditation, and is used when addressing the specificities of the African/Black Diasporas in Europe. Evidence of this can be noted in the establishment of the 2004–6 Black European Studies project at the Johannes Gutenberg University Mainz, Germany, which focused on the history and development of Black people in Europe.[36] Another example of the importance of this term was discernible in the address of Commissioner Spindla to the BEWC's 2008 European Union launch in Brussels. The Commissioner as well as the other invited speakers all referred to the members of the BEWC as 'Black European women'.

However, despite apparent acceptance by this particular group, the label Black European includes a multitude of identities and differences among African immigrants and the nascent Black and dual heritage populations in Europe. Clearly, the concept of what constitutes a Black or African identity was openly and passionately debated at the BEWC Congress in 2007. There was unanimous awareness that in Europe somatic Blackness was readily coupled with the African continent and that individuals were routinely labelled 'African', regardless of their place of birth, parentage, dual heritage or socialisation. Many Black Austrian women pointed out the need to acknowledge the heterogeneity of Black identity in Europe, and argued this point with those who attended the identity and empowerment workshops at the Congress. While many of them claimed Black Austrian identities, there were also some participants who did not consider themselves to be African and strongly argued for use of the term Black European. This is an interesting point worthy of further elaboration. While the Swedish, Polish and Portuguese participants also engaged in the debate about the term, the German-speaking women proved to be the most vocal and challenged the implications of the term African. As mentioned earlier, the issue of a self-ascribed name played a crucial role in the Afro/Black German movement, which also influenced a sense of Black consciousness in Austria. For the Afro/Black German and Black Austrian women, this identity is an African/Black diasporic identity exclusively situated in Europe. This might also have to do with the traditional postwar German and Austrian national attitude that stressed being *European* over being German or Austrian. Ultimately, the women agreed upon the term Black European as a more encompassing one that allows for the diversity of the Black experience in Europe. The term Black European cannot be seen as a panacea for dealing with all identity issues among Europeans of African/Black diasporic heritage. It became apparent in the discussions that coupling the term Black with European also raised questions regarding the efficacy of strategic essentialism and usefulness of identity politics. Despite all this, the interview data do indicate that the majority of BEWC members preferred the term Black European as it underscores the *Hier-Verortung*[37] of the Black experience in Europe rather than stressing the issue of migrancy.[38] The concept of the 'migrant' is one that appears to leave a nearly permanent imprint upon those who have a migration experience. Despite the acquisition of citizenship, it is the persistence of the myth of racial homogeneity that perpetrates the exclusion of Black people from the European self-image.

Within the 'safe space' of the 2007 BEWC conference, the term *Black European* was decided upon as a strategic and political tool for entry into politics on the level of the EU. Defining oneself as a Black European was agreed on as a way to encompass not only the diverse trajectories of Black peoples across the European space, but also the recognition of Black people by EU bodies as empowered players in the struggle to transform the current social, political and economic status quo for now and for future generations.

8.12 Conclusion

I have examined the issues of 'safe spaces', Black feminism, use of the term Black European and Black female subjectivity in relation to political participation in Germany and Austria. The BEWC offers a potential 'safe space' that entails the capacity to support politicised Black women in their efforts to combat the growing delirium of intolerance, and also to position Black women as visible, empowered subjects upon national and EU political stages. The theorisation of space has often been linked to the understanding of space in a geographical sense. My approach to networks as 'safe spaces' takes into account the aspect of a 'virtual' reality for a population where tangible 'Black spaces' are non-existent. 'Safe space' is crucial in sustaining advocacy work, particularly in highly oppositional political times (Katzenstein 1998). These spaces offer real opportunities to develop and institutionalise policies. The BEWC has already exercised its capacity as an official umbrella organisation/TAN and council. In May 2009 an official letter was drafted and sent to the Irish Fine Gael Party in support of BEWC member Benedicta Attoh's[39] candidacy in the municipal elections in the Dundalk South Area of County Louth, Ireland. An excerpt of the letter states: 'We are convinced that the time has come to include visible minorities, especially Black Women in the political arena of the EU [...]'.[40] The BEWC was established in September 2008; however, we have yet to see how developmental processes within the BEWC, and the acquisition of political clout at EU level will ultimately unfold. For this reason, I continue to pose the questions of how the axes of socioeconomic class, 'race'-racism, sexuality, and age/generation will intersect within transborder 'safe spaces'/networks. Specifically, an important question is how entry into local, national and EU-level politics is ultimately to be attained.

While the BEWC is by no means a panacea for all difficulties facing Black women in Germany and Austria, it is a significant step towards creating a 'safe space' where 'Black spaces' are lacking, and towards mobilising a transborder political network that has garnered the recognition of the EU.

Notes

The term Black European refers to individuals with ties to the African Diaspora, who were born and socialised within a European context, and/or self-identify as Black European. There are differing discourses regarding the term Black European and its definition. While it is most commonly employed in reference to individuals socialised within a European frame of reference, many of the participants of the Black European Women's Congress in Vienna in 2007 were not solely socialised in Europe, but view Europe as a central sociocultural point of departure in their lives.

1. Within the frame of this article, the term Black refers to individuals who self-identify as members of the African Diaspora.
2. See Report on the Working Group of Experts on People of African Descent. A/HRC/4/39: [http://daccessdds.un.org/doc/UNDOC/GEN/G07/117/38/PDF/G0711738.pd.], accessed 09.04.2010.
3. While a single, universal definition of this term does not exist, it is commonly employed to designate the practice of stopping and controlling

individuals in the public sphere (pedestrian zones, train stations, urban areas) for no apparent reason other than a statistical profile linked to an individual 'race' or perceived ethnicity. Racial profiling is the result of a systematic and historical practice of targeting African-descended peoples.

4. My use of the term 'in-corporated' relates to my body (corpus). Being Black and female granted me an advantage in terms of access to and participation in the activities of the BEWC.
5. Coined in 1986, the terms Black German or Afro German are the self-ascribed terms (sometimes used interchangeably) by Germans of African diasporic heritage, who claim this identity. Throughout this Chapter, I employ the term Black German. Black German has evolved to include not only individuals with one White German and one African diasporic parent, but also individuals of the African Diaspora socialised in Germany, and people of colour, who regard Germany and aspects of German culture (e.g. language) as central to their lives. However, White German ancestry is not necessarily a prerequisite for Afro/Black German self-identification.
6. My use of the term Black Austrian is in conjunction with the Black Austria media campaign launched in 2007 in Vienna. The goal of the campaign was to dismantle common, stereotypically gendered depictions of Black people living in Austria, such as the 'Black male drug dealer' or 'Black female prostitute'. It remains unclear as to exactly when this term came into use among individuals who identify as Black Austrian. See [http://www.blackaustria.at]. accessed 04.01.10.
7. This chapter deals solely with the sociohistorical developments of African/Black diasporic people in the area of the former Western Germany. For an in-depth history of Blacks in the former German Democratic Republic from a Black perspective, see, Piesche (2002) and Engombe (2004).
8. During the past 20 years, a growing body of scholarship has emerged focusing on and documenting the history of Blacks in Germany and Austria. For Germany, see: Campt 1996, 2003; Campt et al. 1998; El Tayeb 2001, 2004, 2003; Hugel-Marshall 1998; Lemke Muniz de Faria 2002; Massaquoi 1999; Oguntoye 1997; Oguntoye, Opitz et al. 1986; Zöllner 2003. For Austria, see: Johnston-Arthur 2004, 2005, 2007; Unterweger 2005.
9. Unlike many of the European former colonial powers such as the United Kingdom, France the Netherlands or Belgium, Germany's colonial rule in Africa was short-lived (1884/5–1919). The Republic of Austria as successor state of the Habsburg Empire has no colonial or imperial history in Africa. Many of the challenging issues faced by Blacks in these two countries are rooted in and linked to the repercussions of slavery and colonialism/post-colonialism, 'race'-racism and marginalisation. These systems of oppression intersect and have contributed to the current positioning of Black people as foreign, exotic, and excluded from the German and Austrian 'imagined' racial corpus.
10. My use of the term 'dual heritage' refers to individuals of African/Black diasporic and White European descent.
11. I have chosen to couple the two terms 'race'-racism in order to indicate the symbiotic bond between the social construction of race and the actual realities of the racialisation process, racist practices and their subsequent effects (Bacchetta 2009).

12. 'Victim or Suspect – A Question of Colour. Racist Discrimination in the Austrian Justice System', Amnesty International, Index: EUR 13/002/2009 (London: Amnesty International Publications 2009), 11–14. See [http://www.amnesty.org/en/library/info/EUR13/002/2009/en], accessed 01.05.2009.
13. *'Neger raus'* (English: 'Niggers'/Negroes get out). The 'N' word in German is equated with the pejorative term 'N' in English. It is viewed as a racial epithet by many Black Germans as well as Black Austrians. Racial epithets (*'N'-raus*) in graffiti form on the walls of many public spaces in Vienna is a very problematic issue, and causes much distress to Blacks living there. See Johnston-Arthur (2007: 423–42).
14. Marcus Omufuma was a 25-year-old Nigerian asylum seeker, who was scheduled for deportation from Vienna to Sofia, Bulgaria on 1 May 1999. In order to keep him quiet for the flight, Omufuma's mouth and nose were strapped with adhesive tape, which caused suffocation. The death of Marcus Omufuma prompted rage and protest among African migrants, refugees and Black Austrians. The year 1999 was an important one in the political mobilisation of the Black community in Austria.
15. Born in Mozambique, Alberto Adriano came to the former GDR as a contract worker. On 11 June 2000, he was attacked in Dessau, Germany by a group of young White German Right-wing extremists, and was brutally murdered.
16. N'Deye Mareame Sarr migrated from Senegal and was the mother of two small children. Sarr was only 26 at the time of her death. According to various reports, a heated argument erupted between Sarr and her former White German husband in Aschaffenburg, Germany. He alerted the police in order to subdue her. Sarr was shot dead by one of the police officers.
17. I align myself with Bacchetta's (2009) conceptual use of the term of co-formations. Bacchetta asserts that subjects are co-formed through social constructions, i.e. 'race', gender, sexuality etc. When these constructions are blended or overlap, they form inseparable relationships in the production of subjects.
18. Golden was one of the panellists at the 'Becoming Black Europe: Possibilities and Obstacles to a Black Europe' panel (19.09.2004), which was part of the Black Atlantic Project in Berlin (17.09.2004–15.11.2004).
19. AFRA is the acronym for the International Centre for Black Women's Perspectives.
20. See [http://www.verwaltung.steiermark.at/cms/dokumente/10006104_600279/d8a07c82/IF-Folder%200406.pdf], accessed 01.06.2010.
21. The Lisbon Strategy – also known as the Lisbon Agenda, or Lisbon Process – is an action plan for the European Union. Its goal is to make the EU 'the most dynamic and competitive knowledge-based economy in the world capable of sustainable economic growth with more and better jobs and greater social cohesion, and respect for the environment by 2010'. See http://www.europarl.europa.eu/summits/lis1_en.htm], accessed 30.04.2010.
22. Established in 1976, the Commission on Security and Cooperation in Europe (CSCE), also known as the US Helsinki Commission, is an independent agency of the Federal Government created to monitor and encourage compliance with the Helsinki Final Act and other OSCE commitments. See [www.cse.gov], accessed 20.6.2010.
23. During the late 1970s, Black women in Europe began establishing their own organisations and networks. The now defunct Organisation of Women

of Asian and African Descent (OWAAD), founded in 1978 in the UK, was a seminal attempt to bring together women of colour from diverse backgrounds and political views. In the following decades, various other groups emerged, e.g. Brixton Black Women's Group (1970s), or Southall Black Sisters (1979). In the Netherlands, national and local organisations emerged, such as Tiye (1994), Zami (1991) and Sister Outsider (1980s). The European Black Women's Network (1991) also provided Black women, women of colour, migrant and refugee women with the possibility of organising across borders and lines of 'race', ethnicity, legal status and sexuality.

24. Fieldnotes from C. Ellerbe-Dueck (09.04.2009) Utrecht – Soesterberg, NL. See [http://www.bewnet.eu, last accessed 15.7. 2010].
25. EC Article 13 (see Treaty of Amsterdam) constitutes the legal basis for the anti-discrimination measures that were to be adopted and implemented from 2000 onwards by the European Union. Article 13 permits the EU Council of Ministers to take action in order to combat discrimination based on sex, racial origin, religion, disability, age and sexual orientation. See [http://eur-lex.europa.eu/LexUriServ/LexUriServ.do?uri=CELEX:12002E013:EN:HTML], accessed 15.04.2010.
26. Neo-racism, also referred to as 'new racism', is a manifestation of discrimination that is not solely based upon phenotype but also on so-called 'cultural differences'.
27. For details, see Howe and Wilpert (2008).
28. Excerpt from Black European Women's Conference DVD.
29. See e.g. The German *Antidiskriminierungsverband* (advd) [www-anti-diskriminierung.org], accessed 10 July 2010.
30. Social movement theory utilises the term to indicate mobilising structures in organisations and networks. In this case, the BEWC functions as the umbrella organisation/structure (meso-level) that is composed of smaller formal and informal networks (micro-level) (Buechler 1993).
31. Virtcom Consulting is a strategy management consultancy firm that focuses on solving global diversity management challenges. CEO Douglas Freeman is the founder of the World Diversity Leadership Summit and a staunch supporter of the BEWC.
32. Data excerpt from the BEWC General Assembly Meeting, 09–10.04. 2009.
33. See 'The EU is not a Real Partner' [www.normangirvan.info/bananas-eu-not-a-real-partner-joyce-vg-naar/], accessed 23.09.2009.
34. The term *Soldatenkind* is commonly associated with the children of African-American soldiers and White German women.
35. The term 'imagined' refers to the fact that many Afro/Black Germans and Austrians have had to create their own sense of Black identity. In many cases, they did not grow up with their African/Black parent and thus did not experience direct immersion into African/Black diasporic culture.
36. The Black European Studies project was funded by the Volkswagen Foundation, and focused on historical and contemporary perspectives of Black populations in Europe. See [http://www.best.uni-mainz.de/modules/Informationen/index.php?id=13], accessed 20.04.2010.
37. The German term *Hier-Verortung* is nearly impossible to translate. A loose translation could indicate that it points to an individual/collective conscious choice to see oneself geographically grounded within the German-speaking

context, and also as a member of the society in which one was socialised. It suggests, I believe, a politicised, conscious effort to reject an ascribed position of marginality, and to underscore and shed light on the suppressed existence of the Black Diaspora(s) within the German-speaking world.

38. While some of the women of BEWC may have a migrant experience, the migration narrative does not extend itself to the entire Black Diaspora in Europe. Moreover, my research indicates that while some Black Germans and Austrians may have parents who were/are immigrants, many point to Europe as their location of birth and socialisation and as a determining factor in their identity formation. They often express annoyance with constant references to their assumed 'migrant' histories.
39. Benedicta Attoh is an independent cultural trainer and a former Development and Public Awareness Officer with the National Consultative Committee on Racism and Interculturalism in Ireland. She has played a key role in racial integration issues in County Louth and nationally. In June 2009 she ran with Jim D'Arcy for local county elections.
40. Austrian letter of support for Irish candidate Benedicta Attoh. See [http://www.attohdarcy.com/files/afra.pdf], accessed 10.01.2010.

References

Achaleke, B. (2007). 'Chancengleicheit für Alle in der EU: Provokation oder Selbstlüge? In Initiative Minderheiten Peregrina Schwarze Frauen Community', (ed.). *Communicating Equality* (Vienna: Schwarze Frauen Community).

Ahmed, S. (2007) *Queer Phenomenology. Orientations, Objects, Others* (Durham and London: Duke University Press) (second printing).

Amnesty International Report – Austria (April 2009). *Victim or Suspect – A Question of Colour: Racist Discrimination in the Austrian Justice System* (London: Amnesty International).

Bacchetta, P. (2009). 'Co-Formations: Sur les spatialités de résistance de lesbiennes "of color" en France', *Sexualité, Genre et Société*, vol. 1, no.1 http://gss.revues.org/index810.html, accessed 30 June 2010.

Black European Women's Conference Congress Report (2007) (Vienna: AFRA).

Buechler, S. M. (1993). 'Beyond Resource Mobilization? Emerging Trends in Social Movement Theory', *Sociological Quarterly*, vol. 34, no. 2: pp. 217–35.

Campt, T. (1996). '"Afro-German": The Convergence of Race, Sexuality and Gender in the Formation of a German Ethnic Identity', Unpublished Ph.D. Dissertation.

Campt, T. (2003). *Other Germans: Black Germans and the Politics of Race, Gender and Memory in the Third Reich* (Ann Arbor: University of Michigan Press).

Campt, T., Grosse, P., Lemke-Muniz de Faria, Y. (1998). 'Blacks, Germans, and the Politics of Imperial Imagination, 1920–60', in S. Friedrichsmeyer et al. *The Imperialist Imagination: German Colonialism and Its Legacy* (Ann Arbor: University of Michigan Press), pp. 205–29.

Crenshaw, K. (1991). 'Mapping the Margins: Intersectionality, Identity Politics and Violence against Women of Color', in K. W. Crenshaw, N. Gotanda, G. Peller and K. Thomas (eds). *Critical Race Theory: The Key Writings That Informed the Movement* (New York: New Press), pp. 367–84.

Delany, D. (2002). 'Space That Race Makes', *The Professional Geographer*, vol. 54, no. 1: pp. 6–14.
Desai, M. (2005). 'Transnationalism: The Face of Feminist Politics Post-Beijing', *International Social Science Journal*, vol. 57, no. 184: pp. 319–30.
Duncan, N. (1996). *Bodyspace: Destabilizing Geographies of Gender and Sexuality* (New York: Routledge).
Engombe, L. (2004). Kind Nr 95: *Meine deutsch-afrikanische Odyssee* (Berlin: Ullstein Verlag).
El-Tayeb, F. (2001). *Schwarze Deutsche: Der Diskurs um 'Rasse' und nationale Identität 1890–1933* (Frankfurt/New York: Campus Verlag).
El-Tayeb, F. (2003). '"If You Can't Pronounce My Name, You Can Call Me Pride": Afro-Germans, Activism, Gender and Hip Hop', *Gender and History*, vol. 15, no. 3: pp. 460–86.
El-Tayeb, F. (2004) 'Blut, Nation und multikulturelle Gesellschaft', in M.Bechaus-Gerst and R. Klein-Arendt (eds). *Afrikanerinnen in Deutschland und schwarze Deutsche Geschichte und Gegenwart* (Münster: Lit-Verlag), pp. 125–37.
Ferree, M. M. (2008). 'Framing Equality: The Politics of Race, Class, Gender in the US, Germany and the Expanding European Union', in S. Roth (ed.) Gender Politics in the Expanding European Union. Mobilization, Inclusion, Exclusion (Oxford, New York: Berghahn Books), pp. 237–55.
Fischer, T. (2002). 'Black Women, Politics, Nationalism and Community in London', *Small Axe*, vol. 6 (1), no. 11: pp. 135–50.
Fröhlicher-Stines, C. and M. K. Mennel (2004). *Schwarze Menschen in der Schweiz: Ein Leben zwischen Integration und Diskriminierung* (Bern: Eidgenössische Kommission gegen Rassismus (EKR)).
Gummich, J. (1993/1994). 'Als Schwarze diskriminiert – Als Deutsche ignoriert: Schwarze Deutsche', *Perspektiven. Zeitschrift für sozialistische Theorie*, vol. 10 Winter 1993–4: pp. 16–19.
Hanchard, M. (1999). 'Afro-Modernity: Temporality, Politics, and the African Diaspora', *Public Culture*, vol. 11, no. 1: pp. 245–68.
Hill-Collins, P. (2000). *Black Feminist Thought: Knowledge, Consciousness and the Politics of Empowerment* (New York: Routledge).
Howe, C. and C. Wilpert (2008). 'EU 7th Framework Project: Genderace: The Use of Anti-Discrimination Laws, Gender and Citizenship in a Multicultural Context, Country Report – Germany', accessed 31 July 2010. http://genderace.ulb.ac.be.
Hügel-Marshall, I. (1998). *Daheim unterwegs: ein deutsches Leben* (Berlin: Orlanda Frauen Verlag).
Johnston-Arthur, A. (2004) Über die Konstruktion des m*** und der m*** im Kontext epistemischer Gewalt und den traumatischen Charakter neokolonialer Erfahrungen in der modernen afrikanischen Diaspora in Österreich. University of Vienna. Unpublished M.A. Thesis.
Johnston-Arthur, A. (2007). 'Es ist Zeit, der Geschichte selbst eine Gestalt zu geben ... Strategien der Entkolonisierung und Entmächtigung im Kontext der modernen afrikanischen Diaspora in Österreich', in K. Nghi Ha, N. Lauré al-Samurai and S. Mysorekar (eds). *Re/Visionen: Postkoloniale Perspektiven von People of Color auf Rassismus, Kulturpolitik und Widerstand in Deutschland* (Münster: Unrast Verlag), pp. 423–44.
Johnston-Arthur, A. & Ofoedu, C. (2005) "Von kriminalisierten Objekten zu politischen Subjekten. Notizen zu den Realitäten von 'Operation Spring'-sechs Jahre

danach un nach dem neuen Dokumentarfilm von Angelika Schuster und Tristan Sindelgruber" in Stimme von und für Minderheiten, no. 56 (Herbst) pp. 26–27.

Katzenstein, M. F. (1998). *Faithful and Fearless: Moving Feminist Protest Inside the Church and Military* (Princeton: Princeton University Press).

Lang, S. (2007). 'Organizing Political Advocacy: Transnational Women's Networks and Gender Mainstreaming in the European Union', ECREA Brussels Conference paper.

Lemke Muniz de Faria, Y. (2002). *Zwischen Fürsorge und Ausgrenzung: Afrodeutsche 'Besatzungskinder' im Nachkriegsdeutschland* (Berlin: Metropol).

Massaquoi, H. J. (1999). *Neger, Neger Schornsteinfeger: Meine Kindheit in Deutschland* (München: Fischer).

Moghadam, V. M. (2000). 'Transnational Feminist Networks: Collective Action in an Era of Globalization', *International Sociology*, vol. 15, no. 1: pp. 57–85.

Moghadam, V. M. (2005). *Globalizing Women: Transnational Feminist Networks* (Baltimore: Johns Hopkins University Press).

McLaughlin, A. (1995). 'The Impact of the Black Consciousness and Women's Movements on Black Women's Identity: Intercontinental Empowerment: Connecting Across Cultures and Continents', in A. O. Pala (ed.). *Black Women Speak Out on Identity, Race and Development* (New York: United Nations Development Fund (UNIFEM)), pp. 71–85.

Oguntoye, K. (1997). *Eine afro-deutsche Geschichte: Zur Lebenssituation von Afrikanern und Afro-Deutschen in Deutschland von 1884 bis 1950* (Berlin: Hoho Verlag-Christine Hoffmann).

Oguntoye, K., M. Opitz (Ayim) and Schultz, D. (eds) (1986). *Farbe Bekennen: Afro-deutsche Frauen auf den Spuren ihrer Geschichte* (Berlin: Orlanda Frauen Verlag).

Piesche, P. (2002). 'Black and German? East German Adolescents before 1989 – A Retrospective View of a "Non-Existent Issue" in the GDR', in L. Adelson (ed.). *The Cultural After-Life of East Germany: New Transnational Perspectives* (Washington, DC: AICGS), pp. 37–59.

Polletta, F. (1999). 'Free Spaces in Collective Action', *Theory and Society*, vol. 28: pp. 1–38.

Rolandsen Agustin, L. and Roth, S. (2011). 'Minority Inclusion, Self-Representation and Coalition-Building: The Participation of Minority Women in European Women's Networks', in A. E.Woodward, J. M. Bonvin and M. Renom (eds) *Transforming Gendered Well-Being in Europe: The Impact of Social Movements* (Farnham: Ashgate), pp. 231–47.

Silliman, J. (1999). 'Expanding Civil Society: Shrinking Political Spaces – The Case of Women's Nongovernmental Organizations', *Social Politics*, vol. 1: pp. 23–53.

Smith, B. (1983). 'Introduction to Home Girls: A Black Feminist Anthology', in B. Smith (ed.) *Home Girls: A Black Feminist Anthology* (New York: Kitchen Table Women of Color Press), pp. 147–55.

Unterweger, C. (2005). '"Wir greifen Raum", Die Bedeutung von Schwarzen selbstbestimmten Räumen im österreichischen Kontext', *Bildpunkt Zeitschrift der IG Bildende Kunst*, pp. 7–9.

Verloo, M. (2002). 'Gender Mainstreaming: Practice and Prospects', Report prepared for the Council of Europe EG (99) 13, Strassbourg, accessed 30 August 2010.

Zöllner, A. (2003). *Schokoladenkind: Meine Familie und andere Wunder* (Berlin: Rowohlt-Reinbek).

9

Bordering, De-Bordering, Cross-Bordering: A Conclusion

Heidi Armbruster

The *SeFoNe* project that is presented in this book took its departure in the discussion of borders as both physical and mental constructs. The case studies showed that practices of demarcation, differentiation and place-making that invoke nation, ethnicity, history or language and frequently determine bordering practices at the margins of the nation-state can also inform social relations elsewhere, especially in spaces of cultural diversity. The tension between spatial proximity and social distance typically arises in both domains and their academic study. Yet, as Meinhof's introduction in Chapter 1 shows, border studies are usually considered separate from diversity or migration studies, the former conjuring up 'national' communities, periphery, rurality, territorial sides/sites; the latter 'ethnic' communities, centrality, urbanity and cultural sides/sites. By bringing the two fields together this book challenges two assumptions: that people in state border regions are particularly predestined to create cross-border orientations; and that ethnic and cultural boundaries are primarily an effect of migration, or a problem of migrants. The case studies suggested that 'cross-bordering' has become quite generally a vital question, in a situation where people in Europe live increasingly mobile lives and are affected by new forms of cultural diversity and post-industrial change, even in areas outside metropolitan or typically 'multicultural' centres.

In the preceding chapters (cross-)bordering practices involved differences of nationality, ethnicity and history which take effect through their multiple intersections with social class, gender, language and citizenship. They related to institutional and rights frameworks but also hinged on the 'civil sphere' (Alexander 2006) in which citizens generate communities of affinity or solidarity beyond the institutional realm or the national logic of the state. All chapters engaged with resources of the civil sphere, in which people actively mobilise or engage in forms of cross-bordering. While in many cases these are attempts at engaging in a politics of cooperation that recognises (rather than denies) diversity, unequal distributions of power among those involved remain a challenge in all cases, fracturing not only opportunities of cooperation but also often reinstating culture, ethnicity or nation as boundary markers. The civil sphere is rarely far removed from institutional opportunities and constraints, in relation to which citizens' activities take shape. This is a common topos in this book, where authors examine the ways in which the sphere of the everyday relates to the sphere of institutions, policy making, or dominant political or national discourses. The institutional categories radiate from the local to the national and transnational, and frequently address the European Union (EU) as a supranational actor.

In the three chapters on Cypriot, Austrian and diverse Hungarian borders, the authors examined cross-border community processes which imply a relatively strong role of the state, or of state and supra-state institutional actors such as the UN or EU. In all three cases, local communities negotiate state borders that separate a relatively weaker from a relatively stronger state (more economic power often combined with longer EU membership), and that are inscribed with historical or contemporary conflict. However, as the chapters showed, there is evidence that historical, socio-economic and environmental tensions are not simply cast into nationalising scripts by local actors; 'civic action' (Chapter 2) and the emergence of a multinational civil sphere can deflate conflict and forge connections on the basis of common interests and values.

As Chapter 2 on Cyprus showed, this can be a particular challenge when cross-border civic action has to form against a historically entrenched and ongoing 'national' conflict. Demetriou et al. insightfully discuss how local citizens' struggles for bicommunal reconciliation in Cyprus provide real possibilities for change on the one hand, yet have to contend with powerful state, institutional and media actors on the other, who have in some ways monopolised and dominated the tools and resources for negotiating bicommunal relations. By looking at different spheres of 'civic action', the authors showed that the entrenchment of a national if not nationalist logic more generally, and its strong base in the state, in particular, impede the formation of stronger intercommunal relations. The chapter suggested that the Leftist activists who represent 'the least organised' civil sphere challenge state nationalism most openly, and thus provoke the strongest counter-reaction.

Bicommunal issues on the Austrian–Hungarian border which were the topic of Chapter 3 are less fraught by nationalism. Wastl-Walter and Varadi showed how two very unequal opponents that struggle over the legitimacy of a waste incinerator plant on the border are not separated by nationality but by ecological concerns on the one hand and economically driven investment motifs on the other. Ordinary Austrians and Hungarians form coalitions and launch campaigns to defend their natural environment which brings them into opposition with investors, and the regional government in Austria who can muster the most powerful financial, political and scientific resources in this conflict. This border study also addressed the question of democratic legitimacy. It showed that while planning permission procedures for the incinerator have gone through the necessary legal and constitutional process, local citizens remain unconvinced. They challenge institutional decision-making processes that may conform to the regulatory procedures of parliamentary democracy as it stands, but that seem to represent to them the interests of a remote economic and political class which does not have their concerns at heart. This felt lack of democratic participation also conjures up the EU as a symbolically and politically charged participant. It appears as a cofinancier of the industrial park in which the incinerator is to be built, as a supranational legislator of waste management, and, interestingly, as an addressee for the environmental activists and Hungarian politicians who appeal to it as an impartial arbiter of justice. The chapter closed by explaining the ineffectiveness of appeals to the EU, which ultimately came out in support of the powers that be (or, as the authors state, as unable to intervene in such conflicts).

The role of the EU is prominently discussed by Erőss et al. in Chapter 4. The authors examined how historically recent and staggered accessions to the EU and the Schengen accord have modified Hungary's relations to its eastern neighbours. This complexly informed post-Communist but also still relevant post-Trianon legacies that still expose the Hungarian minorities to nationalist bargaining between Hungary and some of its neighbours. However, as the chapter shows, it is mostly the new EU-induced 'Schengen effect' on the Hungarian–Ukraine border that imposes the deepest separating impact on two border communities which have had a long tradition of exchange. Here the nation-state principle enforced by the EU transformed the border, as the authors put it, from a 'bridge to a barrier'. Equally importantly, the chapter showed that sharing Hungarian ethnicity on either side of the border does not translate into unwavering solidarity. Unequal access to socioeconomic opportunities may expose the relationship as one between 'fair weather friends'.

Chapters 5, 6 and 7 took an urban perspective at cross-bordering. Here 'borders' were shown to be the mental barriers between migrants and non-migrants in relatively peripheral cities where multiculturalism is still seen as a new phenomenon. Chemnitz (Chapter 5) and Bayreuth (Chapter 6) in eastern and western Germany, and Catania (Chapter 7) in Italy, all have long-standing immigration histories but only recently started to embrace these as social and political realities. In response to EU and nationally driven 'integration' policies, all three cities have started to implement 'integration' agendas. While boundary constructions are less obviously informed by state borders, the intersections of 'history', 'nation', 'ethnicity', 'religion', 'race' and 'class' shape categories of belonging no less, often as direct manifestations of how institutions, local policies and historical discourses write themselves into people's everyday lives.

In Chapter 5, Carstensen-Egwuom and Holly applied a finely tuned linguistic analysis to interview narratives that speak of immigrant Vietnamese, Jewish and Afro-German experiences of 'integration' in the post-industrial town of Chemnitz. In this process 'integration' emerges as a symbolic, territorial, and affective category of belonging. By closely reading the actual voices of the research participants, the chapter lucidly showed that 'integration' has already become a central discursive force in how migrants think of their status, and that its effects can be constraining. It also showed that 'integration' is still mostly configured as a duty immigrants and those deemed ethnic minorities have to perform, rather than as a process that involves and challenges the dominant majority.

This is also concluded in Chapter 6, where Hauke Dorsch looks more closely at 'integration' in the German town of Bayreuth. By analysing the 'Intercultural Week', an event hosted largely by organisations linked to the Lutheran Church, Dorsch showed why the 'Week's' emphasis on showcasing cultural difference failed to work as a space of intercultural dialogue. He demonstrated that the event exposes the highly elusive meaning of 'integration' on the one hand, while ultimately reproducing an understanding of German society as homogenous on the other. The case study illustrated that the 'to-be-integrated' stayed away from the 'intercultural' event because it denied them equality and symbolic access to 'Germanness'.

In Chapter 7 Orazio Licciardello and Daniela Damigella reported on new processes of neighbouring in the Sicilian port-city of Catania. Often understood as on the outskirts of 'fortress Europe' by those who regard Sicily as a potentially illegal entrance to the EU, the authors remind us that migrants have come to stay and that Italy is slowly recognising itself as a country of immigration. In contrast to the two German examples, though, specifically targeted policy approaches to 'integration' are as yet missing. By selecting different sites of where they see intercultural neighbouring at work, the authors are able to observe different attempts and nascent initiatives, often driven by small civil-society efforts. Comparable to the Chemnitz case study, they also placed a particular emphasis on the importance of educational institutions in developing more intercultural permeability and awareness. The Catania study once again calls to mind the manifold bordering mechanisms that can hinge on 'race' and close vital opportunity structures to new migrants from the start.

The racialisation of boundaries and its effects were more specifically addressed in Chapter 8, where Cassandra Ellerbe-Dueck put yet another perspective on the negotiation of symbolic and geopolitical boundaries as portrayed in the book so far. Women of African descent living in Europe who often find themselves excluded on the basis of gender, race and nation are shown to extend 'neighbouring' practices across local and national boundaries to move them into a virtual and non-virtual space of activism. Here, the EU appears as an enabling force for types of networking that transcend not only the national, linguistic, educational etc. differences of the women themselves but also the limited opportunities of political participation they face within the boundaries of their own European nation-states. Ellerbe-Dueck showed that Black Europeanness is by no means an uncontested category, yet offers a potential site of empowerment and political mobilisation for women who continue to face racist exclusion. She argued that its anti-racism and anti-discrimination policies in particular have made the EU a potential coalition partner for Black Europeans, especially in the face of the slow and reluctant embrace of anti-discrimination legislation in some European nation-states.

All chapters involved bordering and cross-bordering at two intersecting levels: first, at the level of the research participants who engage in practices of in-grouping and out-grouping on the basis of a range of factors such as nationality or ethnicity; second, at the level of governance practices of states, institutions, bureaucracies or corporations which inform, legitimate or even enforce the boundaries of the 'citizen', the 'national', or the 'European'. Most of the preceding chapters showed the relatedness between these two levels to come to the fore in 'discourse' or 'narrative' where individuals talk about their experiences and views but also perceive themselves in the language of a larger social order. The study in the town of Chemnitz, for example (Chapter 5), showed this most effectively with regard to the social proliferation of the politicised term 'integration'; the chapter on the environmental conflict on the Austrian–Hungarian border (Chapter 3) exposed how the struggle of local protestors against a big corporation becomes one against the power of 'expert language' in the institutional planning procedure of the waste plant; and the appropriation of the label 'Black European' as an identity term by Black women activists (Chapter 8) is shown to be a stance against the powerful symbolic association of European with 'white'. All these examples and more across the book showed that studying mental, political, spatial etc. processes of (cross)-bordering means studying the relation between people's languages and performances of (national, ethnic etc.) identity and the claims and conflicts over resources, opportunities and rights they are involved in.

For the remainder of this Chapter, I shall expand on the European dimension that I have already addressed as a crucial context to this book. Europe has a constant, explicit and implicit presence throughout the chapters. Embodied in the 'EU', it has been found relevant by local research participants and in discursive formations across the research sites; through EU funding it has been imparted in the *SeFoNe* study as a 'logic' guiding selection of locales and parameters of comparison. In correspondence with the preceding case studies that examined national borders and immigrant cities, I will read the debate on 'Europe' in parallel with the debate on 'migrants'. Both have been intensely conducted in academic scholarship and policy spheres alike, and both have recently been concerned with notions of 'integration', a term which could in itself be regarded as synonymous with the idea of 'cross-bordering', and which has figured prominently in some of the preceding chapters. Reading the migration debate alongside the EU debate will also illustrate the contradictions that are immanent to the European integration project that is based on both the deflation and inflation of the nation-state and its ideological principles.

9.1 Beyond the nation-state

The EU has been the single most forceful promoter of cross-border cooperation and de-bordering processes in the European space. Some observers have called the EU a 'mixture of supranational, transnational, transgovernmental, and intergovernmental structures' (Erikson and Fossum 2000: 4) that seeks to achieve a dynamic of integration among member states, that is much more than the sum of its parts. Evidently, globalisation and processes of Europeanisation have created a de facto economic and political interdependence between states. Cross-border flows of culture and movements of people have established transnationality as a form of life, and the acute economic and environmental crises and risks of the early 21st century increasingly forge the awareness that humanity shares a common fate. And yet integration among culturally or nationally diverse peoples still often looks like a difficult undertaking.

For some students of the European project, one of the problems lies in the continuous ideological force of the nation-state as a model of territoriality, identity and community. It is the national lens, they argue, that accounts for popular, political and academic insular thinking. Eriksen and Fossum (2000), for instance, speak of the 'tyranny' of the nation-state principle, whose reliance on ideas of independence, territorial boundedness, uniform popular allegiance, and mono-national citizenship adheres to an outdated container model of society. What is more, they align the 'democracy deficit' often attested to the EU as a supranational structure to a perception of democracy that is derived from the nation-state model. This they claim, erroneously, assumes not only that contemporary democratic nation-states actually realise democracy in its most perfected form but also that the EU should be judged like a 'state' in itself rather than considered as a different kind of polity. As they put it:

> The 'tyranny', then, can manifest itself in a certain tendency to graft governance arrangements onto the EU from the actual arrangements of nation-states, without proper attention to democratic principles and whether the arrangements conform with such at a supranational level. [...] For instance, models of representative democracy are based on less stringent popular requirements than are participatory and deliberative ones.
>
> (Eriksen and Fossum 2000: 8)

In other words, for trans-European integration to take shape, they suggest that rather than imposing existing state-centred notions of democracy onto the EU and expecting them to work, democratic principles and their institutionalisations will have to emerge from a deliberative process that is dedicated to such a supranational polity.

In the post-Maastricht era, citizens, politicians and academics have increasingly raised questions about democracy and democratic legitimacy in the EU. Since the early 2000s, political scientists in particular have considered the question of European integration in relation to the question of democracy, and increasingly agreed that democratic governance in the EU has to become 'postnational' in scope, but that this also poses a long-term, transformative challenge which requires an effort of institutional and mental denationalisation akin to the historical process of nation-building itself (e.g., Fabbrini 2005; Hoskyns and Newman 2000; Warleigh 2003). This is not only because the nation-state model has determined Europe's political and symbolic order for nearly two centuries, but also because basic democratic principles – such as equality, citizens' participation in decision making or effective control of elected representatives – are difficult to achieve on a large transnational scale (see Dahl 2005). While the EU has currently 'the only directly elected multinational parliament in the world' (Sbragia 2005: 174), thus comparing relatively well to a whole range of major international institutions that constitute themselves outside the democratic process – such as the United Nations, International Monetary Fund, World Bank, World Health Organisation or North Atlantic Treaty Organisation – citizens' democratic participation in the political process of the EU is hardly developed. Clearly, questions of how citizens (rather than governments or political elites) can effectively be represented in the EU, and how affective patterns of citizenship could 'transnationalise', pose themselves in ever more pressing form.

In addition, Europe presents specific historical and cultural challenges to democratic integration that resonate across the findings of this book. Sbragia summarises them appositely:

> [t]heir linguistic diversity, their history of frequent warfare, their strong links to different parts of the world outside Europe, their negative stereotypes of each other, their different post-war experiences (with the West Europeans experiencing national democracy and prosperity and the East Europeans experiencing the opposite), do not make the path to a democratic EU very easy.
>
> (Sbragia 2005: 170)

This Sbragia quotation also implicitly highlights that 'postnational' democratic participation and integration will have to be negotiated through types of conflict and diversity that are popularly perceived as constituents of – rather than antipodes to – national sentiment and identity.

Extending democracy more effectively across borders, some observers argue, is only one side of the coin. Political equality has to tie in with social equality if integrative capital among citizens but also among economically unequal countries is to be strengthened. Jürgen Habermas, for instance, argues that contemporary forms of global capitalism have already diminished the (European) welfare-state and its 'integration capacity' (Habermas 2000: 29), a thesis that seems to be borne out by the responses to the recent economic crisis. For Habermas, the neoliberal regime of contemporary global capitalism has eroded the welfare state and its ability to act independently to the outside or integratively to the inside. The increasing deregulation and privatisation of national economies, their dependency on deregulated world markets, pressing international competitiveness, the outsourcing of labour and investment-oriented tax regimes have led to a tightening of state welfare provisions and the rolling-out of social risks and costs to the population. Habermas associates the demise of the welfare-state with a 'de-solidarization' of society, the rise of a new excluded 'underclass', and the threat to democratic culture per se (2000: 29–30). He locates effective democratising responses in a postnational scenario in which transnational institutions and political cooperations such as the EU can play a vital role, but only if they are effectively supported by citizens and a strong border-crossing civil society. As he puts it:

> '*Citizens' solidarity* [italics in original], hitherto limited to the nation-state, must be expanded to the citizens of the Union in such a way that, for example, Swedes and Portuguese, Germans and Greeks are willing to stand up for one another, as it is the case now with citizens from former West and East Germany. Only then would it be possible to expect them to accept the same minimum wages, let alone the same opportunities for their different collective forms of life and for their individual life-projects.
>
> (2000: 34)

Similar ideas have been raised by a growing number of scholars who argue that principles of integration that are derived from the nation-state are insufficiently equipped to forge a transnational orientation in citizens and institutional political structures alike. In their view, processes of transnationalisation and cross-border economic, political and ecological interdependence have become such an undeniable fact that domestic political structures and mentalities that insist on self-containment seem unacceptably parochial. Interestingly, scholarly orientations in political science or political philosophy that veer towards cosmopolitan models of cross-border integration and democracy argue for a new type of citizen power, rather than for the political elites as harbingers of change. Transnational openings are envisaged as growing from the social and political resources in grass-roots contexts, social movements and the micro-worlds in which sociality, mentality and identity get shaped. Citizens themselves are seen as enactors of 'cosmopolitan solidarity' (Habermas 2000: 37), 'deliberative democracy' (Warleigh 2003: 31), or 'active citizenship' (Warleigh 2003: 55) in which they keenly participate in the matters that concern their lives, form solidarities and create strong policy-shaping voices.

Scholars who translate these cosmopolitan and grass-roots-based principles of integration into the European project argue that the success of Europeanisation depends on the decoupling of citizenship from ethnicity and nationality and on the investment in civic notions of belonging (e.g. Kuper 2000; Warleigh 2003).[1] For some critical observers, this includes the complete disposal of the idea of a 'European' people, as 'ethnos, demos or nation' (Delanty and Rumford 2005: 103), or of a specific 'European' territory, religion, culture, heritage or identity as interconnecting principles. They argue that inward-looking Europeanness ignores already flourishing global attachments and that Europeanisation is external just as much as internal: 'new European spaces are not necessarily the outcome of the activities of the EU, nor are they limited to a European scope of operation' (Delanty and Rumford 2005: 121).

Others argue that Europe has not yet discovered its own specifically postwar cosmopolitanism, founded in the collective resolve to resist Nazi Germany and in the defiance of perverted nationalisms that have since become part of international legal frameworks (Beck 2003). Beck suggests that the spirit of reconciliation and humanism that emerged in the aftermath of catastrophe and on a continent that carries immense historical responsibility for colonialism, war and terror, needs to be 'excavated'. Europe could renew itself in cosmopolitan fashion if it looked in the mirror of its proven capability for humanism and anti-nationalism.

Habermas similarly appeals to the renewal of a cosmopolitan Europeanness, whose spirit he saw emerging in the pan-European mass demonstrations against the Iraq War in 2003.[2] The ambivalent and post-Holocaust legacies of European history have offered responses that could give shape to a 'European consciousness' (Habermas and Derrida 2003: 295) on which to build greater transnational solidarity. This includes what Habermas considers specifically 'European' civil-society traditions, such as the secularisation of politics, the anti-capitalist class struggles and social justice movements, or critical postcolonialisms (ibid.: 296–7). Habermas's vision of a 'European civil society' in which

Europeans 'rediscover themselves' (Habermas 2003: 98) in the spirit of the above, and form a strong border-crossing public sphere, sounds radically utopian. At the same time, the future visions these intellectual debates espouse convincingly suggest that the transnational perspective is no longer merely optional, that cosmopolitan Europeanness (or merely a cosmopolitan ethics) has yet to be effectively crafted (and promoted by the EU), and that the 'civil sphere' (Alexander 2006) is the indispensable space within which national citizens might become cosmopolitans.

9.2 Migration and methodological nationalism

Debates around civil society represent a major field in which postnational and postwelfare types of European integration have been theorised. European integration is nevertheless conventionally imagined to involve a plurality of nation-states, a relationship to the outside. Clearly, it must equally address the 'inside' of national societies and their increasingly plural cultural fabric. Beck calls the internal diversification of national societies 'globalization from within' (Beck 2002), a process of transformation that works through local lives in often unspectacular and tacit ways:

> [n]ourishment, production, identity, fear, memory, pleasure, fate, can no longer be located nationally or locally, but only globally or glocally – whether in the shape of globally shared collective futures, capital flows, impending ecological or economic catastrophes, global foodstuff chains or the international 'Esperanto' of pop music.
>
> (2002: 30)

In how far these transnational dimensions of personal experience and lived locality are perceived and debated as such, or whether they are discursively and institutionally folded back into the imaginary of the 'nation', is open to question (cf. ibid. 30). For Beck, 'cosmopolitanization' or globalisation 'from within' is an ongoing, profoundly transformative process that requires an altogether new understanding of society (ibid; see also Beck 2007).

Similar voices have been raised from within migration scholarship, where 'integration' has been debated in a way that is not dissimilar to the critical European integration debate discussed further above. In migration scholarship, 'integration' broadly means asking questions about the relationship between migrants and hosts. In applying the critique of 'methodological nationalism', scholars have examined how these questions have evolved and how their assumptions draw on a complicity of science with the political order of the modern nation-state. Just as the naturalisation of the nation-state has clouded the past reality and future potential of cross-border attachments, so, some critics argue, has it determined the epistemological outlook of migration scholars. Wimmer and Glick Schiller (2002) define 'methodological nationalism' as the dominance of the national paradigm in the social sciences, and retrace its specific impact on the theorisation of migration. They show how the equation of society, territory and peoplehood with 'nation' began to reappear in the othering of immigrants as 'antinomies to an orderly working of state and society' (ibid.: 309) from the early 1900s and in concert with the consolidation of European nation-building projects (ibid.: 314–15). By the 1950s and 60s, when new immigrations reach Europe and the US, immigrants have been predominantly configured as national outsiders who potentially challenge the state and society of national insiders. Migration scholars started to occupy themselves with studying immigrant adaptation and integration, and, in alignment with methodological nationalism, assumed that 'integration [...] [was already] established, less problematical, and less fragile among those belonging to the national people' (Wimmer and Glick Schiller 2002: 310). Wimmer and Glick Schiller's thesis goes a long way towards explaining why immigrants have been persistently singled out as a group apart that had a different set of problems and therefore different 'integration' requirements than the national group; why migration of non-citizens has been differently conceptualised to that of citizens (cross-border and internal migration movements are rarely compared) (cf. ibid.: 311); and why nationality or ethnicity has been seen to account for a more fundamental difference between human beings than, say, class, age or political opinion. Glick Schiller has expanded this critique to include 'methodological ethnicity', radically questioning the continued perception of migrants as 'ethnics' who belong to bounded communities and settle in host societies in broadly similar ways (Glick Schiller 2008). Assuming that nationality or ethnicity account for a shared identity of migrants obscures, asserts Glick Schiller, the actual fragmentations moulded by class, educational, familial, religious or political difference, and the diverse routes of incorporation migrants can take within and beyond a given national territory (ibid.).

Abandoning methodological nationalism or methodological ethnicity in studying migration has also meant rethinking what migrant integration or incorporation could actually mean under conditions of globalisation, and in relation to which units of analysis it could be studied. The debate has developed around studies of migrant transnationalism, which opened up a whole new research field on the significance of cross-border practices for social, cultural or economic integration processes. In an effort to shift focus from ethnicity or nationality as principles of affiliation, some scholars have suggested studying 'non-ethnic pathways of incorporation', observable in entrepreneurial, religious or political activity (Glick Schiller 2008); to refocus on locally specific opportunity structures for migrant incorporation (Glick Schiller and Çağlar 2009); on ties that pivot around religious or social institutions rather than around nation or state (Levitt and Glick Schiller 2004); or to reconsider the 'second generation' through which migrant inclusion has been classically discussed (e.g. Levitt and Walters 2002).

While the details of these debates cannot be elaborated here, two conclusions may be drawn at this stage. First, scholars in both European and migration studies have addressed models and potentials of integration through a critique of the nation-state and its principles. This includes theorising visions of cosmopolitanism, both in relations between states and in relations between people. Thus, for instance, cosmopolitans realise that they share experiences, concerns and ideals not by virtue of their nationality but by virtue of being part of similar 'social, economic and political processes, networks, movements and institutions that exist both within and across state borders' (Glick Schiller and Çağlar 2009: 180; see also Vertovec and Cohen 2002). In both scenarios, the post-national, post-ethnic world citizen is primarily defined as a humanist citizen.

Second, in both contexts there has been a critical self-reflection on the ideological assumptions and preconceptions in academic thought. The notion of 'methodological nationalism' captures usefully this embeddedness of academic knowledge in broader political cultures and discourses. From the point of view of the bordered nation-state, the border-crossing subject appears as suspicious, a perspective social science has discursively legitimated, even if it has also challenged it. Knowledge formation about migrants has taken place at the crossroads of science and politics, which involves a broad field in which processes of nation building intersect with immigration policing, media debates, enduring practices of racialisation, and the political economy. While not all of these may directly derive from methodological nationalism, the concept alerts one to the fact that larger political realities do not only permeate the local practices we study but also the questions we ask. In this sense, the utopia of the global citizen has to be read against the ongoing realities of nationalism and racism in political and popular practice.

9.3 EU visions or 'unity in diversity'

The EU applies its motto 'unity in diversity' to the many cultural and political integration processes that continuously animate the European project. However, policy and discourse dynamics generally separate integration domains along EU and non-EU populations despite the fact that the boundaries between these categories have continuously changed. Correspondingly, internal cross-border community building is largely the domain of 'regional policy', whereas multicultural community formation is generally perceived to involve 'third country nationals' and more specifically considered 'integration policy'.

Trans-European integration programmes that involve national borders categorise Europe largely as a universe of 'regions'. These correspond with administrative or historical and cultural regionalisms existent in different nation-states but also with 'Euroregions' that span national borders, EU-devised regional groupings or urban regions. One of the major support instruments in this context is the Interreg programme (currently Interreg 4), whose funding strands comprise 'cross-border', 'transnational' and 'interregional' cooperation, differentiations which may appear confusing to the outsider. They broadly address regions that share a national border; clusters of regions that share a broad geographical area (e.g., 'Alpine', 'Western Mediterranean') without common borders; and geographically disconnected regions that build project-specific networks (European Commission 2004). The reality of Europe as regional emerges as a collage of old and newly formed territorial units that consolidate in concert with EU programmes, policy and funding regimes, guide research interests and shape logics of connectivity that may or may not inform the awareness of local citizens.[3]

Cohesion policy, as regional integration policy is often called – within or across national borders – is largely embedded in the language of economic development. This is based on the understanding that the large disparities of wealth and income across the EU do not only separate countries but also areas within countries, and that more equality will have to be achieved through targeted initiatives and policy programmes (Rumford 2000: 1). The EU's current 'Report on Economic and Social Cohesion' emphasises fostering economic growth and employment as major cohesion-building measures (European Commission 2007a). These are also seen to be under threat from pressures from competitors outside the EU, such as the US, China or India, by globalisation, climate change and a changing and ageing demographic. However, apart from 'growth and jobs', 'development' and 'competitiveness' feature as main concepts in the latest cohesion report, in alignment with the 'Lisbon Strategy' launched in 2000, which boldly proposes to make the EU 'the most competitive economy in the world and achieving full employment by 2010' (Europa Glossary).[4] While the cohesion report clearly addresses the extent of poverty and unemployment across the EU, it leaves little doubt that neoliberal restructuring and competitiveness are where solutions are seen. Some scholars who have closely observed EU cohesion strategies have raised strong doubts in this respect, suggesting that the 'neoliberally inflected EU' (Rumford 2000: 14) does not seek to redistribute wealth or reduce economic inequalities in social democratic fashion but to protect the internal market from outside competitors (ibid.). The tensions of 'social and economic cohesion' that play themselves out in the contradiction between stated aims on the one hand and actual realities on the other are, according to Rumford, explicable by the neoliberal turn itself, that is predicated on the unequal distribution of opportunities and costs (ibid. 69–73).

Without examining this issue further, one of the main points that can be made at this stage is that the narrative of European cohesion and integration follows primarily economic rationales. Broadly speaking, if economic disparities are reduced, more social harmony and community building will follow. While the economic domain is clearly of major relevance, it is nevertheless interesting that people, culture or history are limited to side-effects in these scenarios of 'regional' or 'territorial' union. Relatedly, 'regional' migration is not conceptualised as an issue affecting community cohesion, but as a quasi-natural expression of regional disparities that motivate people to leave in search of employment. This effectively foregrounds the (EU) migrant as *homo economicus* (European Commission 2007a: 42–4). By contrast the narrative of 'immigrant integration' assumes a basic boundary between immigrants as non-EU 'nationals' or 'ethnic minorities' and 'host societies' (Commission of the European Communities 2007: 3), thus highlighting a discourse of group boundaries in which the national difference of one group confronts the national homogeneity or unmarkedness of another. Here, the relevant geographies are not 'regions' but 'the EU' as a whole and its 'member states'. While, in the regional discourse, mobility is an expression of people responding to economic pressures, in the immigration discourse the mobile subject itself comes under suspicion, irrespective of his or her motivations for migration.

Since the late 1990s there has been increasing EU involvement in migration issues. Even though the actual impact of 'Europeanization' in nation-states' migration policies is not straightforward and insufficiently researched (Faist and Ette 2007), all signs point to a more active role for the EU in the shaping of relevant policies, paradigms and discourses in member states. Following on from the Amsterdam Treaty in 1999 which brought international migration into the remit of the EU for the first time, a series of programmes, strategies and agreements have been launched that provide legal and political direction in matters of immigration and asylum, and that are geared towards more policy harmonisation (see Geddes 2007; Bendel 2007).[5] The communications of the Commission place a major emphasis on migration 'management' which is broadly categorised as fighting 'illegal migration' on the one hand and channelling 'legal' immigrants into the sectors of need on the other (European Commission 2007c). While many member states are anxious to remain in charge of regulating migrants' access to their labour markets, and are thus keen not to cede control to the EU,[6] the issue of illegality has led to a widely shared embrace of a securitisation programme, especially in the wake of 9/11 and the attacks in London and Madrid. In fact, some observers have argued that the EU's migration policies have mostly concentrated on 'restriction and control [...] measures that refer to the selection, admission and deportation of third-country nationals' (Bendel 2007: 34–5). This includes visa regimes, the tightening of external borders, border surveillance operations, deportation guidelines ('Return Action Programme'), readmission and assistance agreements with third countries, or the development of shared asylum procedures (European Commission 2007c). The Council's euphemistically termed 'global approach to migration', established in 2005, outlines largely a security and border management framework that seeks to include migrant-sending regions (e.g. Africa, Mediterranean, eastern and south-eastern EU neighbours, Russian Federation) in the effort of limiting 'illegal immigration' into the EU (Council of the European Union 2007: 16–19). In this discursive and political context, the 'third country national's' curbed freedom of movement contrasts sharply with the unbounded mobility of the 'EU citizen',[7] and the diversity of EU regions and populations transforms into the uniformity of a superstate that pulls up the bridges at its external frontiers.

The emphasis on a more tightly 'managed' exclusion to the outside is mirrored by a heightened ambition of (an equally 'managed') inclusion to the inside. Here, 'integration' has become a major pillar of the EU migration and cultural diversity strategy, shaping discursive approach and policy recommendations.[8] The European Council agreed on 11 'Common Basic Principles' (CBPs) on integration in 2004. These are primarily addressed at member states, invoking their responsibility to integrate immigrants and providing specific guidelines for the development of integration policies (Council of the European Union 2004: 15–17).[9]

Clearly implicit in the formulation of the CBPs is the acknowledgement of an immigrant/non-immigrant divide that has worked to the disadvantage of immigrant citizens in all European societies. 'Integration' is thus associated with greater immigrant 'participation' and equal access in key social, political and economic spheres. Comparable to the EU gender mainstreaming programme,[10] the 'Principles' call for 'mainstreaming integration policies in all relevant policy portfolios and levels of government and public services' (ibid., 18), thus reinforcing the correlation between integration and the promotion of equality. What is more, the CBPs recognise that integration is a 'two-way process' involving 'immigrants' and 'national citizens' alike (ibid., 19). While 'immigrants' are asked to 'adapt' to the host society, 'receiving societies' are asked to provide the opportunities for full immigrant participation (ibid.). The 'methodological nationalisms' in these discursive framings notwithstanding, the CBPs represent a degree of ambition and progressiveness that surely outperforms the status quo in many member states. The Commission's publications such as the 'Handbook on Integration'[11] or the 'Annual Report on Migration and Integration'[12] assess and compare integration policies in member states according to the CBPs, thus strengthening their specific discursive input; yet, their implementation on the ground remains a different issue, and is ultimately dependent on the political will of the individual member state.

EU funding for integration measures is highly limited, and mostly administered by national governments.[13] The progressive, universalist, anti-discriminatory rhetoric on immigration and integration to be found in the CBPs and in many of the Commission's communications and publications, is likely to be related to its distance from national contexts and the non-binding nature of many of its proposals. At the same time, the Commission seeks to legitimise its own role in the highly contentious immigration policy field, where national governments seek to safeguard their own control and many civil-society actors strive for legitimacy (Boswell 2009: 203). Boswell argues that the Commission's strategy has largely focused on 'talk', or on the proliferation of 'rationalist, universalist argument [...] based on expert knowledge' (ibid.: 201), thereby shaping a discourse that seeks to substantiate policy with research and academic expertise (ibid.: 201–3). Funding academic research on migration issues has clearly developed into a major field of Commission activity, and one that is expected to yield policy-relevant knowledge. The project presented in this book is one such example, as it was funded under the EU Framework Programme and thus tied into a commitment to delivering academic knowledge that holds out relevance for policy making. The growth of EU-sponsored migration research has evidently built capacity in expanding cross-border research communities and in informing media debates and policy making. However, there are important questions to be asked about the instrumentalisation of social research for policy, both in the light of an ever growing migration research 'industry' and an increasingly restrictive European migration policy.[14]

At any event, the EU's presence as a policy player in the field figures differently in different European countries, yet notions of 'integration' or 'social cohesion' have increasingly moved to the forefront of priority issues when European governments address immigration. While the meaning of 'integration' is elusive, its usage frequently revolves around the risks and problems that are understood to be associated with multicultural societies. Integration ministries and integration commissions have sprung up in many places, making integration subject to public policy and immigration legislation. Access to citizenship or admission to countries are now often directly tied to immigrants passing 'integration courses' or 'integration tests'. While these are discursively framed as means of enabling more social justice and inclusion for migrants, some observers have argued that the new integration policies have largely become instruments of assimilation, or serve as a 'juridical and policy mechanism of control by which the state may better manage who enters and who is included inside its territory' (Carrera 2006: 2).

In the post 9/11 world, European-wide debates have particularly singled out 'Muslims' as a 'difficult to integrate' group, giving rise to a discourse about segregation and 'parallel societies', and informing an anti-immigrant – or what Beck might call an 'anti-cosmopolitan' – backlash. Some of the chapters in this book address integration debates and policies in specific national contexts. They illustrate the implications 'integration' has for those categorised 'immigrant', but also how 'integration' often works to draw boundaries between 'immigrant' and 'citizen' – rather contrary to the aim of inclusion which the EU's CBPs ambitiously espouse.

The discussion above indicates that both domains of European 'integration' sustain the ideology of nationality as a basis for dis/integrative practice. Crossing the boundary from region to state or from immigrant to citizen presupposes rights and entitlements which are ultimately tied in to notions of citizenship and belonging that are exclusively derived from nationality. The question remains as to how far the culture of nationhood is still a powerful idiom of social and political perception among European citizens (both old and new), or whether alternative modes of belonging and affiliation become thinkable that engender forms of democratic inclusion at the same time.

In exploring the ethnographic realities of 'national' and 'ethnic' border crossings in different European sites, we have seen that the preceding chapters also address this question. Their findings suggest that nationality may have run its course as an instrument for forming solidarity and civic networks. Instead, other types of connections, networks and affiliations are called for in culturally diverse contexts in which nationality may neither be a vehicle for solidarity nor a useful category for explaining actual processes of inequality.

Notes

1. The ways in which citizenship can be configured as culturally universalist while accommodating minority rights has been subject to extensive debates in social and political theory (e.g. Benhabib 2004; Kymlicka and Norman 2000; Modood et al. 2006). This debate shows the problematic of societal integration through 'nationhood' from the perspective of societies which are increasingly diverse and multicultural.
2. Evidently, these demonstrations took place globally which makes the specific 'European' dimension that Habermas's text suggests somewhat debatable.
3. For the conceptualisation of space and spatial politics in the EU context see Scott (2002).
4. For more recent developments in EU cohesion policy and its implementation in specific member states, see e.g. Baun and Marek (2008).
5. Within the EU, the European Commission develops policy documents and proposals for legislation, directly responding to the directives of the Council. Migration is part of the remit of the Commission's Directorate-General Justice, Freedom and Security. Relevant policy directions have been laid out in a range of five-year programmes, the most recent being the *Stockholm Programme* (2009–14) (see e.g. European Commission 2009: 10–13; Collett 2010). Since 1 July 2010, the Directorate has been transformed into two directorates, one of which, the Directorate-General for Home Affairs is now responsible for 'internal security', 'immigration and asylum' and 'migration and borders'. See [http://ec.europa.eu/dgs/justice_home/index_en.htm], accessed 28.08.2010.

6. EU member states have long been reluctant to agree on a common labour migration policy or to harmonise their legislation in this context. The new Blue Card system for highly skilled non-EU nationals, coming into force in 2011, is the only commonly agreed measure to date (Collett 2010).
7. The principle of 'free movement' in the EU applies to EU nationals. This may, however, exclude the right to work in another member state. Some member states imposed restrictions of access to their labour markets for workers from countries that joined the EU in 2004. In 2014 this transition period is due to end (see Brady 2008).
8. See also European Commission (2007d).
9. Migrant generations are cursorily addressed in the explanatory framework of the CBPs. Strictly speaking, it defines only non-EU (i.e. third-country) nationals as 'immigrants' and thus as target groups for integration. This can be considered a paradoxical effect of the 'methodological nationalism' of the EU which defines migrant categories according to nationality. Migrant exclusion and discrimination in Europe are related to, but not reducible to, citizenship, nor can it be assumed that all descendants of immigrants hold EU passports. Collett suggests that second- and third-generation migrant concerns are allocated to the Directorate- General Employment and Social Affairs and its 'social inclusion and anti-discrimination' portfolio, assuming that nationals' access to integration works through the labour market. As an expression of this logic, the *Racial Equality and Employment Equality Directives* consequently 'exclude nationality as a ground for discrimination' (Collett 2008).
10. Gender mainstreaming, formally adopted by the EU in 1996, seeks to achieve equality between the sexes by integrating a gender perspective into policy making. See e.g. Mazey (2001).
11. To date published in 2004 and 2007. See European Commission (2007b) for latest edition at time of writing.
12. To date published in 2004, 2006 and 2007.
13. The Integration Fund (2007–13) aims to support the integration of newly arrived non-EU nationals; the European Social Fund and PROGRESS (2007–13) provide funding for integration projects (see Collett 2008).
14. The Commission sponsors specific research initiatives in the field, such as the European Migration Network founded in 2002; an increasing number of studies under the Framework Programmes, or the so-called Networks of Excellence, such as the International Migration, Integration and Social Cohesion network (IMISCOE) launched in 2004 (for details see European Commission 2009; see also Penninx et al. 2008).

References

Alexander, J. C. (2006). *The Civil Sphere* (Oxford: Oxford University Press).

Baun, M. and D. Marek (eds) (2008). *EU Cohesion Policy after Enlargement* (Basingstoke: Palgrave Macmillan).

Beck, U. (2002). 'The Cosmopolitan Society and its Enemies', *Theory, Culture & Society*, vol. 19, no. 1–2: pp. 17–44.

Beck, U. (2003). 'Understanding the Real Europe', *Dissent*, Summer 2003, http://www.dissentmagazine.org/article/?article=483 (accessed 10 June 2010).

Beck, U. (2007). 'The Cosmopolitan Condition: Why Methodological Nationalism Fails', *Theory, Culture and Society*, vol. 24, no. 7–8: pp. 286–90.

Bendel, P. (2007). 'Everything under Control? The European Union's Policies and Politics of Immigration', in T. Faist and A. Ette (eds). *The Europeanization of National Policies and Politics of Immigration: Between Autonomy and the European Union* (Basingstoke: Palgrave Macmillan), pp. 32–48.

Benhabib, S. (2004). *The Rights of Others: Aliens, Residents, and Citizens* (Cambridge: Cambridge University Press).

Boswell, C. (2009). *The Political Uses of Expert Knowledge: Immigration Policy and Social Research* (Cambridge: Cambridge University Press).

Brady, H. (2008). *EU Migration Policy: An A–Z Centre for European Reform (CER)* (London), http://www.cer.org.uk.

Carrera, S. (2006). 'Introduction: Towards and EU Framework on the Integration of Immigrants', in S. Carrera (ed.). *The Nexus between Immigration, Integration and Citizenship in the EU: Challenge. Collective Conference Volume*, April 2006: 1–5, http://www.ceps.eu/book/nexus-between-immigration-integration-and-citizenship-eu (accessed 20 June 2010).

Collett, E. (2008). 'What Does the EU Do on Integration?' Brussels: European Policy Centre, http://www.migrationinformation.org/integration/files/EUIntegrationPolicyFactsheet-04-2008.pdf (accessed 10 June 2010).

Collett, E. (2010). 'The European Union's Stockholm Program: Less Ambition on Immigration and Asylum', Migration Policy Institute, 12 January 2010, http://www.migrationinformation.org/Feature/display.cfm?ID=768 (accessed 10 June 2010).

Commission of the European Communities (2006). *Commission Staff Working Document: Second Annual Report on Migration and Integration* (Brussels: Commission of the European Communities), SEC (2006) 892.

Commission of the European Communities (2007). *Communication from the Commission to the Council, the European Parliament, the European Economic and Social Committee and the Committee of the Regions: Third Annual Report on Migration and Integration* (Brussels: Commission of the European Communities), COM (2007) 512 final.

Council of the European Union (2004). *Press Release: 2618th Council Meeting: Justice and Home Affairs, Brussels, 19 November 2004* (Brussels), 14615/04 (Presse 321).

Council of the European Union (2007). *Press Release: 2807th Council Meeting: Justice and Home Affairs, Luxembourg, 12–13 June 2007* (Brussels), 10267/07 (Presse 125).

Dahl, R. A. (2005). 'Is International Democracy Possible? A Critical Review', in S. Fabbrini (ed.). *Democracy and Federalism in the European Union and the United States* (London: Routledge), pp. 194–204.

Delanty, G. and C. Rumford (2005). *Rethinking Europe: Social Theory and the Implications of Europeanization* (London: Routledge).

Eriksen, E. O. and J. E. Fossum (2000). 'Post-national Integration', in E. O. Eriksen and J. E. Fossum (eds). *Democracy in the European Union: Integration through Deliberation?* (London: Routledge), pp. 1–28.

Europa Glossary: Lisbon Strategy, http://europa.eu/scadplus/glossary/lisbon_strategy_en.htm (accessed 29 May 2010).

European Commission (2004). *Communication from the Commission to the Member States of 2 September 2004: Laying down Guidelines for a Community Initiative*

Concerning Trans-European Cooperation Intended to Encourage Harmonious and Balanced Development of the European Territory, INTERREG III, Official Journal of the European Union C 226/2.

European Commission (2007a). *Growing Regions, Growing Europe: Fourth Report on Economic and Social Cohesion* (Luxembourg: Office for Official Publications of the European Communities).

European Commission (2007b). *Handbook on Integration for Policy-Makers and Practitioners, 2nd edition.*

European Commission, Justice and Home Affairs (2007c). *Towards a Common European Union Immigration Policy*, Update September 2007 http://ec.europa.eu/justice_home/fsj/immigration/fsj_immigration_intro_en.htm (accessed 10 June 2010).

European Commission, Justice and Home Affairs (2007d). *A Common Framework for the Integration of Third-Country Nationals*, Update: September 2007, http://ec.europa.eu/justice_home/fsj/immigration/integration/fsj_immigration_integration_en.htm (accessed 10 June 2010).

European Commission (2009). *Moving Europe: EU Research on Migration and Policy Needs* (Luxembourg: Office for Official Publications of the European Communities), EUR 23859.

Fabbrini, S. (ed.) (2005). *Democracy and Federalism in the European Union and the United States: Exploring Post-national Governance* (London: Routledge).

Faist, T. and A. Ette (2007). 'The Europeanization of National Policies and Politics of Immigration: Research, Questions and Concepts', in T. Faist and A. Ette (eds). *The Europeanization of National Policies and Politics of Immigration: Between Autonomy and the European Union* (Basingstoke: Palgrave Macmillan), pp. 3–31.

Geddes, A. (2007). 'The Europeanization of What? Migration, Asylum and the Politics of European Integration', in T. Faist and A. Ette (eds). *The Europeanization of National Policies and Politics of Immigration: Between Autonomy and the European Union* (Basingstoke: Palgrave Macmillan), pp. 49–70.

Glick Schiller, N. (2008). 'Beyond Methodological Ethnicity: Local and Transnational Pathways of Immigrant Incorporation', *Willy Brandt Series of Working Papers in International Migration and Ethnic Relations*, Malmö University, no. 2/08.

Glick Schiller, N. and A. Çağlar (2009) 'Toward a Comparative Theory of Locality in Migration Studies: Migrant Incorporation and City Scale', *Journal of Ethnic and Migration Studies*, vol. 35, no. 2: pp. 177–202.

Glick Schiller, N. , A. Çağlar and T. C. Guldbrandsen (2006). 'Beyond the Ethnic Lens: Locality, Globality, and Born-again Incorporation', *American Ethnologist*, vol. 33, no. 4: pp. 612–33.

Habermas, J. (2000). 'Beyond the Nation-State? On Some Consequences of Economic Globalization', in E. O. Eriksen and J. E. Fossum (eds). *Democracy in the European Union. Integration through Deliberation?* (London: Routledge), pp. 29–41.

Habermas, J. (2003). 'Making Sense of the EU: Toward a Cosmopolitan Europe', *Journal of Democracy*, vol. 14, no. 4: pp. 86–100.

Habermas, J. and J. Derrida (2003). 'February 15, or What Binds Europeans Together: A Plea for a Common Foreign Policy, Beginning in the Core of Europe', *Constellations*, vol. 10, no. 3: pp. 291–7.

Hoskyns, C. and M. Newman (eds) (2000). *Democratizing the European Union: Issues for the Twenty-First Century* (Manchester: Manchester University Press).

Kuper, R. (2000). 'Democratization: A Constitutionalizing Process', in C. Hoskyns and M. Newman (eds). *Democratizing the European Union* (Manchester: Manchester University Press), pp. 156–75.

Kymlicka, W. and W. Norman (eds) (2000). *Citizenship in Diverse Societies* (Oxford: Oxford University Press).

Levitt, P. and N. Glick Schiller (2004). 'Conceptualizing Simultaneity: A Transnational Social Field Perspective on Society', *International Migration Review*, vol. 38, no. 3: pp. 1002–39.

Levitt, P. and M. C. Waters (eds) (2002). *The Changing Face of Home: The Transnational Lives of the Second Generation* (New York: Russell Sage Foundation).

Mazey, S. (2001). *Gender Mainstreaming in the EU: Principle and Practice* (London: Kogan Page).

Modood, T., A. Triandafyllidou, R. Zapata-Barrero (eds) (2006). *Multiculturalism, Muslims and Citizenship: A European Approach* (London: Routledge).

Penninx, R., D. Spencer and N. van Hear (2008). *Migration and Integration in Europe: The State of Research*, Report commissioned by the ESRC for NORFACE, ESRC Centre on Migration, Policy and Society (COMPAS), University of Oxford.

Rumford, C. (2000). *European Cohesion? Contradictions in EU Integration* (Basingstoke: Macmillan).

Sbragia, A. M. (2005). 'Post-national Democracy as Post-National Democratization', in S. Fabbrini (ed.). *Democracy and Federalism in the European Union and the United States* (London, New York: Routledge), pp. 167–82.

Scott, J. W. (2002). 'A Networked Space of Meaning? Spatial Politics as Geostrategies of European Integration', *Space and Polity*, vol. 6, no. 2: pp. 147–67.

Vertovec, S. and R. Cohen (eds) (2002). *Conceiving Cosmopolitanism. Theory, Context, and Practice* (Oxford: Oxford University Press).

Warleigh, A. (2003). *Democracy in the European Union* (London: Sage Publications).

Wimmer, A. and N. G. Schiller (2002). 'Methodological Nationalism and Beyond: Nation-State Building, Migration and the Social Sciences', *Global Networks*, vol. 2, no. 4: pp. 301–34.

Index

Page numbers followed by 'n' indicate notes.

N

O

P

R

S

T

Made in the USA
Las Vegas, NV
28 October 2024

10601791R00127